JACOBY
ON
CARD
GAMES

"A bible for cardplayers . . . a well-written, authoritative book and a desirable addition to any cardplayer's library."

—*Contract Bridge Bulletin*

OSWALD JACOBY, author of the bestselling classics *How to Win at Canasta* and *Oswald Jacoby on Poker*, was a passionate gamesman from his early years until his death in 1984. He formulated many bridge techniques in use today, and was the first bridge player to earn 1,000 master points in a year and 10,000 master points overall. For more than thirty years, he wrote the popular, nationally syndicated, daily bridge column "Jacoby on Bridge." Oswald was also a World Backgammon Champion.

JAMES JACOBY, a world-renowned bridge expert (surpassing even his father's records), has earned enough points to be a Life Master forty times over! He is the author of the successful column his father originated, which now reaches more than 600 newspapers and is today's most popular column on bridge. Jim continues to play (and win) on the world-class bridge circuit.

Books by James Jacoby

Jacoby on Bridge
Jacoby on Card Games
   (with Oswald Jacoby)

Published by POCKET BOOKS

JACOBY
ON
CARD
GAMES

**Oswald Jacoby
and
James Jacoby**

POCKET BOOKS

New York London Toronto Sydney Tokyo

POCKET BOOKS, a division of Simon & Schuster Inc.
1230 Avenue of the Americas, New York, NY 10020

Published by arrangement with Pharos Books
Library of Congress Catalog Card Number: 85-52402

ISBN: 0-671-66883-8

First Pocket Books printing December 1989

10 9 8 7 6 5 4 3 2 1

POCKET and colophon are registered trademarks
of Simon & Schuster Inc.

Printed in the U.S.A.

Acknowledgments

We gratefully acknowledge the valuable contribution of the late Capt. W. T. Benson (retired) to the preparation of this book. Capt. Benson, colleague of my father's during his naval service in the Korean War, helped with several of Oswald Jacoby's later books. Without his assistance, completion of *Jacoby on Card Games* would have been considerably delayed.

We also thank Richard T. Frey, who edited the final manuscript, and Beverly Jane Loo, our editor at Pharos Books. Their cooperation and help made our work much easier.

Contents

RUMMY 145

SOLITAIRE WITH TWO DECKS 229

INDEX 249

Introduction

My father, Oswald Jacoby, was an unquestioned mathematical genius. His genius was mainly directed at mastering intellectual games. Most of these games involved cards, but my dad was also an excellent chess player, and he won several world championships of backgammon. His primary love was card games, though, and his expertise in bridge, poker, canasta and gin rummy led to bestselling books by him on these games.

Dad told me that he started playing whist—the forerunner of bridge—at the age of six, when he played with his parents and the family doctor. At 15, he lied about his age and spent two months in the army during the First World War. While in the army, he played poker well enough to later pay for his college tuition out of his winnings. At Columbia University, Dad became a member of his college chess team, and years later he played the Russian master Petrossian to a draw in lightning chess, albeit with a slight handicap. In 1929 Dad won the first contract bridge championship held in the United States.

Writing a bestselling book on poker in 1940, my father followed up after World War II with books on gin rummy, canasta, and a guide to gambling probabilities entitled *How to Figure the Odds*. Later came the *Backgammon Book*, *Oswald Jacoby on Gambling*, and a book on mathematical puzzles. Dad won world championships at backgammon and bridge, as well as countless United States and North American bridge championships, and he was the captain of the American bridge team that twice (in 1936 and 1970), won the world championship. I had the good fortune to be a playing member of the latter team.

Over 50 years after my dad won his first national bridge championship, he won his last one. In late November, 1983, shortly before his 81st birthday, we won the Reisinger Trophy. His remarkable feat was even more striking because he was battling terminal cancer at the time.

His mathematical mind was legendary. At 21, Dad took his actuarial examinations while working for Metropolitan Life; he was the youngest person ever to pass. Because of the skills he honed as an actuary, he received a naval commission early in World War II. Not many months later he became a key member of the team that deciphered the Japanese code.

Lest anyone think that games were central to my father's life, I can proudly affirm that love of country came first. On December 7, 1941, he was leading a national bridge championship in its final afternoon. When the Japanese attack on Pearl Harbor was announced, Dad walked away from the table to offer his services in Washington, giving up his chance for yet another national bridge title. Some years later, when asked to return to naval service during the Korean War, he did so immediately, although he had to then resign from the U.S. bridge team playing for the world championship in Bermuda in 1950.

He loved games with the same devotion that he loved his country. In March and April of 1984, weak from cancer, Dad struggled to play both the North American Team Championship and the Texas District Grand National Team final. Although his team did not win either competition, his own play was of top caliber. Dad wouldn't give up.

Throughout the last year of his life he worked daily at the material in this book. He would type up sections and mail them to his good friend and frequent collaborator, W. T. Benson, who would return clean manuscript copy. Dad then made further additions and modifications. Toward the end, too weak to sit at a typewriter, Dad would dictate his work to my mother. Some months earlier, I had begun contributing a small effort in this process. *Jacoby on Card Games* is the result of this collaboration.

Oswald Jacoby was quoted in *Sports Illustrated* in 1978 as saying, "A games expert probably does more for the country than a second vice president of a bank, whose contribution is turning down loans." What I am sure he meant to say was this: "Writing about games does something for others that more mundane activities cannot do. It gives your fellow man a perspective and a way of responding to the tedium of his everyday existence. If it entertains and amuses him, then I have accomplished something that I hold to be quite important in our mortal scheme of things."

My dad believed that. He fiercely loved playing games. Those of us who knew him and loved him regret that he did not live to see this book in print. But we have to believe he is still entertaining and instructing those who love the thrill and excitement of the turn of cards and rush to learn how best to play them.

JAMES OSWALD JACOBY
February 20, 1986
Richardson, Texas

Bridge

WHIST[1]

PRELIMINARIES

Number of players Four players, playing as two pairs of partners. When five or six players wish to play, all cut cards; the top four play in the first game and the others sit out. After the first game is finished, the inactive players replace those of the top four who cut lowest. This process is continued. For example, if players A, B, C, D, E, and F cut in that order, then A, B, C and D would play in the first game; A, B, E, and F would play in the second game; and C, D, E, and F would play in the third game. This process would repeat as long as necessary. In each case the four players cut again for cards and seats.

The pack Two standard 52-card packs, one being shuffled while the other is being dealt and played with.

Rank of the cards In play, ace (highest), K, Q, J, 10, 9, 8, 7, 6, 5, 4, 3, 2 (lowest). In cutting for partners and deal, the ace is lowest and the king is highest.

The draw Cut or draw from a spread pack for partners and seats; the two highest play against the two lowest. Low card has choice of cards and seats.

---

[1] The history of whist goes way back into the early 17th century. From it developed Bridge about 1896, then Auction Bridge about 1904, and finally Contract Bridge in 1927.

The shuffle and cut   Any player may shuffle; however, the dealer has the right to shuffle last. The player at the right must cut the cards after the last shuffle and before the deal begins.

The deal   The dealer gives one card at a time, face down, to each player in a clockwise direction beginning with the player to his or her left, until the last card, which is the trump card.

The trump card   The dealer must place the last card of the pack, face up, on the table in front of him or her; it and all cards of the same suit become trump cards. When it is the dealer's turn to play to the first trick, he picks up the exposed trump and it becomes a part of his hand.

Object of the game   The object is to win tricks.

THE PLAY

The turn to play is from player to player in clockwise rotation, the first player (the leader) to the first trick (the player to the left of the dealer). He or she may lead any card desired. Each player in turn thereafter must play a card, following suit if able to do so; if not able to follow suit, he may play any card that he wishes. Four cards so played, including the card led, constitute a trick.

A trick containing any trump is won by the player who played the highest trump; a trick not containing a trump is won by the player who played the highest card in the suit led. After the first trick, the winner of each trick leads to the next trick.

SCORING

Each odd trick (trick in excess of six) counts one point to the side winning it.

GAME

A game consists of seven points.

IRREGULARITIES

New deal   There must be a new deal by the same dealer:

1. If any card except the last is faced in the deal.
2. If during the deal or during the play of the hand the pack is proved incorrect or imperfect, but any prior score made with that pack shall stand.
3. If anyone deals out of turn or with the adversaries' deck, that person may be stopped up to the point that the trump card is turned, after which the deal is valid and the packs, if changed, so remain.

Misdeal   It is a misdeal (after a misdeal, the deal passes to the player to the left unless either of the adversaries touches a card or in any other manner interrupts the dealer):

1. If the dealer fails to have the deck cut and it is discovered before the trump card is turned and before anyone has looked at his or her cards.
2. If the dealer deals a card incorrectly and fails to correct the error before dealing another card.
3. If the dealer looks at the trump card before the deal is completed.
4. If having a perfect deck, the dealer has not dealt to each player the proper number of cards and the error is discovered before all have played to the first trick.
5. If the dealer places the trump card face downward upon his own or any other player's cards.

Irregularities in the hands   If at any time after all have played to the first trick (the pack being perfect), a player is found to have either more or less than his or her correct number of cards, and his or her adversaries have their correct number, the latter (upon discovery of such surplus or deficiency) may consult and shall have one of the following choices:

1. To have a new deal;
2. To have the hand played out, in which case the surplus or missing cards are not taken into account.

If either of the adversaries also has more or less than the correct number of cards, there must be a new deal.

If a player is short because he failed to play to a trick, his adversaries can exercise the foregoing privilege only after the offender has played to the trick following the one in which the omission occurred.

Leading out of turn If a player leads out of turn, a suit may be called from either her or her partner the first time it is the turn for either of them to lead. The penalty may be enforced only by the adversary on the right of the player from whom a suit can rightfully be called.

If a player so called on to lead a suit has no cards in the suit, or if all have played to the false lead, no penalty can be enforced. If all players have not played to the false lead, the cards which have been played may be picked up without a penalty.

Playing out of turn If the third hand plays before the second hand, the fourth hand may also play before the second hand. If the third hand has not played and the fourth hand plays before the second hand, the latter may be called upon by the third hand to play the highest or lowest card of the suit led; or, if he has none, to trump or not to trump the trick.

If a player leads a card better than one that either of her adversaries holds in that suit, and then leads one card or more without waiting for partner to play, either adversary may call upon the latter to take the first trick, and the other cards improperly played are liable to call. It makes no difference whether they are played in sequence or are all thrown on the table at once.

A player having a card subject to call must not play another until the adversaries have had an opportunity to say whether or not they wish to call the subject card. If he leads a card other than the card subject to call without waiting for the adversaries to make their decision, such other card also is subject to call.

Abandoned hands If all four players throw their hands upon the table, face up, no further play of that hand is permitted. The result of the hand as then claimed, or admitted, is then established provided that, if a revoke is discovered, the revoke penalty applies. (See below.)

Cards liable to be called   The following cards are liable to be called by either adversary:

1. Every card that is put face up on the table and that is not part of the regular course of play.
2. Any extra card or cards that a player inadvertently plays to a trick. The player must indicate the card he intended to play; the other card or cards become subject to call.
3. Every card so held by a player that her partner may see any portion of its face.
4. Any card named by a player holding that card.

All cards liable to be called must be left face upwards on the table. A player must lead or play them, when they are called, provided that he follows suit when he plays them. The call may be repeated at each trick until the card is played. A player may not be prevented from playing a card subject to call; once it is played, no penalty remains.

Revoke   Player who fails to follow suit when able to do so is said to have revoked. A revoke may be corrected by a player before the trick in which it occurs has been turned and quitted, unless either he or his partner, whether in his right turn or otherwise, has led or played to the following trick, or unless his partner has asked whether or not he has any cards in that suit and he has answered, "No." This is a perfectly proper question which a partner should always ask.

If a player corrects his revoke in time, there is no penalty other than the fact that the card improperly exposed becomes subject to call and must be placed face up on the table in front of the offender.

If the revoke becomes established (that is, if it is not corrected in time), the penalty is that two tricks must be transferred from the offender's side to that of the nonoffender. It can be enforced as many times as the offending side revokes. Also, the revoking side cannot win the game in that hand. If both sides revoke in the same hand, neither side can win the game in that hand. The hand should be played out.

The offending side may score any points which it wins (after transferring two tricks per revoke to the adversaries) up to a total of six points.

A revoke may be claimed at any time up to when the cards are cut for the following deal, but not thereafter.

STRATEGY

There is considerable strategy in the play of the cards. A major tactic concerns the opening lead. Generally, when the leader would like to win tricks by ruffing with low trumps, he leads a short suit. When the leader would like to establish a long suit, he leads that suit. When the opener has high cards in several suits, he leads trumps in order to try to prevent his high cards from being ruffed.

A bridge player can use this strategy to advantage.

♣ ◇ ♡ ♠

CONTRACT BRIDGE[2]

PRELIMINARIES

Players Four players usually; however, five or six may play by cutting in as in Whist.

----

[2] It is not possible in the few pages available to cover the play of Contract Bridge in any depth. There are many excellent books available on this subject. However, by far the best way to learn is to play it!

It is our hope to cover the essential rules in a simplified form to enable you to grasp the essential elements of the game. Although they are not a part of the laws of the game, conventions have become an essential feature of it. We shall, therefore, discuss some of the more common ones.

For more information about the laws of Contract Bridge, see page 42.

The pack Two standard 52-card packs are invariably used. While one player is dealing, his partner is shuffling the second pack for the next hand.

Rank of cards Ace (highest), K, Q, J, 10, 9, 8, 7, 6, 5, 4, 3, 2 (lowest).

Rank of suits Spades (highest), hearts, diamonds, clubs (lowest).

The draw After the deck is spread face down, fan-fashion, on the table, each player draws one card, being careful not to draw one of the last four cards at either end of the deck. If a player draws more than one card inadvertently, they are put aside and he draws again. Preferably no one exposes the card that he has drawn until all are ready to show their cards simultaneously. Many localities do not bother with this refinement; each player merely draws and then turns the card face up.

The player drawing the highest-rank card is the first dealer, who also chooses a seat and the cards with which to deal. The player drawing the card next highest in rank becomes his partner, who sits in the opposite seat.

The shuffle The player to the dealer's left shuffles the deck and puts it to the dealer's left. The dealer, after reshuffling the deck if he so wishes, presents it to the player on his right for cutting.

The cut The player at the dealer's right then lifts off the top portion of the deck (not less than four cards or more than 48 cards) and sets it down on the table toward the dealer. The dealer then picks up the remainder of the deck and places it on top of the portion the player to his right had lifted off.

The deal The dealer then deals one card at a time, clockwise, beginning with the player to his left, until each player has received thirteen cards.

Rotation The turn to deal, bid, and play always passes clockwise to the left.

THE AUCTION

Calls Each player, in turn, beginning with the dealer, must make a call (pass, bid, double, or redouble). If all four players pass on the first round, the deal is "passed out" and there is a new deal by the next player to the original dealer's left. If any player makes a bid in the first round, the bidding is opened.

Passing A player who does not wish to bid, double, or redouble passes. A pass is not considered a bid.

Bidding When a player wishes to bid, that player, in proper turn, must name a certain number of tricks (called odd tricks) in excess of six, which the bidder proposes to win, and a suit which will become the trump suit if the bid becomes the contract (that is, if the bid turns out to be the highest bid made by any of the players). Thus, two hearts is a bid to make eight tricks $(6+2=8)$ with hearts as trumps. If the bid is made in no-trump, it means that there is no-trump suit. The lowest possible bid is one and the highest permissible bid is seven. As the players bid or pass in turn, each bid must be for a higher number of tricks or, if for the same number of tricks, in a higher-ranking suit or in no-trump. No-trump is the highest-ranking bid, outranking spades. As stated previously, the ranking of the suits is spades (highest), hearts, diamonds, clubs (lowest). Thus a bid of three no-trump will overcall three spades, but a bid of four of a suit is necessary to overcall three spades.

Doubling and redoubling Any player may, at his turn, double the last bid made, provided it was made by an opponent. A player may not double a bid made by partner, nor double a pass. The effect of doubling is to double the value of odd tricks, overtricks, and undertrick penalties, if the doubled bid becomes the final contract (see Scoring, page 27).
    Either of the doubler's opponents may, at his turn, redouble a previous double provided there has been no intervening bid. Note that no player may redouble partner's double. A redouble again increases the scoring values.

Doubling or redoubling does not affect the size of a bid necessary to overcall. Thus, if the last bid was three hearts, doubled or redoubled, it could be overcalled by three spades, three no-trump, four clubs, four diamonds, or any higher bid.

Information as to previous calls Any player may, when it is her turn to bid, ask to have the bidding reviewed. She should ask for this information only for her own benefit; she should not ask for it in order to call partner's attention to some part of the previous bidding.

Final bid and the declarer When a bid, double, or redouble is followed by three consecutive passes, the auction is closed. The final bid in the auction becomes the *contract*. The player who, for his side, first bid the suit or no-trump named as the final contract becomes the *declarer*. If the contract names a suit, every card of that suit becomes a trump. The declarer's partner becomes the *dummy*, and the other two players, the *defenders*.

PLAY

Leads and plays A play consists of taking a card from one's hand and placing it, face up, in the center of the table. Four cards so played, one taken from each hand in clockwise rotation, constitute a *trick*. The first card played to a trick is called the *lead*.

The leader to a trick may lead any card. The other three players must follow suit if they can, but if any are unable to follow suit, they may play any card they wish from those remaining in their hand.

Opening lead; facing the dummy The defender on the declarer's left makes the first lead. Dummy then spreads his hand face up, with the cards separated into suits. The trump suit is placed at the dummy's right.

Winning of tricks A trick containing a trump is won by the hand playing the highest trump. A trick which does not contain a trump is won by the hand playing the highest card of the suit led. After the opening lead has been made, the winner of a trick leads to the next trick.

Dummy Declarer plays both her and the dummy's cards, but each in proper turn. Dummy may reply to a proper question, but may not comment or take an active part in the play, except to call attention to an irregularity, and may warn the declarer (or any other player) against infringing a law of the game. For example, dummy may say, "It's not your lead," or ask, "No spades?" when a player fails to follow suit to a spade lead.

Played card Declarer has officially played a card when he removes it from his hand and places it, face up, on the table or when he names the card as the one he intends to play. A card is considered played from dummy when declarer touches it (except to rearrange dummy's cards) or names it. A defender has played a card when it is exposed, with apparent intention to play it, so that partner can see its face. A card, once played, cannot be withdrawn except to correct a revoke or other irregularity.

Taking in tricks won A completed trick is gathered and turned, face down, on the table. A trick is then said to be quitted. Declarer and the partner of the defender winning the first trick should keep in front of him all the tricks won by his side, so arranged that it is apparent how many tricks the side has won and the order in which they were won.

Claim or concession of tricks by the declarer If a declarer claims or concedes one or more of the remaining tricks, or otherwise suggests that play be curtailed, play should cease and the declarer, with his or her hand face up on the table, should indicate the intended line of play. If both defenders concede, play ceases and the declarer is considered to have won the tricks claimed.

If a player disputes declarer's claim, declarer must play on, adhering to any statement made as to the intended line of play. Declarer may not, in the absence of such a statement, make any play the success of which depends upon finding one of the defenders with any particular card. A defender may face his or her hand and may suggest a line of defense to partner.

Claim or concession of tricks by a defender To claim or concede any part of the remaining tricks, a defender should show his hand, or part of it, to the declarer. A defender's concession is not valid unless his partner also concedes.

Trick conceded in error The concession of a trick which cannot be lost by any play of the cards is void.

Inspecting tricks during the play Declarer or either defender may, until his side has led or played to the next trick, inspect a quitted trick and inquire which hand contributed any card to it.

SCORING

When the last (13th) trick has been played, the tricks taken by each side are counted and agreed upon. (See Scoring Table on page 29 for point values.) The points earned by each side are not entered on the score sheet.

Any or all of the players may keep score. When there is only one scorekeeper, all players are responsible to see that he or she makes the entries properly.

Each side has both a premium and a trick score. The scorekeeper draws a vertical line to keep his score separate from that of the opponents. He also draws a horizontal line to keep the point score and the premium score separate.

Trick score If declarer made her contract, the trick-point value of the odd tricks that she contracted for is added to the previous total of points, if any, on her side of the vertical line and *below* the horizontal line.

Premium score Odd tricks won by the declarer in excess of the contract are known as *overtricks* and are scored to the credit of that side in the premium column *above* the horizontal line. Premiums for honors held in one hand, for slams bid and made, for rubbers made, and for undertricks scored against the opponents are scored in the premium score column to the credit of the side earning them.

Undertricks When a declarer wins fewer odd tricks than contracted for, the opponents score in their premium score column the undertrick premium for each trick by which she fell short of her contract.

Slams   If a side bids and makes a contract of six-odd tricks (all but one trick), it receives the premium for a small slam; if the contract is for seven-odd tricks (all of the tricks), it receives the premium for a grand slam.

Vulnerable   A side which has won its first game toward a rubber becomes *vulnerable*. It is exposed to increased undertrick penalties if it fails to make a subsequent contract, but receives increased premiums as well for slams and for overtricks made in doubled or redoubled contracts.

Honors   When there is a trump suit, the A, K, Q, J, and 10 of that suit are *honors*. If a player holds four-trump honors in his hand, his side receives a 100-point premium whether he is the declarer, the dummy, or a defender; for five-trump honors in one hand or for all four aces in one hand at a no-trump contract, his side receives a 150-point premium.

Game   When a side has won a total of 100 or more in trick points below the line, whether or not these points are scored in one hand or more than one, it wins a game. Both sides then start the next game with a zero score.

Rubber   When a side has won two games, it wins a premium for the rubber—500 points if the other side has also won a game, 700 points if the other side has not won a game. The scores of the two sides are then totaled, including both trick points and premium points, and the side which has scored the most points wins the rubber. The players then either draw again for partners and seats or they may rotate.

Summary score   Usually, but not necessarily the difference in the totals for the two sides is computed and rounded to the nearest 100 points; 40 points or less being dropped and 50 points or more being changed to 100 points. Thus a net score of +740 is treated as +700 and a score of −660 as −700. Normally, individual summary scores are kept for each player.

Irregularities   See page 42 and the excerpt from "Proprieties" on page 47.

SCORING TABLE

TRICK SCORE

Scored below the line by declarer's side if contract is fulfilled.

For each trick over six bid and made	If trumps are			
	♣	◇	♡	♠
Undoubled	20	20	30	30
Doubled	40	40	60	60
Redoubled	80	80	120	120

	At a no-trump contract		
	Undbld	Dbld	Rdbld
For the first trick over six bid and made	40	80	160
For each addit'l trick over six bid and made	30	60	120

The first side to score 100 points below the line in one hand or more, wins a game When a game is won, both sides start without a trick score toward the next game First side to win two games wins the rubber

PREMIUM SCORE

Scored above the line by declarer's side

For winning the rubber, if opponents have no game	700
For winning the rubber, if opponents have one game	500
Unfinished rubber—for having won the only game	300
For having the only part-score in an unfinished game	50
For making any doubled or redoubled contract	50

SLAMS

For making a slam	Not Vul	Vul
Small slam (12 tricks) bid and made	500	750
Grand slam (all 13 tricks) bid and made	1000	1500

SCORING TABLE
(continued)

OVERTRICKS

For each overtrick (tricks made in excess of the contract)	Not Vul	Vul
	Trick Value	
Undoubled		
Doubled	100	200
Redoubled	200	400

HONORS

Scored above the line by either side·

For holding four of the five trump honors (A, K, Q, J, 10) in one hand	100
For holding all five trump honors (A, K, Q, J, 10) in one hand	150
For holding all four aces in one hand in a no-trump contract	150

UNDERTRICK PENALTIES

Tricks by which declarer fails to fulfill the contract, scored above the line by declarer's opponents.

	Not Vul		
	Undbld	Dbld	Redbld
For first undertrick	50	100	200
For each additional undertrick	50	200	400

	Vul		
For first undertrick	100	200	400
For each additional undertrick	100	300	600

STRATEGY

Of course, there is much more to Contract Bridge than a mere recital of the laws and rules! It should be obvious that one of the most important features of the game is accurate bidding.

Valuing the hand   Every player, upon picking up his hand, makes some rough estimate of its value. Using the point-count system popularized by Charles Goren, a player values his hand as follows:

Four points for each ace
Three points for each king
Two points for each queen
One point for each jack

(One point should be deducted when these honors are insufficiently guarded: blank K, Q, or J.)

There are 40 points in all. Usually the two partners together must hold 26 points to make a game, 33 points to make a small slam, and 37 points to make a grand slam.

For no-trump bidding, only high cards are counted. For opening suit-bids, a player adds the following points based on the distribution of his hand:

Three points for each void suit
Two points for each singleton
One point for each doubleton

After the first player was able by his bidding to accurately describe his hand to his partner, he must assume a supporting role and thereafter accept his partner's decision as to whether the partnership should try for part-score, game, or slam.

It is almost self-evident that you should:

1. Force to game and invite slam when your hand has sufficient strength to make slam a possibility if your partner holds slightly more than the minimum of the range of hands his bidding to date has indicated.
2. Bid game, or force to game, if your hand has sufficient strength to make game a probability under the assump-

tion that your partner holds the minimum of the range of hands that his bidding has indicated.

3. Invite game if your hand has sufficient strength to make game a probability if your partner holds slightly more than the minimum of the range of hands that his bidding has already shown.

4. Failing a hand strong enough for any of the above, keep the bidding open with a bid of a minimum nature if your hand has sufficient strength to indicate the possibility of game and if your partner holds the maximum of the range his bidding has already shown.

5. Sign off, or pass, as soon as it becomes evident that there is no game in the combined hands.

It is not the intention of this book to attempt to cover the broad aspects of bidding and play of the game of Contract Bridge. There are many excellent books on the market which are designed for this purpose.

CONVENTIONS

Although you are not permitted to tell your partner what cards you hold or, in fact, to give any specific information about your hand, over the years various conventions have been developed which assign a specific meaning to the bids when they are made in a certain situation. Here again, it would be impossible to cover all the existing conventions, but it is possible to cover the more important ones—those which should be understood even if not used by everybody. We shall try to cover these conventions; understanding them is essential to any good game of Contract Bridge.

Strong two-bids   This is one of the earliest of the bidding conventions. A player using it opens the bidding with a two-bid in any of the four suits, announcing to his partner (and, naturally, to the opponents) that he has a hand so strong that he insists that his partner (the responder) keep the bidding open until either game is reached or until the opponents enter the auction. This is a *business double* (a double made for the purposes of inflicting penalties for undertricks as differentiated from a takeout double; see below).

The question the opener is looking for the responder to answer is, "Have you any interest in slam?" The responder answers this question by bidding two no-trump with a poor hand (six points or less). Holding the equivalent of an ace and a king, responder makes the encouraging response of two in his longest suit or of three no-trump with flat distribution and sufficient high-card strength. Even when holding three or more trumps, responder should bid two no-trump before showing trump support if he does not have good side-card strength.

The forcing two-club bid The forcing two-club bid is used in conjunction with the weak two-bid. This artificial bid replaces the strong two-bid; the fact that all forcing suit bids are opened in clubs rather than mentioning a natural suit at the first opportunity is little real loss. Two clubs followed by two hearts (or three hearts, if necessary) is, for all practical purposes, equivalent to an opening two hearts. In addition to losing little, it has two real advantages, namely:

1. It releases the opening bids of two spades, two hearts, and two diamonds for weak two-bids. (See below.)
2. It makes the bidding of no-trump much more accurate by reducing the spread of each bid (except one no-trump) to two points.

Bid	High-card points
One no-trump	16–18
Two no-trump	21–22
Two clubs followed by two no-trump	23–24
Three no-trump	25–26
Two clubs followed by three no-trump, etc.	27–28

After partner has opened two clubs, responder, desiring to show a poor hand, bids two diamonds. This has an additional advantage in that it leaves the bid of two no-trump open for the strong hand rather than by the weak hand.

Weak two-bids The purposes of a weak two-bid are to accomplish the following:

1. Make it difficult for the opponents to find their best contract if they hold most of the missing strength.
2. Make it easy for your partner to compete if the strength is fairly evenly divided.
3. Make it easy for your side to find the final contract if your partner has a good hand.

Remember that a weak two-bid is essentially a preemptive bid. You should have sufficient playing tricks not to be set more than 500 points if your partner's hand is worthless and the opponents double. Also, the general rule for preemptive bidding is to bid as high as the number of playing tricks in your hand will support. You do not wish to be down more than two tricks vulnerable or three tricks not vulnerable if the opponents double and your partner has no assistance for you. However, if your partner has a good suit, he should bid it, since the higher you can bid, the greater your interference in the opponent's bidding. Do not open a weak two-bid if your hand will warrant a regular opening bid of one.

Game-forcing bids   In addition to strong forcing opening two-bids and opening two-club bids, the following bids are forcing to game or to a penalty double of an opponent's bid:

1. A double raise of partner's bid. Note that some players play this as a limit bid; check to see how your opponents use it.
2. A jump bid of one more than necessary in a new suit by either the opener or by the responder.
3. A cue-bid in the opponent's suit.

One-round forcing bids   The following bids are forcing for one round:

1. Any bid in a new suit by a responder who has not previously passed.
2. Any double of an opponent's bid at the one- or two-level. This double is usually for takeout and asks the doubler's partner to make a bid. This request should be complied with. The weaker the partner's hand the more urgent the need for him to bid, unless the intervening opponent has inserted a bid, thereby reopening the bidding for the doubler. The only excuse for a pass is

when you hold considerable strength in the opponent's suit and you wish to convert the takeout double into a penalty double. Do not pass a double of one in a suit unless you are prepared for your partner to lead a singleton trump. After all, passing a double of one in a suit is equivalent to your bidding one in that suit and passing the opponent's double.

Doubles of preemptive bids.   Doubles of preemptive bids are usually optional; that is, the doubler's partner may pass or bid depending upon the defensive and offensive qualities of his hand.

Special cases   The above situations cover most of the cases where you wish to force your partner to bid. There are, of course, special cases where you must be alert to forcing inferences. Suppose you have doubled your right-hand opponent's four-spade bid for penalty and your left-hand opponent makes an obvious rescue bid of five clubs. Your partner, who has been supporting your hearts strongly, passes. Clearly, she expects you either to double the five-club bid or to go on to five hearts; she is making what is known as a "forcing pass."

Stayman   In addition to those conventions which ask your partner to make one bid or more, there are conventions designed to elicit certain specific information. Experience has shown that it is better to play a hand in a four-four fit in the major than in no-trump. One of the most efficient ways of locating such combinations is the Stayman convention.

It consists of bidding two clubs in response to partner's opening bid of one no-trump. Some players also use it by bidding three clubs over an opening two no-trump. When first devised, it asked partner to respond two spades if he held a four-card spade suit; two hearts if he held a four-card heart suit but no four-card spade suit; two no-trump if he held the maximum count of 18 high-card points and did not hold any four-card major suit; otherwise to bid two diamonds. This has been modified to require the responder to bid spades with four spades, hearts with four hearts and fewer than four spades, and diamonds with no four-card major.

This has the very real advantage of allowing the responder to make the no-trump opener the declarer when responder holds a perfectly worthless hand, say a four-four-four-one distribution and a count of zero to three points in high cards with a singleton club. With such a worthless hand it would be fatal if the no-trump bidder should rebid two no-trump to show a count of 18! Responder is not at all interested in the 18-point count; all he wants is to get out of no-trump and into a suit in which the partnership has at least eight trumps.

An added benefit of this convention is that although it leaves the opener somewhat in the dark as to the strength of the responder's hand (he may be interested in slam, game, or merely getting out of no-trump), it also leaves the opponents completely in the dark. Until the responder rebids, the opponents have no idea who has the balance of power, and sometimes when they find out, it is too late.

This convention has many advantages and few, if any, disadvantages. Note, however, that it cannot, except with special partnership agreement, be used after an intervening bid or double by the opener's left-hand opponent.

Jacoby transfer This is another convention designed to permit the responder to make the no-trump opener the declarer in a major suit of the responder's choosing. It works very nicely in conjunction with the Stayman convention. It is simplicity itself in its operation. After an opening bid of one no-trump followed by an opponent's pass, a bid of two diamonds demands that the no-trump opener rebid two hearts. Similarly, a bid of two hearts demands that the no-trump bidder rebid two spades; no other rebids are permitted. Again, the responder makes no commitment as to the strength of his hand. If he rebids, it will be to invite or force to game or to invite or force to slam. If he passes, obviously, all he wants is to get out of no-trump and to have the no-trump opener become the declarer.

This ability to control the direction of partner's bidding after opener has made a strength-defining bid, such as one no-trump (or two no-trump, if the partnership has agreed to use the Jacoby transfer over an opening bid of two no-trump), without disclosing anything about the strength of responder's hand is a great advantage.

Texas transfer This convention is quite similar to the Jacoby transfer except that it operates at the four-level. If, after an opening bid of one no-trump by her partner, the responder bids four diamonds, she demands that her partner bid four hearts. Similarly, if the responder bids four hearts, she demands that the opener rebid four spades.

This convention may be used in conjunction with the Jacoby transfer if both partners have agreed to it. When so used it has the advantage of allowing the responder to force the no-trump bidder into a game contract in responder's long major suit and still prevent the opener from making any attempt toward slam. For example, one no-trump—pass— four hearts (Texas transfer)—pass—four spades—pass— pass—pass. Unless the opponents come into the auction, a very remote probability, your partner will not be able to make any try for slam regardless of how much she may want to. It follows that this convention must be used with care if it is to be an asset.

Other refinements open to you when you play both Jacoby transfer and Texas transfer are the following:

1. *One no-trump—pass—two diamonds (Jacoby transfer)—pass—two hearts—pass—three spades*, showing a good six-card heart suit and a singleton spade, with slam possibilities; or four diamonds, showing a good six-card heart suit and a singleton diamond, with slam possibilities. Note: Be sure to reach an agreement with your partner about whether a rebid of four clubs would show a singleton club or be a Gerber bid. (See page 39.)

2. *One no-trump—pass—two diamonds (Jacoby transfer)—pass—two hearts—pass—four hearts*, showing a good six-card heart suit with slam possibilities but no singleton.

3. *One no-trump—pass—four diamonds (Texas transfer)—pass four hearts—pass—pass*, showing a game-going hand but no interest in slam.

4. If you and your partner agree to use one no-trump—pass—two diamonds (Jacoby transfer)—pass—two hearts—pass—four clubs to indicate a good six-card heart suit, a singleton club, and slam possibilities, then the only way to ask for aces without any chance of confusion is to use the Texas transfer followed by four no-trump (Blackwood, see below); that is, *one no-trump—pass—four diamonds (Texas transfer)—pass—*

> *four hearts—pass—four no-trump* would be Black-wood.

Blackwood convention   This convention is the most popular slam-bidding device, and properly used, it is one which few players can afford not to adopt. It permits a player, by bidding four no-trump under the proper circumstances, to ask partner the question, "Partner, how many aces do you hold?" Partner replies according to the following schedule:

Response	Number of aces shown
Five Clubs	None
Five Diamonds	One
Five Hearts	Two
Five Spades	Three
Five Clubs	Four

Two questions immediately arise:

1. What are the "proper circumstances" under which the bid of four no-trump is Blackwood?
   (a) *Has no-trump been bid previously?* If so, the bid of four no-trump is a normal raise in no-trump asking partner to bid six no-trump if he holds better than a minimum hand for his previous bidding.
   (b) *Is this the first no-trump bid?* If so, it is probably the first part of the Blackwood convention; it surely is if the bidder has jumped past three no-trump.
2. How does the four no-trump bidder tell whether his partner has zero or four aces? The answer to this lies in the partner's previous bidding; it must show whether he has a hand with no aces or one with four aces. Why introduce even this little chance for confusion? The answer lies in the fact that it is very convenient, under admittedly rare conditions, to be able to use the bid of five no-trump for the following convention.

The Blackwood five no-trump convention   Here the Blackwood five no-trump bidder is asking, "Partner, how many kings do you have?"

Response	Number of kings shown
Six Clubs	None
Six Diamonds	One
Six Hearts	Two
Six Spades	Three
Six no-trump	Four

When should this bid be used? Clearly, not unless you have a real interest in bidding seven if your partner has the necessary number of kings. Be certain you do not use it when your agreed suit is, say, diamonds, and you need three kings in your partner's hand to make a grand slam; he may have two kings and reply six hearts and you are out on a limb.

Secondly, never bid Blackwood five no-trump unless you are certain that your side holds all of the aces.

The Gerber convention The Gerber convention is similar to Blackwood except that it uses the bid of four clubs to ask for aces in accordance with the following schedule:

Response	Number of aces shown
Four Diamonds	Zero
Four Hearts	One
Four Spades	Two
Four no-trump	Three
Four Diamonds	Four

The same questions arise here as in Blackwood.

1. When is four clubs Gerber? There is no consensus as to the answer to this question. Almost all players who use Gerber agree that, under conditions when four no-trump would not be Blackwood, four clubs is Gerber; that is, after the partnership has made a no-trump bid. In addition some play Gerber "when obvious"; that is,

they play when clubs have not been bid previously as a suit, and either there is an agreed suit or the bid of four clubs is a jump bid.

2. The answer to how do you tell zero from four aces is the same as in Blackwood—the previous bidding should make it quite clear.

The king-asking Gerber convention   Originally the king-asking Gerber convention required the four-club bidder to make the lowest possible bid available to him over partner's response. Partner replies to indicate the number of kings to go on from there. For example, one spade—pass—three spades—pass—four clubs (Gerber, ace-asking)—pass—four hearts (one ace)—pass—four spades (lowest possible bid, king-asking)—pass—five diamonds (two kings).

Because this sometimes caused confusion, some players have adopted the five-club bid as the king-asking Gerber bid, just as the five no-trump is the king-asking Blackwood bid. Here is how this convention would change the bidding sequence in the previous example: One spade—pass—three spades—pass—four clubs (Gerber, ace-asking)—pass—four hearts (one ace)—pass—five clubs (Gerber, king-asking)—pass—five spades (two kings).

Note that the king-asking Gerber bid does not guarantee that the partnership holds four aces. There are conditions, particularly when spades are the agreed suit, under which it is convenient for the Gerber bidder to ask for kings before deciding whether or not to bid a small slam.

Cue-bidding to suggest a slam   Neither Blackwood nor Gerber is of much help when you hold a worthless doubleton in an unbid suit or when the answer to the question will not surely help you in picking the final contract. Under these conditions, it will probably be of value to use a cue-bid. Space does not permit a proper discussion of the merits of cue-bidding as opposed to those of Gerber. Suffice it to say that I, personally, do not usually employ the Gerber convention. I prefer the normal meaning to the bid of four clubs.

Refinements to the Blackwood convention   There are several refinements to the Blackwood convention which you should know about even though you may not wish to use them yourself. The firm rule of the Blackwood convention is that the player who asks the question is the captain of the team. Because the captain of the team will know the count of the aces but his partner will not, it is the captain who will place the final contract. There are two situations under which this rule may be disobeyed:

1. Let us say that you hold a void and wish to bid a gambling small slam. If your normal response would be, say, five hearts, showing two aces, bid six hearts showing two aces and a void. This jump response should be made only when the responder is afraid that his normal response of five hearts could be passed; that is, when his normal response happens to be in the agreed trump suit. Otherwise, he can afford to make his normal response at the five-level, confident that he will have one more opportunity to decide whether or not to show his void after he hears one more bid from his partner.

2. After his partner has bid five no-trump, asking for kings, he knows that the partnership holds all four aces and that his partner believes that he can make seven if he holds enough kings. However, if the responder holds the king of trumps, clearly one of the vital kings, plus a long solid side-suit upon which the declarer can discard any losers in the other two suits, he then must take the initiative and bid seven!

The effect of a cue-bid   If a player makes a cue bid and later makes a Blackwood four no-trump bid, she is asking her partner not to count any ace she may hold in the cue-bid suit in making her reply. For example:

South	West	North	East
One club	One spade	Two hearts	Pass
Two spades	Pass	Three clubs	Pass
Four-no trump	Pass		

Here it is clear that South is interested only in aces other than spades; she wishes her partner to base her reply on how many aces she holds other than the ace of spades. The

Blackwood bidder may hold a hand such as: ♡K, ♡Q, ♡7, ♡3, ◇K, ◇Q, ◇5, ♣A, ♣K, ♣J, ♣9, ♣6, ♣4

Playing at five no-trump　Although the situation does not often arise at rubber bridge, at duplicate bridge, where five no-trump will probably bring in a top score and five hearts an average score, the question arises, "How does the four no-trump bidder get to play five no-trump when his partner's response is an ace short of what he had hoped for?" The answer is usually quite simple. The four no-trump bidder (who cannot bid five no-trump himself—that would be asking for kings) bids any previously unbid suit at the level of five; this bid demands that the responder bid five no-trump, which becomes the final contract.

IRREGULARITIES IN CONTRACT BRIDGE

This digest of the most frequently invoked laws of Contract Bridge (Copyright © 1981 by the American Contract Bridge League) has been prepared with the valued assistance of Edgar Kaplan, co-chairman of the National Laws Commission. The most important changes—the first since 1963—involve the penalties for revokes; for cards exposed (penalty cards) before, during, or after the auction, whether inadvertently or through error; for calls out of turn; and for leads out of turn. For the complete laws, see the *Laws of Contract Bridge*, published by the ACBL, copies of which may be obtained at your local bookseller, or by writing the ACBL, 2200 Democrat Road, Memphis, TN 38116.

Prior to the bidding
NEW SHUFFLE AND CUT　Before the first cut is dealt, any player may demand a new shuffle and cut. There must be a new shuffle and cut if a card is faced in shuffling or cutting.

DEAL OUT OF TURN　The correct dealer may reclaim the deal before the last card is dealt; thereafter, the deal stands as though it had been in turn and the correct dealer loses his right to deal in that round.

REDEAL　There must be a redeal if the cards are not dealt correctly; if the pack is incorrect; if a card is faced in the pack or elsewhere; if a player picks up the wrong hand and looks at it; or if at any time during the play one hand is found to have too many cards and another too few (and the discrepancy is not caused by errors in play). When there is a redeal, the same dealer deals (unless the deal was out of turn) and with the same pack, after a new shuffle and cut.

INCORRECT HAND   If a player has too few cards and the missing card is found (except in a previous trick), it is considered to have been in the short hand throughout. If it cannot be found, there is a redeal. If it is found in a previous trick, see *Defective Trick* on page 50).

During the bidding

WAIVER OF PENALTY   When a player calls or plays over an illegal call or play by his right-hand opponent, he accepts the illegal call or play and waives a penalty. The game continues as though no irregularity had occurred. However:

RETENTION OF THE RIGHT TO CALL   A player cannot lose his only chance to call by the fact that an illegal pass by his partner has been accepted by an opponent. The auction must continue until the player has had at least one chance to call.

BARRED PLAYER   A player who is barred once, or for one round, must pass the next time it is his turn to bid; a player who is barred throughout must pass in every turn until the auction of the current deal is completed.

CHANGE OF CALL   A player may change an inadvertent call without penalty if he does so without pause for thought. Any other attempted change of call is canceled. If the first call was an illegal call, it is subject to the applicable law; if it was a legal call, the offender may either:

1. Allow his first call to stand, whereupon his partner must pass at his next turn; or
2. Substitute any legal call (including a pass, double, or redouble) whereupon his partner must pass at every subsequent turn.

INSUFFICIENT BID   If a player makes an insufficient bid, he must substitute either a sufficient bid or a pass (not a double or redouble). If he substitutes:

1. The lowest sufficient bid in the same denomination, there is no penalty.

2. Any other bid, his partner must pass at every subsequent turn.

3. A pass, his partner must pass at every subsequent turn, and declarer (if an opponent) may impose a lead penalty. A double or redouble illegally substituted is penalized the same as a pass and is treated as a pass.

The offender need not select his final call until the law has been stated; previous attempts at correction are canceled.

INFORMATION GIVEN BY CHANGE OF CALL   In the case of an illegal call which has been canceled, if an opponent becomes declarer, the illegal call may be subject to the special lead penalty described hereafter.

A CALL OUT OF ROTATION ("out of turn")   may be accepted by the player next to call. If it is not accepted, the illegal call is canceled and the auction reverts to the player whose turn it was. Rectification and penalty depend on whether it was a pass, a bid, or a double or redouble, as follows:

A call is not out of rotation if made without waiting for the right-hand opponent to pass, if that opponent is legally obliged to pass; nor if it would have been in rotation had not the left-hand opponent called out of rotation. A call made simultaneously with another player's call in rotation is deemed to be subsequent to it.

PASS OUT OF TURN   If it occurs before any player has bid, or when it was the turn of the offender's right-hand opponent, the offender must pass when his regular turn comes. If it occurs after there has been a bid and when it was the turn of the offender's partner, the offender is barred throughout; the offender's partner may not double or redouble at that turn; and if the offender's partner passes and the opponents play the hand, declarer may impose a lead penalty.

CALL OUT OF TURN   Any player may call attention to such a call, but the player to offender's left may accept it, in which case the auction continues without penalty. If it is not accepted, the following penalties apply:

1. If the illegal case was a pass:
   (a) When it was the turn of the right-hand opponent, or before any player has bid, offender must pass at his first opportunity.

(b) If any player has already bid, and it is the turn of the offender's partner, the partner may pass, bid a suit or no-trump, but may not double or redouble. Offender is then barred for the balance of the auction.

2. If it was an illegal bid of a suit or no-trump:

(a) At partner's turn or at the turn of the dealer at offender's left, the illegal bid is canceled but partner must pass throughout. Should an opponent become declarer, lead penalties may apply.

(b) At the right hand opponent's turn and:

    (i) Opponent passes, the bid out of turn stands and there is no penalty. (An insufficient bid must be corrected.)

    (ii) Opponent makes any call other than a pass and offender then bids a sufficient number of the same suit, offender's partner must pass at his next turn. If offender substitutes any other bid, his partner must pass throughout. (Lead penalties may apply.)

Double or redouble out of turn:

1. When it was partner's turn to bid, offender's partner is barred (must pass) throughout the action. Offender may not double or redouble the same bid which he illegally doubled or redoubled. (Lead penalty may apply.)

2. When it was the turn of offender's right-hand opponent, if that opponent passes, the double or redouble may be repeated without penalty.

3. When it was the turn of offender's left-hand opponent, who then makes any call except a pass, offender may make any legal call but offender's partner must pass at his next turn. (Lead penalty may apply.)

IMPOSSIBLE DOUBLES AND REDOUBLES   If a player doubles or redoubles a bid that his side has already doubled or redoubled, his call is canceled; he must substitute any legal call, in which case his partner is barred throughout and if he becomes the opening leader, declarer may prohibit the lead of the doubled suit; or a pass, in which case either opponent may cancel all previous doubles and redoubles, the offender's partner is barred throughout, and if he becomes the opening leader, he is subject to a lead penalty.

If a player doubles his partner's bid, redoubles an un-doubled bid, or doubles or redoubles when there has been no bid, he must substitute any proper call, and his partner is barred once.

OTHER INADMISSIBLE CALLS　If a player bids more than seven, or makes another call when legally required to pass, he is deemed to have passed and the offending side must pass at every subsequent turn; if they become the defenders, declarer may impose a lead penalty on the opening leader.

CALL AFTER THE AUCTION IS CLOSED　A call made after the auction is closed is canceled. If it is a pass by a defender, or any call by declarer or dummy, there is no penalty. If it is a bid, double, or redouble by a defender, declarer may impose a lead penalty at the offender's partner's first turn to lead.

A CARD EXPOSED DURING THE AUCTION　becomes a penalty card (primary—an honor; or secondary—a spot card, as defined in the penalty card law). In addition, the partner of the player with a primary penalty card must pass at his next turn to bid.

REVIEW OF THE BIDDING　may be requested:

1. When it is a player's turn to bid. (The review should be given by an opponent, but if erroneous, it may be corrected by any player.)
2. After the final pass, by any player (except dummy) *at his turn to play to the first trick.*
3. Any player may ask to have a call repeated if it is not heard distinctly.

Play

DUMMY'S RIGHTS　Dummy may give or obtain information regarding fact or law, ask if a play constitutes a revoke, warn any player against infringing a law, and, only when the play is over, may draw attention to an irregularity. Dummy forfeits these rights if he looks at a card in another player's hand.

If dummy has forfeited his rights, and thereafter is the first to draw attention to a defender's irregularity, declarer may not enforce any penalty for the offense; and thereafter warns declarer not to lead from the wrong hand, either defender may choose the hand from which declarer shall lead; and thereafter is the first to ask declarer if a play from declarer's hand is a revoke, declarer must correct a revoke if able, but the revoke penalty still applies.

REVOKE   A revoke is the act of playing a card of another suit, when able to follow suit to a lead. Any player, including dummy, may ask whether a play constitutes a revoke and may demand that an opponent correct a revoke. A claim of revoke does not warrant inspection of turned tricks, prior to the end of play, except by consent of both sides.

CORRECTING A REVOKE   A player must correct his revoke if aware of it before it becomes established. A revoke card withdrawn by a defender becomes a penalty card. The non-offending side may withdraw any cards played after the revoke but before attention was drawn to it.

ESTABLISHED REVOKE   A revoke becomes established when a member of the offending side leads or plays to a subsequent trick (or terminates play by a claim or concession). When a revoke becomes established, the revoke trick stands as played (unless it is the twelfth trick).

REVOKE PENALTY   The penalty for an established revoke is one trick (if available), in addition to the trick on which the revoke occurred if won by the revoking side, transferred at the end of play from the revoking side to the opponents. This penalty can be paid only from tricks won by the revoking side after its first revoke, including the revoke trick. If no trick is available, there is no penalty. (But see excerpt from "Proprieties" below.)[3]

---

[3] The laws cannot cover every situation that might arise, nor can they produce equity in every situation covered. Occasionally, the players themselves must redress damage. The guiding principle: The side that commits an irregularity bears an obligation not to gain directly from the infraction itself. For example: South, declarer at three no-trump, will have nine tricks available if the diamond suit—ace-king-queen-sixth in dummy opposite declarer's singleton—divides favorably. The six missing diamonds are in fact split evenly, three-three, between East and West. However, West, who holds jack-third, shows out on the third round of diamonds, revoking. Thus, declarer wins only three diamond tricks instead of six, for a total of six tricks instead of nine. The established revoke is later discovered, so one penalty trick is transferred after play ends. But declarer is still down two. Here, East-West gained two tricks as a direct consequence of their infraction. The players should adjudicate this result, scoring the

REVOKES NOT SUBJECT TO PENALTY   A revoke made in the twelfth trick must be corrected, without penalty, if discovered before the cards have been mixed together. The nonoffending side may require the offender's partner to play either of two cards he could legally have played. A revoke not discovered until the cards have been mixed is not subject to penalty, nor is a revoke by any faced hand (dummy, or a defender's hand when faced in consequence of a claim by declarer). A revoke by failure to play a penalty card is not subject to the penalty for an established revoke.

LEAD OUT OF TURN   Defenders may accept declarer's lead out of the wrong hand, or request declarer to lead from the correct hand (if he can) a card of the same suit. If it was a defender's turn to lead, or if there is no card of that suit in the correct hand, there is no penalty.

If a defender is required to retract a lead out of turn, declarer may either treat the card so led as a penalty card, or impose a lead penalty on the offender's partner when next he is to lead after the offense.

LEAD   If a defender leads out of turn, declarer may accept the lead, treat the card led as a penalty card, require the lead of that suit from the proper leader, or forbid him to lead that suit for as long as he holds the lead at that turn.

PREMATURE PLAY   If a defender leads to the next trick before his partner has played to the current trick, or plays out of rotation before his partner has played, declarer may require the offender's partner to play his highest card of the suit led, his lowest card of the suit led, or a card of another specified suit. Declarer must select one of these options, and

---

deal as three no-trump making three. (Note: Declarer is not given a penalty trick in addition; the object is to restore equity, to restore the result likely to have occurred had the infraction not been committed.)

There is no penalty for a subsequent established revoke in the same suit by the same player.

A transferred trick ranks for all scoring purposes as a trick won in play by the side receiving it. It never affects the contract.

(For example, if the contract is three hearts and declarer wins nine tricks plus one trick as a revoke penalty, total 10 tricks, he can score only 90 points below the line and the other 30 points go above the line.)

if the defender cannot comply, he may play any legal card. When declarer has played from both his hand and dummy, a defender is not subject to penalty for playing before his partner.

EXPOSED CARDS   Declarer is never subject to penalty for exposure of a card, but intentional exposure of declarer's hand is treated as a claim or concession of tricks.

A defender's card is exposed if it is faced on the table or held so that the other defender may see its face before he is entitled to do so. Such a card must be left face up on the table until played and becomes a penalty card.

PENALTY CARD   In the case of a card prematurely or illegally exposed there are now two types of penalty card:

1. If the card is one of "secondary significance," i.e., a card below honor rank, that is inadvertently exposed, the offending player may substitute an honor card of that suit (or any legal card in another suit), but may not play any other card below honor rank in this suit until the penalty card has been played.

2. If the card is one of "primary significance," i.e., an honor card not inadvertently exposed by a defender during the bidding or play, it must be played at the first legal opportunity. When offender's partner first obtains or holds the lead, declarer may demand or prohibit the lead of that suit, in which event the penalty card may be picked up and the offender may choose to play any card in the suit led. If declarer does not impose a lead penalty, the exposed card remains as a primary penalty card. (Note that under the revised laws declarer may no longer call for the lead of any other specified suit.)

SPECIAL PENALTY   A lead penalty incurred in the bidding: If the offender's illegal call was other than in a suit (i.e., a bid of no-trump or a double or redouble), the declarer may bar the lead of a specified suit. (But he may NOT call for the lead of a particular suit.)

TWO OR MORE PENALTY CARDS   If a defender has two or more penalty cards that he can legally play, declarer may designate which one is to be played.

FAILURE TO PLAY A PENALTY CARD   Not subject to penalty, but declarer may require the penalty card to be played, and any defender's card exposed in the process becomes a penalty card.

INABILITY TO PLAY AS REQUIRED   If a player is unable to lead or play as required to comply with a penalty (for lack of a card of a required suit, or because of the prior obligation to follow suit), he may play any card. The penalty is deemed satisfied, except in the case of a penalty card.

DEFECTIVE TRICK   A trick containing more or fewer than four cards. When one player is found to have more or fewer cards than the other players, the previous tricks should be examined, face down. If a defective trick is discovered, the player with a correspondingly incorrect hand is held responsible. The defective trick is then inspected.

Unless all four hands have played to a subsequent trick, the defective trick is rectified thus: If offender has failed to play a card, he adds to that trick any card he can legally play; if he has played more than one card to that trick, he withdraws all but one card, leaving one which he can legally play. After all four hands have played to a subsequent trick, the defective trick is considered won by the nonoffending side, but the offender either adds a card he could legally have played or the offender leaves the highest card he could legally have played and withdraws the other, which may be considered a penalty card and may constitute a revoke if he could have played it to a subsequent trick but did not.

DECLARER CLAIMING OR CONCEDING TRICKS   If declarer claims or concedes one or more of the remaining tricks (verbally or by spreading his hand), he must leave his hand face up on the table and immediately state his intended plan of play.

If a defender disputes declarer's claim, declarer must play on, adhering to any statement he has made, and in the absence of a specific statement he may not "exercise freedom of choice in making any play the success of which depends on finding either opponent with or without a particular unplayed card."

After curtailment of play by declarer, it is permissible for a defender to expose his hand and to suggest a play to his partner.

DEFENDER CLAIMING OR CONCEDING TRICKS   A defender may show any or all of his cards to declarer to establish a claim or concession. He may not expose his hand to his partner, and if he does, declarer may treat his partner's cards as penalty cards.

CORRECTING THE SCORE   A proved or admitted error in any score may be corrected at any time before the rubber score is agreed, except as follows: An error made in entering or failing to enter a part-score, or in omitting a game or in awarding one, may not be corrected after the last card of the second succeeding correct deal has been dealt (unless a majority of the players consent).

EFFECT OF INCORRECT PACK   Scores made as a result of hands played with an incorrect pack are not affected by the discovery of the imperfection after the cards have been mixed together.

Miscellaneous

OPENING LEAD OUT OF TURN   When the error occurs because of misinformation from an opponent, there is no penalty.

If, after an opening lead out of turn, declarer exposes one or more of his cards as if he were dummy, partner then becomes declarer.

Declarer may accept an incorrect lead by playing a card or, if he accepts it verbally, he may see dummy before playing from his own hand.

SIMULTANEOUS LEADS

1. By defender:
   (a) If only one card of two is visible, it is played.
   (b) If two or more cards are exposed, the offender may name which one is played, but the other card so exposed becomes a penalty card.
2. By declarer: He designates which card is played; the other card is returned to the proper hand.

♣   ◇   ♡   ♠

TWO-HAND BRIDGE

GENERAL

There are about as many forms of two-hand bridge as there are bridge players! About the only point on which all two-hand bridge players agree is the rank of the cards!

BASIC TWO-HAND BRIDGE

The dealer deals out all 52 cards in four piles of 13 cards each, all face down. Then he turns the last card dealt face up, as in whist, to determine the trump suit.

His opponent meanwhile has looked at all 26 cards in the first and third hands dealt. Play now starts with a lead by the hand to the left of the dealer. Meanwhile the dealer has looked at the 13 cards in the hand opposite him and plays one of them. The dealer's opponent now plays from the third hand and the dealer from his own hand.

The high card of the suit led wins the trick unless some player is out of that suit and chooses to trump it. Play continues with the winner of each trick leading to the next trick.

Variation In many two-hand games there is never any trump suit. In other words, all hands are played in no-trump.

BIDDING

Most two-hand games are played without bidding. You score one for every trick over six tricks. When there is bidding, it follows standard four-hand bridge, as does the scoring.

STRATEGY

This is a tough game. You should tend to play your long suit, but if you have a bad hand, you should try to find a way to collect as many tricks as you can right away.

OTHER FORMS OF TWO-HAND BRIDGE

In almost all variations all 52 cards are dealt. Here is a game I learned when I was eight years old. The dealer deals himself and his opponent 13 cards each. The remaining 26 cards become the stockpile with the top card turned face up.

The nondealer leads a card. The dealer must follow suit if he can. High card of the suit led wins the trick, which has no value at all except that the winner must take the face-up card from the top of the stockpile and place it in his hand. His opponent must take the next card and place it in his hand. The next card on top of the stockpile is then turned face up. Play continues in this fashion, with the winner of the last trick leading to the next one, until all cards in the stockpile are exhausted. Bidding now starts with the winner of the last trick bidding first. Bidding follows the rules of four-hand Contract Bridge. In the play of the first 13 cards, if you have a good hand, you play to build up your good suit and high side-cards, and with a poor hand, you tend to lead your opponent's suit.

Gamblers have developed a lot of exciting two-hand games. Here is an example. The cards are dealt as in four-hand bridge. Thus each player controls 26 cards. The first 13 are his hand; the remaining 13 are his reserve pile and are used to improve his hand. Each player plays as rapidly as he can, taking a card from the reserve pile and discarding one from his hand, face down, in front of himself until all the 13 cards in the reserve pile are used up. Once a card is placed in the discard pile, it is irrevocable—you cannot change your mind!

BIDDING

The bidding proceeds as in four-hand bridge.

PLAY

Your play is based upon how you discarded. You might end up with a sure grand slam in diamonds or clubs only to find that your opponent has a grand slam in a major suit! There can be considerable jockeying in the bidding. Thus you can open seven clubs as if you had discarded for a good hand, and instead you hope that your opponent will bid seven hearts or spades, which you will kill because you have protected yourself in the majors by your discards.

♣   ◇   ♡   ♠

THREE-HAND BRIDGE

Strangely enough, three-hand bridge is usually played by four players. The players cut for seats—high card is the dealer, second high sits to the dealer's left, third high chooses one of the other two seats, and fourth high takes the remaining seat.

Cards are dealt as in regular bridge—the fourth hand becomes the dummy. The dummy has no interest in that hand.

After the first hand is completed, the deal rotates counterclockwise and the hand opposite the last dealer becomes the dummy. This process is repeated after each hand is completed.

BIDDING

The dummy is face down during the bidding. The dealer must bid at least two no-trump. She cannot pass. Second hand can pass, double, or bid at least three no-trump. The bidding then continues as in four-hand contract bridge, the third hand having all options open to her.

PLAY

Unless the dummy is already opposite the declarer, it is moved there before play begins. Play is the same as in Contract Bridge. Declarer plays dummy's hand. Dummy cannot revoke.

SCORING

The scoring is the same as in Contract Bridge, except if declarer is set. In this case each opponent scores the full penalty. This looks unfair, but if the declarer makes her contract, she collects from both opponents.

STRATEGY

Strategy is most concerned with the first two bids. If dealer has a good hand, she opens with a game bid. She does not want to play two no-trump undoubled. If second hand has a good hand, she doubles or bids game. If two no-trump is passed around to the third hand, she bids as second hand would have bid with the same cards.

Variation 1 In some localities if two no-trump is passed out, the hand is thrown in and the deal rotates.

Variation 2 Of course, the above game could have been played with only three players, with the fourth hand being dealt to the right of the dealer.

♣   ◊   ♡   ♠

TOWIE

This three-hand game was invented by the late Leonard Replogle about 1920. The word towie stands for 1000, which was a frequent penalty. The deal is the same as in regular three-hand Contract Bridge, except that, when the deal is completed, the dealer turns five of the dummy's cards face up.

BIDDING

Dealer must open with at least two no-trump; the rest of the bidding is normal. Naturally, with five of the cards face up, there is room to speculate on the other eight. With five bad cards faced up, the chances are that the unfortunate player forced to bid two no-trump will be really hurt.

The real interest in the bidding is when good cards are faced up in the dummy. Thus, with three aces faced up, the bidding might go three no-trump, four no-trump. If four or five spades or hearts are faced up, the bidding might go four hearts, six hearts.

We have devoted this space to Towie for nostalgic reasons. I just loved this game.

AUCTION BRIDGE

Auction Bridge follows the same rules as Contract Bridge except in the scoring. There is one big difference (other than the values assigned to tricks and bonuses), namely, when a bid is made in Contract Bridge, only the amount of the bid is scored "below the line." On the other hand, when a bid is made in Auction Bridge, all the tricks won in play (and not merely those bid for) contribute toward points below the line and thus toward winning the game.

Auction Bridge scoring is as follows:

TRICKS

As mentioned above, if declarer's side makes its contract, it scores all odd tricks won below the line.

AUCTION BRIDGE TRICK SCORE

	Trick Value per Odd Trick		
Declaration	Undoubled	Doubled	Redoubled
Clubs	6	12	24
Diamonds	7	14	28
Hearts	8	16	32
Spades	9	18	36
No-trump	10	20	40

The side that first accumulates 30 points below the line wins the game. Another horizontal line is then drawn on the score sheet to indicate that a game has been won. Both sides start the new game with an accumulated score of zero. The side that first wins two out of three games wins a rubber bonus of 250 points.

BONUSES

If a side wins a doubled contract, it scores, above the line, 50 points for making the contract plus 50 additional points for each overtrick. If a redoubled contract is made, these bonuses are raised to 100 points each. These bonuses are in addition to the score for odd tricks but do not count toward game.

UNDERTRICKS

If a side fails to make its contract, that side scores nothing for tricks and the defenders' side scores above the line for each undertrick. An undoubled contract scores 50 points, a doubled contract 100 points, and a redoubled contract 200 points.

SLAMS

If either side makes 12 tricks—a little slam—it scores 50 points above the line. If either side wins all the tricks—a grand slam—it scores 100 points above the line. These bonuses are independent of the contract and whether or not it was fulfilled.

HONORS

At a suit declaration, the honors are A, K, Q, J, and 10 of the suit bid. At no-trump, the honors are the four aces. The side to whom three or more honors were dealt (regardless of which side was the declarer) scores the following values above the line:

HONORS

Combination	Premium Value
Three honors	30
Four trump honors, divided	40
Five trump honors, divided	50
Four trump honors in one hand	80
All trump honors, divided 4-1	90
Four aces in one hand	100
All five trump honors in one hand	100

♣ ◇ ♡ ♠

DUPLICATE BRIDGE

Duplicate Bridge is the only form of Contract Bridge played in tournaments, but it is equally adapted to play in homes or clubs. The laws of the game differ little from the official laws of Contract Bridge. Such differences mostly pertain to destroying the way the cards are dealt (each hand has to be played repeatedly) and pertain to etiquette and irregularities.

♣ ◇ ♡ ♠

PROGRESSIVE CONTRACT BRIDGE

When a bridge party is given for 16 or more guests, especially when it is a mixed party, the best game is Progressive Contract Bridge.

The hostess prepares in advance two sets of tally cards (a combination of score sheets and seating arrangements), one for each group of guests (usually one for the men and one for the women). Usually the two sets differ in color to assist her in passing them out to the guests prior to the start of the game. The hostess announces the scoring and any special rules regarding progression.

The card tables are all numbered, and when the hostess is ready, she asks all guests to go to their assigned seats. There will be one player in each group assigned to table 2, couple 1. These two players play as partners for the first round.

The players cut for deal. One player (North) remains seated at each table. The other players pivot around him or her after each round is played. Nonstationary players then move to the next table in accordance with the progression usually shown on the tally card. The scoring is almost always the same as in regular Contract Bridge, except that there are no rubber bonuses; when a player makes her contract, she adds one of the following bonuses to her trick score:

50 points for a part-score;
300 points for a nonvulnerable game scored on just one deal;
500 points for a vulnerable game scored on just one deal.

Four hands are played on each round: on the first hand neither side is vulnerable; on the second and third hand the dealer's side is vulnerable; finally, on the fourth hand, both sides are vulnerable.

♣   ◇   ♡   ♠

PROGRESSIVE AUCTION BRIDGE

In Progressive Auction Bridge, the Auction Bridge scoring schedule is followed, except that there is no bonus for rubber. Instead, each time a side scores a game on one deal, they also score a bonus of 125 points.

When the fourth hand is completed each player enters on her tally sheet the total of the points that her side has won on the four hands. At each table (other than table 1) the winning pair advances to the next lower-number table, where the two pairs shift partners before starting to play. As an exception to this general shift, at table 1 the winners stay and the losers go to the highest-number table to join the losers who are already there. Whether or not the players at table 1 shift partners depends on the rules made by the hostess.

Play continues for the number of rounds previously determined by the hostess. Then all players total the scores on their tally sheets. The hostess usually has prizes to give to the player with the best score, to one with the poorest score, to the guest of honor, etc.

♣   ◇   ♡   ♠

PROGRESSIVE RUBBER BRIDGE

This differs from Progressive Contract Bridge only in that six hands are played in each round with regular Contract Bridge scoring. After the sixth hand the play ceases, regardless of whether or not a rubber has been completed. There is a bonus of 300 points for having a game in an unfinished rubber and a bonus of 50 points for having a part-score in an unfinished game.

In some localities it is common procedure to place a limit on the maximum score that can be made on a single hand (except for slam bonuses) or even to prohibit doubling or redoubling altogether.

Cribbage

Like many other games, Cribbage is believed to be an improvement of an older game about which little is known. Sir John Suckling (1609–1642) is credited with having invented it.

Cribbage is an excellent two-hand game combining, as it does, a high degree of skill with a certain amount of chance in the deal.

PRELIMINARIES

Players Two players, although there are modifications which permit three or five players (playing independently) or four or six players (playing as pairs of partners) to play.

Cards The standard 52-card pack, with the cards ranking: K (highest), Q, J, 10, 9, 8, 7, 6, 5, 4, 3, 2, A (lowest). The king, queen, jack, and ten count ten, with the remaining cards counting the number of spots. Suits play little part in the game.

The cribbage board A special board, known as a *Cribbage board*, is used for scoring. This board (see Figure C-1) may vary from very crude unfinished pieces of wood to elaborate fine inlaid objects of precious woods, ivory, etc. Smaller boards have two rows of 30 holes for each player (requiring two round trips to complete the game), whereas larger boards have one row of 120 holes for each player. Most boards are designed for two players only, but boards for three and four players are available.

The draw For the first hand the players cut for the deal, the player cutting the lower card (ace low) winning the deal.

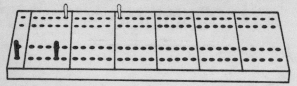

Figure C-1

The shuffle and cut Both players have the right to shuffle the cards, with the dealer having the right to shuffle last. The dealer must then offer the pack to his opponent for cutting. The cut must leave not less than four cards in either packet.

The deal The dealer deals six cards, one at a time, to each player.

The crib Each player, after looking at his cards, selects two and places them face down in a pile (known as the *crib*) which belongs to the dealer. The crib plays no part in the actual play of the hand.

The starter After the four cards forming the crib have been laid away, the nondealer cuts the remaining deck and the dealer turns the top card of the lower portion of the deck. This card is placed, face up, on the deck. It is called the *starter*. If it is a jack (called *His Nibs*) the dealer *pegs* (scores) two points. The starter takes no part in the play of the remaining four cards in each player's hand.

Pegging Each player has two pegs (usually those of each player differ in color). When a player makes his first score, he enters one of his pegs in the corresponding hole in the outer row of holes.[1] When he makes his second score, he enters his second peg in the hole which has the corresponding number of holes in front of his first peg. When he makes his third

---

[1] The pegging method described assumes use of a smaller board, requiring two trips to complete a game. Obviously, larger boards requiring only a single circuit are advantageous, particularly for beginners, who are apt to forget which way they are headed on the small boards and inadvertently peg backward!

score, he picks up his back peg and advances it the corresponding number of holes in front of the peg which had previously been in front. The front peg thus shows the total number of points scored by that player.

When he reaches the end of the outer row, he merely goes around the corner and comes back toward the starting point using the inner row. When he reaches the end of this row (having a score of 60 or more points), he goes around the corner and again advances along the outer row to the end, where he once more turns and comes back along the inner row.

The first player to reach a total of 121 points or more places his peg in the game hole. The game stops immediately with no more points being scored by either player. If at this time the loser has not passed the three-quarter point (that is, has scored less than 91 points), he is *skunked* or *lurched* and loses a double game. If the loser has not reached the halfway point (61 points), he loses a triple game.

PLAY

After the crib is formed and the starter cut, play begins. The players play their cards alternately, the nondealer playing first. As a player exposes her card, face up in front of herself, she announces the total of her card and those previously played, if any.

This process continues until the player whose turn it is to play has no card in her hand which she can play without exceeding a total of 31. In this case she says "go," and if her opponent also cannot play without exceeding a total of 31 points, the last player to have played a card scores one point; she scores two points if the sequence had ended at exactly 31 points.

However, if the total is less than 31 points, and the opponent holds any card or cards which she can play without exceeding the 31 limit, she must play them before she pegs the point for having played the last card (again she scores two points if the final total is exactly 31). In addition, she may peg any points to which she is entitled for pairs or sequences (see page 64). This is one condition under which a player plays two or more cards in succession.

The player who called "go" now starts a new series of plays, starting again from zero. This lead may not be combined with any cards previously played to form a scoring combination (see below), because the call "go" has interrupted the sequence of play. The player playing the last of the eight cards in the two hands pegs one point for the last card, two if it brings the count to exactly 31.

Scoring during the play Points may be scored during the play for the following combinations or sequences, in addition to those scored for "go."

Fifteen For playing a card that makes the total 15, peg two points.

Pair For playing a card of the same rank as the card previously played, peg two points. Note that face cards pair only by actual rank; that is, king with king but not king with queen, even though both cards count as ten.

Threes For playing (in proper sequence) the third card of the same rank, peg six points.

Double Pair For playing (in sequence) the fourth card of the same rank, peg 12 points.

Note that three or four cards of the same rank count only when played in sequence. For example, 7-7-7 would entitle the player of the second seven to peg two points (pair) and the player of the third seven to peg six points (threes). On the other hand, three sevens played in the sequence 7-7-2-7 would entitle the player of the second seven to peg two points (pair), but would not entitle the player of the third seven to any points, the play of the 2 having interrupted the sequence.

Run or sequence For playing a card which forms, along with those played previously, a sequence of three or more cards, peg one point for each card in the sequence. Runs are independent of suit; they go strictly by rank: 10-Q-J is a run but 10-J-K is not a run. The order of play is immaterial: 5-7-8-6 is a run but 5-7-8-2-6 is not a run. Again the two has interrupted the sequence.

In scoring during the play, all points are pegged immediately. Thus if the play has gone 5-5 (pair, two points) and the first player plays another five for fifteen, he pegs a total of eight points (fifteen, two points; and threes, six points). As another example, the play has gone 3-3-4. If the next player puts down a five, he pegs five points (fifteen, two points; and run of three, three points).

Counting the hands After play is completed, the two hands and the crib are counted in the following order: first, the non-dealer's hand; second, the dealer's hand; and finally, the crib (which, of course, belongs to the dealer). The order of counting may be important toward the end of the game, for it is entirely possible for the nondealer to *count out* (go over 120) and thus win the game, even though the dealer might have achieved a higher total than the nondealer if he had been able to count his hand and the crib.

It is now that the starter comes into its own. It is considered to be a part of each of the three hands, so that, in effect, both hands and the crib are composed of five cards. The basic combinations of scoring values are as follows:

Fifteen Each combination of cards which totals fifteen counts two points.

Pairs Each pair of cards of the same rank counts two points. Note that three-of-a-kind can be made into three different pairs and scores six points, while four-of-a-kind can be made into six different pairs and scores twelve points.

Runs Each combination of three or more cards in a sequence counts one point for each card in the sequence.

Flush Four cards in the same suit, not counting the starter, in either the dealer's or nondealer's hand count four points. If the starter is also the same suit, count five points. If the crib and the starter are all one suit, count five points.

His Nibs (Nobs) If either of the hands or the crib contains the jack of the same suit as the starter, it counts one point.

In the above list, the word "combination" is used in its strictest sense. For example, a hand with the starter of 5-5-8-Q-K would be counted as follows, with the amounts showing a running total: fifteen (2 for the 5-Q), fifteen (4 for the 5-K), fifteen (6 for the other 5-Q), fifteen (8 for the other 5-K), and a pair makes ten. Note that counting is usually done aloud, taking the categories in the above order and giving the opponent an opportunity to verify the count before it is pegged.

It is proper to announce the total for certain common combinations in toto:

Three of a kind   6-6-6 scores six points.
Four of a kind   6-6-6-6 scores twelve points.
Double run   8-9-10-10 scores eight points.
Double run of four   8-9-10-10-J scores ten points (plus one if the jack is His Nibs and not the starter).
Triple run   8-9-10-10-10 scores fifteen points.
Quadruple (double-double) run   8-9-9-10-10 scores sixteen points.

Muggins (optional)   Each player must count his hand and crib aloud. If he overlooks any points, the other player may call "Muggins" and take the overlooked score for himself. Muggins should be used only when both players are of equal skill. It is an excellent teaching tool for beginners.

IRREGULARITIES

New deal   There must be a new deal by the same dealer if:

1. The deck was not cut by the nondealer (provided the nondealer calls attention to the fact before she looks at her hand). This is waived in many localities.
2. A card is exposed in the dealing of the cards or the deck is found to be imperfect.
3. It is found that *both* hands have an incorrect number of cards, except in the case where both hands are short by the same number of cards. In this case it is corrected by the dealer dealing as many more cards as necessary.

Wrong number of cards   If a player has the wrong number of cards in his hand while the other player and the crib have the correct number, his opponent may elect to have a new deal, or to let the deal stand and the incorrect hand be corrected by drawing cards from the deck in the case of a deficient hand, or by the nonoffender drawing a card or cards from the hand with an excess number. In the latter case the nonoffender pegs two points.

If the crib has the wrong number of cards and the other hands are correct, it is corrected in a similar fashion and the nondealer scores two points.

If the crib is found to be one card long and one of the players one card short, the player whose hand is correct shall temporarily withdraw his two cards from the crib and the other player shall pick up the remaining three cards and make a proper discard of two cards to the crib.

Failure to play If a player calls "go" when able to play or fails to play after an opponent calls "go," the card or cards she should have played are dead. Dead cards are unplayable; the offending player must complete her play with a short hand. However, the cards are playable when counting the hand after the play is completed.

Error in scoring A player may correct her own error in pegging provided she does so before she plays again. An opponent may demand that a score be corrected provided that she does so before she plays her next card.

STRATEGY

Basic strategy in Cribbage consists in selecting the right cards to go into the crib and in the play of the hand so as to optimize the opportunity to score points during the play. Advanced strategy includes playing to the score. Late in the game, if the dealer has 97 or 98 points, he expects to go out on the next deal. Remember the nondealer scores first. If both hands are about 91, the nondealer with a good hand plays to score points during the play, with the hope of going out on the next hand. With a poor hand, he tries to keep the dealer from scoring points during the play in the hope of getting to play two more hands. The dealer with a good hand tries to score points. With a poor hand he tries to keep the scoring as low as possible in the hope of getting to play a third hand.

The selection of cards to place in the crib is frequently easy. Just examine the six cards in your hand and select the four which have the largest count—the remaining two go into the crib. If the crib belongs to you, this usually works fine. But when it belongs to your opponent, it may present a problem. Normally, it is preferable to deplete your hand somewhat rather than to put dangerous cards in your enemy's crib. Such cards as fives, sevens, and eights are very dangerous; fours, sixes, and nines are also dangerous. In addition, adjacent cards, or cards in sequence but one, are undesirable. The best cards to put in your opponent's crib are very high, very low, or widely separated.

In my Navy days, particularly during the Korean War, we played a lot of Cribbage and named the two best discards "kay nine" the dog (the king and the nine), and "quinine" the medicinal discard (the queen and the nine). Queen-eight is almost as good as queen-nine but king-nine (K-9) the dog, is the best to put in an opponent's crib.

In play, the general principal is to try to prevent your opponent from scoring 15 or a run, unless you feel you can score some points yourself by continuing the run. Obviously, the safest lead is A, 2, 3, or 4, because your opponent can neither make 15 nor pass 15 and thus deprive you of a chance to make it. He might pair you, but against pairs there is no defense. A lead from any two cards totaling 15 is usually a good one. If your opponent scores 15, you will be able to make a pair. Note that a lead of seven from 7-8 may prove to be disastrous. Suppose the play goes 7-8, which is 15, two points to your opponent; 7-8-8, two points to you for a pair; 7-8-8-8, eight points to your opponent (including two for 31).

On the other hand 6-9, which is 15, two points to your opponent followed by 6-9-9, two points to you for a pair, makes it impossible for your opponent to score six because another 9 would put the total over 31.

After a lead, the question sometimes arises as to whether or not to *play* on or to *play off*; that is, to play a near card making a sequence possible or to play a wide card. Naturally you should play "on" only when you have hope of being able to continue the sequence when it is your next turn to play.

When there are no other considerations, play your higher cards first and save your lower cards to eke out a "go." For example:

Nondealer	Dealer
3-5-6-6-6-10	3-3-4-5-7-8

(These hands are better than average, but were chosen to show the various options in discarding and playing.)

The nondealer has the kind of hand she would like to have if she were the dealer. She would then be very happy to put the 5-10 in her own crib and retain the 3-6-6-6 (counting 15 two, 15 four, 15 six, and threes for a total of 12 points), an excellent hand which would improve greatly if the starter turned out to be a 3, 6, or 9. But the discard of 5-10 would be much too dangerous, so she does the best she can by putting the 3-10 into the crib.

The dealer is quite happy. He has one of those hands where the discard to his own crib is a natural one, namely the 7-8. If he had held this hand as nondealer, he would have had to compromise by discarding something else, the 3-8 being probably the best choice.

Assume that the starter is a 6, a highly improbable chance, but one which delights both players at the moment.

Nondealer	Starter	Dealer
5-6-6-6	6	3-3-4-5

The play could proceed in various ways, but let us assume that the nondealer starts with a 6, thus presenting a small problem to the dealer. The play of the 5 would give the nondealer a chance at both a sequence and a 15. The same is true of the play of a 4. It follows that both of these plays are highly undesirable: therefore, as the least of three evils, he plays a 3 for a total of nine. Here again the nondealer has a choice. However, a little reflection will show that the play of a 5 for a total of 14 is quite dangerous.

This is a most complicated hand. We're going to leave you right here to work out the future plays yourself. Remember, you have another card in your hand.

After the play of the four cards in each hand is completed, it is time to count the hands and the crib. Now the starter comes into its own.

First the nondealer counts her hand (5-6-6-6 plus the starter 6) as 12 points for a double pair.

Assuming that the nondealer has not already won the

game, the dealer next counts his hand (3-3-4-5 plus the starter 6) as 15 two, 15 four, plus ten for a double run of four, making a total of 14 points.

The dealer next counts his crib (3-7-8-10 plus the starter 6) as 15 two, plus three for a run of three, making five points.

THREE-HAND CRIBBAGE

Three-hand Cribbage is played by three players, each playing for himself. It is similar to two-hand Cribbage with the following exception:

Draw for the first deal; thereafter the deal rotates to the left, clockwise.

Deal five cards, one at a time, to each person and then deal one card to the crib (which, of course, belongs to the dealer). Each player then discards one card to the crib.

Eldest player (the player to the left of the dealer) cuts for starter and leads first. On the call "go" the players continue to play in turn, if possible. The last person to play scores the "go."

The player to the left of the last to play leads to the next series of plays.

After the play is completed, the hands are counted in this order: eldest, then the player to his left, then the dealer, and finally the dealer counts his crib. Special boards with three pairs of rows (each containing 30 points per row) are used for scoring. Sometimes these boards are triangular. Lacking such a board, players can use two regular Cribbage boards.

FOUR-HAND CRIBBAGE

Four-hand Cribbage is played by two partnerships, which may be determined by mutual agreement or by cutting the cards—the two players cutting the lowest cards playing against the two players cutting the highest cards. One of the players cutting the lowest card deals first. Five cards are then dealt to each player. Finally, each player discards one card to form the dealer's crib.

Eldest hand cuts for starter and makes the first lead. On the call of "go" the other hands continue to play if able—the last side to play scoring the "go." As before, the new lead is made by the player to the left of the last to play on the preceding series. Only one score is kept for each side. After the play is completed, the hands are counted in this order: eldest hand, dealer's partner, the other nondealer, dealer, and finally the crib, which, as usual, belongs to the dealer's side.

♣   ◇   ♡   ♠

FIVE-HAND CRIBBAGE

Five-hand Cribbage is played as in three-hand Cribbage, except that the dealer receives only four cards and does not contribute to the crib.

♣   ◇   ♡   ♠

SIX-HAND CRIBBAGE

Six-hand Cribbage may be played as three two-player partnerships or as two three-player teams. In any event, play is as in four-hand Cribbage, except that dealer and dealer's right-hand opponent are dealt only four cards and do not contribute to the crib.

Eights—Crazy Eights

PRELIMINARIES

Players   Two to seven players.

Cards   Regular pack of 52 cards with two to five players; two such packs with six or seven players.

The deal   With two players, deal seven cards to each player; with more than two players, deal five cards to each player. The rest of the pack is placed, face down, in a pile in the center of the table to form a *stockpile*. The top card of the stockpile is turned face up and placed alongside the stockpile as a *starter*.

PLAY

The player to the left of the dealer plays first. After he completes his play the turn to play moves to the left (clockwise). A play consists of placing one card on top of the pile begun by the starter. The first player must match the starter in either suit or rank. Subsequent players must match the last card played in either suit or rank. For example, if the previous player had played a five of diamonds, the next player may play any five-spot, any diamond, or any eight (see below).

If at any time when it is her turn to play, a player does not hold a card that she wishes to play, she must draw from the stockpile (one card at a time) until she draws a card that she does wish to play. Note that a player may draw from the stockpile even when she holds a playable card. Cards drawn which the player does not wish to play are placed in her hand. After the stockpile is exhausted, a player passes if she does not hold a playable card.

Eights   The eights are wild. An eight may be played upon any preceding card, regardless of its suit or rank. The owner of an eight must specify a suit (not necessarily the same suit as the eight) which the eight calls for. The next player must follow with a card of that suit or with another eight.

SCORING

Play ends when any player gets rid of all the cards in his hand. He scores the total of the cards remaining in the other hands: 50 points for an eight, 1 point for an ace, 10 points for each face card, and the number of pips for all the spot-cards. Each hand may be treated as a separate game, but when there are only two players, it is usual to play until one of them scores 100 points or more.

VARIATIONS

Some or all of the following features may be added to the basic game:

1. When a two is played, the next player must draw two cards from the stockpile. If this player plays another two, the following player must draw four cards; if he, in turn, plays a third two, the next player must draw six cards; a fourth two in succession calls for eight cards.
2. When the queen of spades is played, the next player must draw five cards from the stockpile.
3. The play of a jack causes the next player to lose his turn.
4. If more than two play, the play of a king reverses the order of play.
5. When a player cannot play, he draws one card only and the turn then passes to the next player.
6. A player must announce to the other players when he plays his next-to-last card (saying "last card") or forfeit his right to play at his next turn, drawing a card instead.

STRATEGY

Eights should be saved for special purposes; they should not be played merely to prevent drawing. In fact, in a two-hand game, it is good strategy to draw a few extra cards at times. It is often best to play one's long suit. Also it is a good plan to play a suit that the opponent has refused.

Euchre

PRELIMINARIES

Players   Four players in two partnerships.

Cards   A pack of 24 cards, A, K, Q, J, 10, 9 of four suits.

Rank of cards   In general, the cards rank ace (highest), K, Q, J, 10, 9; but in the trump suit the highest card is the jack (the *right bower*), followed by the jack of the same color (the *left bower*), followed by A, K, Q, 10, 9.

The deal   Five cards are dealt to each player in two rounds of 3-2 or 2-3 as the dealer chooses. The cards are dealt in rotation to the left, then clockwise.

After dealing the last packet to himself, the dealer places the remaining four cards face down on the table and turns the top card face up. This *turnup* proposes the trump suit for the deal.

Choosing trump   Left-hand opponent may pass or accept the turnup for trump by saying "I order it up." If he passes, each player in turn has the same options. Should any player, including dealer, accept the turnup as the trump suit, the dealer at once discards one card from his hand, and the turnup becomes part of his hand. (By custom the turnup is left on the pack.)

If all four hands pass, the dealer places the turnup card face down on the pack, and his left-hand opponent then has the right to name a trump suit or pass. If he passes, each player again, in turn, has the same options. Note that no player may name the suit of the turnup as trump.

If all four hands pass again, the deal is thrown in, and the cards are dealt by the next dealer.

Playing alone The hand that makes the trump, in either round, has the right to *play it alone*. If he so declares, his partner does not participate in the play.

PLAY

If the maker plays alone, the lead is by the player at her left; otherwise the lead is by the player at the left of dealer. Each player must follow suit, if able. If unable, he or she may play any card. A trick is won by the highest trump or, if there are none, by the highest card of the suit led. The winner of a trick leads to the next.

The object of the play is to make at least three tricks. If the making side fails to do so, it is *euchred*. If all five tricks are taken by the making side, it is called *march*.

SCORING

The maker of trump, playing with a partner: for making three or four tricks, one point; for march, two points. Maker playing alone: for three or four tricks, one point; for march, four points. In any case, if opponents make three or more tricks (euchre), they score two points.

Four-hand euchre is usually played to ten points.

IRREGULARITIES

Misdeal There must be a new deal by the same dealer if a card is exposed in dealing, or the pack is found to be imperfect. In the latter case all previous scores stand. A deal by the wrong player (stealing the deal) may be stopped before a card is turned up; after that, the deal stands.

Error in bidding If a player names for the trump the suit of the turnup after it has been turned down, or orders it up, or names a suit trump when it is not his turn, then his declaration is void and his side may not make the trump.

Fan Tan

PRELIMINARIES

Players   Three to five players, but best with four.

Cards   Regular pack of 52 cards. In each suit the rank is K, Q, J, 10, 9, 8, 7, 6, 5, 4, 3, 2, Ace (low).

The deal   All cards are dealt out, one at a time. It does not matter that some players have one more card than some of the other players.

The pool   Before starting the game, all players receive an equal number of poker chips. Before each game, a *pool* is started, each player with an extra card anteing one chip and each other player anteing two chips.

PLAY

The player to the left of the dealer plays first. He or she must play a seven, or else pass and pay a forfeit of one chip to the pool. Each player, in turn (clockwise), must play if able. If unable to play, the player passes and must, as before, pay a forfeit of one chip to the pool.

Sevens are always playable. When played, they are placed in a row in the center of the table as a starting point for the four center *stack piles*. Once a seven is played, it forms a starting point for play of other cards in the same suit; the eights are placed in a row on one side of the sevens and the sixes in a row on the other side of the sevens. Additional cards may be played on these cards (in suit and in sequence), upward on the eights to the kings and downward on the sixes to the aces.

OBJECT OF PLAY

The object of play is to get rid of all the cards in one's hand. The first player to do so wins the game. Once play has stopped, each player puts one chip in the pool for each card remaining in his hand. The winner then takes the entire pool.

IRREGULARITIES

If a player passes and is later found to have a seven in his hand, he must pay three chips to the pool and three chips each to the holder of the six and eight of that suit. If a player passes and later is found to have a playable card other than a seven, he must pay three chips to the pool. It is highly irregular for a player to deliberately pass when able to play.

STRATEGY

Given a choice, a player should:

1. Play a card higher (lower) than a seven whenever she holds another card in the same suit which is still higher (lower) but not in direct sequence. It never pays to block a card in one's own hand.
2. Play a card from a sequence in which she holds higher (lower) cards in order to retain future plays for herself and still block that particular side of the suit in question. When she has to choose between two or more cards, which are the last she holds in that direction of sequence, she should play the one which is nearest to a king or ace, so as to minimize the number of plays that she opens up to her opponents.

Five Hundred[1]

THREE-HAND FIVE HUNDRED

PRELIMINARIES

Players Two to six players, but best for four playing as partners.

Cards Thirty-three cards, the A, K, Q, J, 10, 9, 8, 7, plus the joker.

Rank of cards The highest trump is the joker. The next highest is the jack of the trump suit (the *right bower*). Third best is the jack of the suit of the same color as the trump suit (the *left bower*). The remaining trumps rank A, K, Q, 10, 9, 8, 7. In each of the other two suits, the rank is A, K, Q, J, 10, 9, 8, 7. In bidding, no-trump ranks highest, then hearts, diamonds, clubs, and spades, in that order.

The cut Cards are cut for the deal. The joker counts lowest. The next lowest is the ace, and the series then continues in normal ascending order. The player cutting the lowest card becomes the dealer. Any player may shuffle, the dealer having the right to shuffle last. After the shuffle is complete, the dealer offers the pack to the player on his right for the final cut before starting the deal.

---

[1] This game was devised and introduced to card players by the United States Card Playing Company, which has kept the copyright for over 50 years without charging anyone for its use. It became instantly popular and for years shared, with Auction Bridge, the lead among trick-taking games. The aim was to provide Euchre enthusiasts with a similar game having greater opportunity for skill.

The deal Beginning with the player on his or her left, the dealer gives each player three cards. He or she then deals three cards, face down, in the center of the table to form the *widow*. Then the dealer deals each player four cards and, finally, three cards each. This exhausts the deck; each player has received ten cards and the widow three.

BIDDING

Each player, beginning with the player to the dealer's left and proceeding clockwise, has one and only one opportunity to bid. If he does not bid, he must pass. If all players pass, the hand is abandoned without a score. If he bids, he must bid a number of tricks from six to ten and name a suit. If there was a previous bid, his bid must be for a higher number of tricks or, if for the same number of tricks, in a higher denomination. The highest bid becomes the contract, and the suit that the *bidder* named becomes trumps.

PLAY

The other two players combine in temporary partnership against the bidder. The bidder picks up the widow and, without showing those three cards to her opponents, puts them in her hand. She then discards any three cards she wants to, again without showing them.

The bidder leads to the first trick. After that, the winner of the previous trick leads. The leader may lead any card that she desires from those remaining in her hand. After the lead is made, each of the other players must follow suit, if able. If not able to follow suit, a player may play any card in her hand that she desires. A trick not containing a trump is won by the player who played the highest card in the suit led. If a trick does contain a trump, it is won by the player who played the highest trump.

Each player should keep in front of her the tricks she has taken, segregated in piles, so that any possible irregularity in play may be checked later.

The joker When there is a trump suit, the joker is the highest trump. It belongs to the trump suit and must be played, if necessary, to follow suit. it may be played only when it is legal to play a card of the trump suit. In no-trump. the joker is a suit by itself. It is also the highest card of any suit and takes any trick to which it may legally be played. The holder of the joker may not play it when he can follow suit to the card led. On the other hand, if he cannot follow suit, he may play the joker and, of course, win that trick. If a player leads the joker when playing a no-trump contract, he must specify the suit to which the other players must follow, if they are able.

SCORING

If the bidder wins as many tricks as he has bid, he scores the number of points called for in the following table. He does not score any bonus for tricks taken over the amount of the bid except that, if he takes all 10 tricks, he scores a minimum of 250 points (more if the table calls for more).

AVONDALE SCHEDULE

(GAME OF FIVE HUNDRED)

Tricks	6	7	8	9	10
Spades	40	140	240	340	440
Clubs	60	160	260	360	460
Diamonds	80	180	280	380	480
Hearts	100	200	300	400	500
No Trump	120	220	320	420	520

If a player fails to make the number of tricks that he contracted for, the value of the bid is subtracted from his score. Thus it is possible for a player to have a minus score. He is then said to be *in the hole*, an expression stemming from the common practice of circling minus scores. Whether the contract is made or not, each of the opposing players scores 10 points for each trick that he took.

GAME

The player to first reach a score of plus 500 points wins the game. If a player scores minus 500 points, he loses the game. He cannot win but continues to play until someone reaches plus 500 points. If this happens to be the player who had been minus 500 points, no one wins the game. If the bidder and an opponent reach 500 points on the same deal, the bidder wins the game.

If the bidder does not reach 500 points, but both of the opponents do, the opponent first to reach plus 500 points wins the game. If the bidder's score would not reach plus 500 points (assuming that the bidder makes his contract), the opponent to first reach plus 500 points may claim the game as soon as he takes the trick which brings his score to plus 500 points. At the time of making his claim, he must show his remaining cards. If he does not have the plus 500 points that he claimed, play continues; all his remaining cards become exposed cards (see below).

IRREGULARITIES

New deal There must be a new deal by the same dealer if a card is found exposed in the pack, or if the dealer gives the wrong number of cards to any player; or if, before the last card is dealt, attention is called to the fact that there had been no cut.

Bid out of turn In a three-hand game there is no penalty for a bid out of turn. The call is void and the offender may make any legal call at his or her next regular turn to bid. In partnership play, a bid (not a pass) out of turn is void and that side may make no further bid, although a bid previously made by the partner of the offender is not canceled.

Exposed Cards If a card falls face up on the table, or is held so that its owner's partner can see its face, or is named by the owner as being in his hand, it is an *exposed card*. An exposed card is left face up on the table and must be played at the first legal opportunity thereafter. The bidder is not penalized for an exposed card if he is playing alone, except in the case of a corrected revoke (see page 82).

Wrong number of cards If, during the bidding, two hands are found to have the wrong number of cards, there must be a new deal by the same dealer. If the widow and one hand are incorrect, they must be rectified. Another player draws out the excess card and gives it to the short hand (or widow). The player whose hand was incorrect is barred from bidding.

If, during the play, the bidder and one opponent are found to have an incorrect number of cards, or if there is one incorrect hand because of an incorrect pack, there must be a new deal by the same dealer. If two opponents have incorrect hands, the bidder's hand being correct, the bid is assumed to have been made and the opponents score nothing. The bidder may continue to play in an effort to win all 10 tricks. He wins all of the final tricks to which the short hand cannot play. If the opponents' hands are correct and the bidder's hand and the discard incorrect, the bid is lost. The hand is played out to determine how many tricks should be credited to the opponents.

Lead or play out of turn If an opponent requests it before the trick is completed, a lead out of turn must be corrected. Any cards played on it may be retracted without penalty, but the card led in error is treated as an exposed card. If it was the offender's partner's turn to lead, the opponent to his left may require him to lead a given suit or not to lead the suit of the exposed card.

If a player, not the leader, plays out of turn, the card is an exposed card.

If an error in leading (or in playing) out of turn is not found until the trick is quitted, the trick stands as played.

Revoke Failure to follow suit to a lead when able to do so is a *revoke*. A revoke may be corrected any time before the offender or her partner plays to the next trick; otherwise it stands as established. When a revoke is corrected, the incorrect card is treated as an exposed card, including the case where it belongs to the bidder playing alone. If an established revoke is claimed and proved before the cut to the next deal, and the revoking hand was on the contracting side, the contract is scored as lost. If the revoke was committed by an opponent, the contract is scored as made and the opponents score nothing.

Error in score   Upon request, a proved error in recording scores must be corrected, provided that the request is made before the first bid (not pass) of the next deal after that to which the error pertained. In any other case, recorded scores may not be changed.

STRATEGY

As there are only 10 trumps, the average hand contains three or four trumps. The minimum recommended trump length for a bid is four, and then only when the trump suit includes at least two of the three top trumps and the hand has considerable side-strength. Most contracts go to the hands with five or more trumps.

An approximate method of hand evaluation is to count one trick for each trump over three, one for each top trump as good as an ace, and one for each side ace or guarded king.

Since each player has only one opportunity to bid, it is important to bid the full value of a hand; however, be conservative in higher bids.

With five or more trumps the bidder should lead trumps at once in order to draw two of the opponent's trumps for one of his own. Even with only four trumps, the bidder should lead them if his other suits are stopped.

Do not bid in the hope of finding a specific card, say the joker, in the widow. On the other hand, you are entitled to count on some help.

To bid no-trump without the joker is speculative. With the joker a poor suit is acceptable if the rest of the hand is solid in top cards. At no-trump, you should normally open your longest suit, regardless of its top strength, and should continue it at every opportunity. With no real long suit (five cards or more), you should try to force out the adverse aces and kings that stand in the way of your lower-card tricks.

As an opponent, your strategy should be to try to develop your longest and strongest suit. When you find the bidder void in a suit, force him with it at every opportunity.

The opponents should try to get the bidder in the middle by letting the lead come from his right rather than from his left.

♣   ◇   ♡   ♠

TWO-HAND FIVE HUNDRED

The play and the deal are the same as in three-hand Five Hundred, except that the hand to the dealer's left is dealt face down and is dead; that is, out of the play. This makes the bidding largely guesswork; you have to be a bit bold to make progress. If one player's score reaches minus 500, the other wins the game.

Two-hand Five Hundred may also be played with a 24-card deck; A, K, Q, J, 10, 9 of each suit, the other spot-cards and the joker being deleted from the pack. The widow is four cards and the play, otherwise, is as in three-hand Five Hundred.

♣ ◇ ♡ ♠

FOUR-HAND FIVE HUNDRED

Four-hand Five Hundred is usually played with fixed partnerships, partners sitting opposite each other as in bridge. The pack contains 43 cards made by deleting the twos, threes, and black fours from the deck of 52 cards plus the joker. Each player receives 10 cards, the remaining three going to the widow. Play proceeds as in three-hand Five Hundred. Sometimes it is played without the joker, and the widow has only two cards.

♣ ◇ ♡ ♠

FIVE-HAND FIVE HUNDRED

Five players use the standard 52-card pack, usually with the joker added. It follows that each player has 10 cards and the widow three cards. After the bidding, the high bidder selects any of the other four players to be her partner; if she has bid eight or more tricks, she may select two partners.

♣ ◇ ♡ ♠

SIX-HAND FIVE HUNDRED

For six players a 62-card pack is available which has, in addition to the regular 52 cards, an 11-spot card and a 12-spot card in each suit and a 13-spot card in two of the suits; this pack, with the joker, permits dealing 10 cards to each player and three cards to the widow. The six players play as two sets of partners of three each—seated alternately—so that each player has an opponent to his right and to his left.

Hearts

PRELIMINARIES

Players   Two to seven players, but best with four.

Cards   A standard 52-card pack.

Rank of cards   The cards rank ace (highest), K, Q, J, 10, 9, 8, 7, 6, 5, 4, 3, 2 (lowest).

The deal   Cut the cards for deal; the player with the lowest card deals first. The deal rotates to the left, clockwise. The cards are dealt one at a time as far as they will go equally. Any remaining cards are placed on the table, face down. They are taken by the player who takes the first trick. Usually only that player may look at these cards.

The pass   After looking at his hand, each player selects three cards and passes them to his right-hand opponent. Each player must select his three cards and pass them on before he looks at the cards he receives from his left-hand opponent.

Variation 1   The cards are passed to the left-hand opponent.

Variation 2   The direction in which the cards are passed is alternated, first to the right, then to the left.

Variation 3   As in variation 2, but no pass is made every third hand.

PLAY

The player to the left of the dealer makes the first lead. Each player in turn, clockwise, must follow suit to the lead if he can. If a player cannot follow suit, he may play any of the cards remaining in his hand except that the holder of the queen of spades must discard it at his first legal opportunity. A trick is won by the player who plays the highest card of the suit led. The winner of a trick leads to the next trick. The object of the game is to avoid winning any trick with a heart on it and, particularly, to avoid winning any trick containing the queen of spades (known as the *Black Maria*).

Take all or slam One player takes all 13 hearts and the queen of spades.

SCORING

At the end of the play of each hand the number of hearts on the tricks taken by each player is totaled. Each heart counts one point. The player who took the queen of spades adds 13 points to the number of hearts that he took. If a player has a take all, 26 points are added to each of the opponents' scores (variation: 26 points are subtracted from the player's score). A separate cumulative score is kept for each player. After an agreed number of hands, or after an agreed time is reached, or when any player has reached an agreed score, the final scores are computed by one of the following methods:

Method 1 Each player settles with each other player. The payment is made on the difference of their totals—the player with the lower score being the winner.
Method 2 Only the winner (the player with the lowest score) collects from the other players.

For example:

Player	Final Total
A	42
B	13
C	15
D	34

Using method 2, player A would lose 29 points, player B would win 52 points, player C would lose 2 points, and player D would lose 21 points.

Using method 1, player A would lose 64 points ($-29-27-8=-64$); player B would win 52 points (as in method 2); player C would win 44 points ($+27-2+19=44$), and player D would lose 32 points ($+8-21-19=-32$).

Note that the aggregate of all scores at any time must be a multiple of 26.

IRREGULARITIES

Misdeal If the dealer exposes a card in dealing or deals a player an incorrect number of cards, it is a misdeal and the next player in line deals.

Play out of turn A lead or play out of turn must be corrected if noted before all players have played to the trick. After all players have played to the trick, the play out of turn stands without penalty.

Quitted tricks Each trick taken must be placed in front of the winner. Tricks must be kept separate, face down. If a player keeps her tricks so that it is not possible to check a claimed revoke (see below), she is charged with all 26 points for the deal, regardless of whether she, or someone else, was charged with the revoke.

Revoke Failure to follow suit, when able, or to discard the queen of spades at the first opportunity (when playing this variation) constitutes a revoke. A revoke is established when the trick is turned and the player winning it leads to the next trick. If a revoke is called and established, play immediately ceases on that hand and the player revoking is charged with all 26 points for that hand. If a revoke is established against more than one player, each player who has revoked is charged with 26 points. A penalty for a revoke may not be enforced after the deck is cut for the next deal.

A player discovered to have too few cards must take the last trick. If more than one card short, he must take each trick to which he cannot follow.

Hearts may be played with some or all of these variations:

Variation 1 The player who captures the jack of diamonds scores—10 points.

Variation 2 The lead to the first trick is always the club two by whomever holds it.

Variation 3 Hearts may not be led until a trick has been taken containing a heart or the queen of spades, unless the player on lead has only hearts.

Variation 4 The queen of spades is not required to be discarded at the first opportunity. This allows some possibility of dumping it on the low scorer, but also allows some amount of "ganging up," which may cause ill feelings.

♣ ◇ ♡ ♠

CANCELLATION HEARTS

PRELIMINARIES

Number of players Seven to ten players.

Cards Two full 52-card packs.

The deal As in regular hearts.

The pass No cards are passed before the play.

PLAY

Play is the same as in regular hearts except that two cards of the same rank on the same trick cancel each other; neither can win the trick. If all of the cards played to a trick are paired, the trick goes to the winner of the next trick.

Michigan

PRELIMINARIES

Players   From three to seven players, but four is best.

Cards   A regular deck of 52 cards. Cards rank ace (highest), K, Q, J, 10, 9, 8, 7, 6, 5, 4, 3, 2 (lowest).

Layout   Take the ace of hearts, the king of clubs, the queen of diamonds, and the jack of spades from another deck and place them in a horizontal line in the middle of the table. These cards, and the corresponding cards in the deck used for play, are known as the *boodle* cards. (These layouts may be purchased in game stores.)

Tokens   At the start of a game all players are given an equal number of chips, matches, buttons, or other tokens. Before each deal the dealer places two chips on each boodle card in the center of the table, and each of the other players places one chip on each boodle card.

The deal   The turn to deal passes in rotation to the left (clockwise). The dealer, starting with the player to his or her left, deals the cards (one at a time) until the deck is exhausted. Thus some hands may have one more card than other hands. One extra hand, known as the *widow,* is dealt. It is placed to the dealer's immediate left.

AUCTION

After looking at his hand, the dealer may discard it and play the widow instead of the hand originally dealt to him. If he elects to keep his original hand, he must auction off the widow. The other players, after looking at their hands, may bid for it, the highest bidder getting the widow after paying the dealer the number of chips that he has bid. The widow may not be seen by anyone other than the one who takes it.

PLAY

The player to the left of the dealer plays first. He may lead any suit that he wishes, but must lead the lowest card he holds in that suit. Cards, as played, may be thrown into a common pile or may be kept in separate piles in front of their owners. The player holding the next higher card of the same suit then plays it, and so on. Note that the turn to play does not rotate but passes to whomever can play the next higher-ranking card in the same suit.

This sequence of plays is eventually stopped, either because it reaches the ace or because it is not available (being either in the dead hand or having been played earlier). The last player to play is then entitled to start a new sequence. He must choose a new suit and must play his lowest card in that suit. (Some say that the suit must be of another color.) If he only holds cards in the old suit, the privilege of starting the new sequence shifts to the player to the left. The play ends as soon as any player gets rid of the last card in his hand. He then collects one chip for each card remaining in the other players' hands.

Boodle cards When a player is able to play one of the boodle cards, she collects all of the chips on that card. It frequently happens that not all of the boodle cards are played during a deal. Uncollected chips, swelled by further antes, remain on the boodle cards until finally won.

IRREGULARITIES

A player who violates a rule may not win a deal or collect by playing a boodle card. If she goes out first, the others continue to play. If the offender holds but fails to play, when it was playable, the next card below a boodle card, and that boodle card is not played during the play of the hand, she must pay the owner of that boodle card the number of chips on it. The error of leading the same suit rather than shifting to a new suit is not subject to penalty; however, it must be corrected. If the next hand plays before the error is noted, it stands as played. Here again, it is quite improper for any player to violate this rule intentionally.

STRATEGY

If you hold a boodle card or have average high-card strength, keep your hand—do not speculate on the widow. The time to exchange your hand for the widow or to bid for it is when you hold a hand with an above-average number of low cards. Even then it is not a paying proposition to bid more than five chips for the widow. As dealer, however, you may gain an advantage by interchanging an indifferent hand, for then you will know in advance all of the natural stops. In play keep track of the initial cards led. Each such card becomes a blank card. When you gain the lead, first play those cards which are stopped or begin a sequence that you can stop, so that you may hold, or quickly regain, the lead.

Oh Hell

This is one of the best games for sheer relaxation; also it is comparable to Hearts in the opportunity for skillful play.

PRELIMINARIES

Players Three to seven players, but is best four-hand. Each player plays for himself.

Cards A regular pack of 52 cards. In each suit the cards rank ace (highest), K, Q, J, 10, 9, 8, 7, 6, 5, 4, 3, 2 (lowest).

The game There are a fixed number of deals to a game. In the first deal, each player receives one card; in the second deal, two cards, and so on. In a three-hand game, there are 15 deals; in a four-hand game, 13; in a five-hand game, 10; in a six-hand game, 8; in a seven-hand game, 7. The number of deal may be reduced, by agreement, to make the game shorter.

The deal The turn to deal rotates to the left (clockwise). The dealer distributes the cards, one at a time (clockwise), up to the number due in that deal. She then establishes the trump suit for that hand by turning the next card in the deck face up on the table. The rest of the pack is laid aside: it is dead for that deal. In the last hand of a game, no card is faced; it is played at no-trump.

BIDDING

The bidding proceeds clockwise, beginning with the player to the left of the dealer. Each player must bid the number of tricks that he expects to take. The possible bids are, of course, limited by the number of cards in that particular hand. Thus in the first deal the only possible bids are one and zero. In the last deal of a four-hand game, the bids may range from zero to thirteen.

The scorekeeper   One player should be appointed *score-keeper*. The score is kept on paper, usually with two columns for each player. The scorekeeper must keep a record of each bid and furnish information, upon request, about the bids. After the bidding is over, the scorekeeper should announce whether the total is overbid, even, or underbid; that is, if the total of all bids exceeds the number of cards in the hand, equals it, or is less than it.

PLAY

The player to the left of the dealer makes the opening lead. The cards are played out in tricks. A player must follow suit, if able. If unable to follow suit, he may play any card that he wishes. A trick is won by the highest trump on it. Otherwise, if it does not contain a trump, it is won by the highest card of the suit led. The winner of a trick leads to the next trick. Each player must keep his tricks segregated so that his opponents may readily ascertain their number.

SCORING

In Oh Hell, as differentiated from Bridge, Pinochle, etc., a player who makes more tricks than her contract does not fulfill her bid; she must make the exact number of tricks that she has bid. A player who makes more, or less, than the number of tricks that she has bid, *busts*. After the hand is over, the player who makes her bid scores the amount of her bid plus 10. Some players prefer that a player who bids zero receive five plus the number of cards in the hand, on the theory that a bid of zero becomes progressively more difficult to make as the hand grows in size. A player who busts scores nothing.

At the end of the game the player with the highest score wins.

IRREGULARITIES

Irregular bid If a player bids out of turn, his bid stands, but the turn to bid reverts to the proper player. If a player who has bid in his proper turn attempts to change his bid, he may do so provided the next player to his left has not bid.

Exposed card If a player shows a card from his hand, or leads or plays out of turn, that card is *exposed*. Exposed cards must be left on the table, face up, and must be played at the first legal opportunity thereafter.

Revoke Failure to follow suit when one is able is a *revoke*. A revoke may be corrected before the lead to the next trick, and any cards played to the trick may be retracted without penalty, but the card played by the offender becomes an exposed card. If a revoke is established, the deal is void. There must be a new deal of the same number of cards by the same dealer. Also 10 points are deducted from the score of the offender.

STRATEGY

As a general rule it is easier to lose tricks than to win them, especially when there are fewer than five cards in the hand. It follows that it is better to bid one less than the number of tricks you estimate you can make. Unless he has a hand whose trick value is clear cut, the dealer, who bids last, should try to make a bid which will make the total of all bids equal to the number of tricks in the hand for that deal. He hopes that he will benefit from all the other players trying to make their exact bids.

The ideal suit is one with both high and low cards in it. You can go either way, depending upon the circumstances. The poorest suit is one with several intermediate cards. You are more or less at the mercy of your opponents in such a suit.

Once you have taken more tricks than you bid, try to take as many more tricks as possible; every excess trick that you take is one less available to the opponents, who are trying to make their bid.

Pinochle

PRELIMINARIES

Cards A Pinochle pack of 48 cards. There are two cards in each rank running from 9 to ace, inclusive, in each of the four suits. They rank ace (highest), 10, K, Q, J, 9 (lowest). When duplicates are played to the same trick, the first-played card ranks as higher.

Card values The higher cards have scoring values when taken in tricks, as shown in the table below. (Note that points are counted on all tricks taken at any time.)

Winning the last trick counts 10 points. The total number of points at stake on each deal thus becomes 250.

Card	Original count	Simplified count
Ace	11	10
Ten	10	10
King	4	5
Queen	3	5
Jack	2	0
Lower Cards	0	0

MELDS

Certain combinations of cards, known as *melds,* have additional values, as shown on page 97. A card may be used in two or more melds, provided that the melds are made of different classes. For example, the same queen of spades may be used in a marriage, 60 queens, and pinochle. However, it is necessary that a royal marriage be melded before you meld a flush, if you wish the royal marriage to count separately.

MELDS

Sequences	Values
A-Q-J-10- of trumps (flush)	150
K-Q of trumps (royal marriage)	40
K-Q of any other suit (simple marriage)	20

Groups	
♠A-♡A-◇A-♣A (100 aces)	100
♠K-♡K-◇K-♣K (80 kings)	80
♠Q-♡Q-◇Q-♣Q (60 queens)	60
♠J-♡J-◇J-♣J (40 jacks)	40

Special	
♠Q-◇J (pinochle)	40
9 of trumps (dix, pronounced "deece" most circles do not count dix)	10

♣ ◇ ♡ ♠

TWO-HAND PINOCHLE

PRELIMINARIES

Cards Either the 48-card pack described above or a 64-card pack, which is the same deck with eight eights and eight sevens added. With the 64-card pack the seven of trumps rather than the nine of trumps is the dix.

The deal If the game is for 1000 points, the deal alternates. If each hand is treated as a separate game, the winner deals. Cards are cut for the first deal.

The dealer deals each player 12 cards, three at a time, when the 48-card pack is being used; 16 cards, four at a time, when the 64-card pack is being used. The rest of the pack is

placed, face down, in the center of the table as the stockpile.
The dealer then turns the top card of the stockpile face up
and slides it partway under the pile. This card establishes the
trump suit for that deal.

PLAY

The play falls into two parts, namely:

Part I   This portion of the game covers the period during
which there remain cards in the stockpile. Play starts with
the non-dealer making the first lead. The winner of each trick
(the player who plays the highest trump, or if there is no
trump on the trick, the highest card of the suit led) draws the
top card from the stockpile; his opponent draws the next
card. The winner of a trick leads to the next trick. During this
part of the play the second player to a trick need not follow
suit. He may play any card he wishes. Also, it is during this
period that melds (which count toward the score in accordance with the previous table) may be made by placing any
of the combinations listed in the table face up upon the table,
provided the conditions listed below are met.

1. A player may meld only after winning a trick and before
   leading to the next trick.
2. Except as noted in item 3 below, a player may make
   only one meld at a time.
3. The holder of dix may, after winning a trick and before
   leading to the next trick, exchange it for the trump card
   and thus obtain a higher trump and score 10 points for
   dix, assuming that it was agreed upon that the dix
   counts 10 points. This exchange, and also the melding
   of the second dix which is accomplished by merely
   showing it, may be made in the same turn as another
   meld.

A card of a meld on the table may be used as a part of a
new meld provided the player uses at least one new card from
his hand and the melds are of different classes. Thus, a player
having melded a royal marriage (and having scored 40 points
for it) may, at a later turn, add the trumps A-J-10 and score
150 points for a flush. If the new card the player is adding to

the table could be used with the cards already on the table to form two new melds, the player may score only one of them. For example, suppose a player who has previously scored pinochle now melds 80 kings; he or she cannot also score for the spade marriage.

Melded cards remain on the table but may be played in tricks; that is, they remain a part of the player's hand.

A combination of four kings (also of different suits) and four queens (also of different suits) is called a *roundhouse*. In three-hand pinochle they may be melded all at once, scoring 240 points. In two-hand pinochle it must be treated as separate melds, scoring at the most 220 points. When the stockpile is exhausted (after the 12th trick when playing with a 48-card pack; after the 16th trick when playing with a 64-card pack), part I ends and part II begins.

Part II After the players have picked up their melds (they should have 12 [16] cards in their hands), the hand is played out in tricks. No further melds may be made. Also, the second player to a trick must follow suit, if able; if void in the suit led, he must trump, if able. If a trump is led, his opponent must win the trick, if able.

SCORING

The scores for melds are accumulated during part I of the play. After part II has been completed, each player totals the values of the cards that she has won in tricks and adds it to her previous total. The player taking the last trick adds 10 points to her total.

GAME

The player who first reaches a total of 1000 points or more wins the game, provided the other player has less than 1000 points. If both players have over 1000 points, the game continues, with a new total required to win of 1250 points (1500 points, and so on, if there is no clear winner).

At any point in the game a player may *declare himself out*. At that point play ceases and the total point value of the cards in his tricks, plus the value of his melds, plus his previous score, is calculated. If his total score is 1000 points or more (or whatever the agreed total for the game happens to be), he wins the game regardless of what the total value of his opponent's score may be. If his total score is less than the necessary 1000 points, he loses the game.

IRREGULARITIES

Misdeal   The nondealer may call for a new deal if, before playing to the first trick, any of her own cards or those in the pack are exposed in dealing. Either player, before playing to the first trick, may demand a new deal if she has less than the required number of cards. There must be a new deal if, before both players have played to the first trick, it was discovered that either player was dealt too many cards. The same dealer redeals.

Exposed cards   If more than one card is exposed in turning the trump card, they must be put back into the stockpile and the pile reshuffled. The dealer's opponent then draws out a card which establishes the trump suit. If, after play has started, a card is found face up in the stockpile, the card is placed in the stockpile, the pile reshuffled, and play is continued.

Wrong number of cards   If a player's hand is found incorrect after play has begun, play continues, and the error is corrected as follows: A short hand draws extra cards at once from the stockpile; a long hand omits drawing from the stockpile until his hand is correct. (He may not meld until his hand is correct.)

Incorrect stock   If at any time the stockpile is found to have an incorrect number of cards, play continues, and the error is corrected as follows: When there are only three cards left, the winner of the last trick takes the top card; the other player may take either the stock card or the trump card. The remaining card is discarded, being considered dead. If it is the stock card, it is exposed before being discarded.

Lead out of turn If a player leads out of turn, her opponent may accept it or require it to be withdrawn. There is no penalty.

Revoke (renege) In part II, a *revoke (renege)* is failure to follow suit when able, failure to trump when so required when able, or to win a trump ticket when able. A player may correct his revoke without penalty provided he does so before he plays to the next trick; otherwise it stands as established. Play continues in order to determine the non-offender's score. The offender scores nothing for the value of the cards he has taken in tricks after the revoke. He does not lose the value of the cards he took in tricks before the revoke or the value of his melds.

STRATEGY

At the beginning, save cards for valuable melds by letting go of jacks and lower cards. Save for marriages when you can, but try to keep track of the combinations which have become impossible or unlikely. Use tens to capture the lead. A lead of a ten will often permit you to retain the lead, because your opponent cannot win the trick without (usually) impairing his chance of forming and melding 100 aces or a flush.

If you have several melds available, play the one with the least number of cards, so that you will have some left for future melds, thereby making the excess cards available for play. However, play a royal marriage as soon as possible with the hope of being able to complete a flush later.

Toward the end of a hand, give thought to the possibility of defending against a possible flush meld by your opponent by keeping him out of the lead. Lead trumps in the hope that he will be unable to take a trick without giving up one of his essential trumps.

Make it more difficult for your opponent to obtain the lead by leading your longest suit and continuing to lead it. When possible save trumps and aces to build up a strong hand for part II.

The best players invariably know all 12 of the cards held by their opponent when play to part II begins. If you are unable to carry so many cards in your mind, at least keep track of his trumps and aces. During this period it is usually more important than ever to lead your longest suit and force the opponent to use trumps. When you have any chance to reach game in a deal, try to build up everything you can by melding. Keep an accurate mental count of the cards that you capture so that, at all times, you know your total score.

♣   ◇   ♡   ♠

AUCTION PINOCHLE

This is one of the best of the three-hand games in opportunities for skill. However, it has been more or less superseded by Bridge and the various forms of Rummy.

PRELIMINARIES

Players   Although only three are active at a time, the game is an excellent one for four. Five may also play. With four players the dealer gives himself no cards; with five, he neither deals himself any cards nor the second player to his left.

Cards   The standard 48-card Pinochle deck.

The deal   Each player receives 15 cards dealt in batches. After the first round has been dealt, the dealer places three cards, face down, in the middle of the table. These three cards are known as the *widow*.

BIDDING

Each player, beginning with the player to the left of the dealer, must bid or pass. A player may continue bidding at her turn, but may not bid after passing. No suit is mentioned. Usually, the player to the left of the bidder is required to make a minimum bid of 300 points (250, or 200 points in some circles). The other players may bid or pass, as they prefer.

Widow The bidder turns the widow face up for all to see. He then puts the cards into his hand. Next he faces the melds he holds; no other player melds.

The meld The bidder then places, face up, all his cards that form proper melds (see table on page 97). The bidder may change his melds and the trump suit at any time before he makes the opening lead.

Concession The bidder may concede defeat before making an opening lead. In this event he loses *single bete* (pronounced "bate"). Or the opponents may concede that he will surely make his bid, in which case there is no play. One opponent's concession is not binding on the other opponent. If the bidder's melds total as much as (or exceed) his bid, his contract is made and there is no play. (The bidder need not take a trick to score his melds.)

Burying If the bidder needs some points to make his bid, and he decides to play, he *buries* (discards) any three cards from his hand face down. However, he may not bury any card which he used in a meld. The buried cards belong to the bidder, and after the play, he counts them along with the cards in his tricks. After burying these three cards, the dealer picks up his melds and names the trump suit, if he has not already named it by melding a royal marriage or a flush.

PLAY

The bidder makes the opening lead. She may lead any card, not necessarily a trump. All players must follow suit to a lead, if able; if unable to follow suit to a nontrump lead, he or she must trump, if able. Note a player need not overtrump a trump previously played upon a nontrump lead. When a trump is led, however, he or she must play a trump higher than any trump already on the trick, if able. A trick is won by the highest trump on it, or if there is no trump on it, by the highest card played in the suit led. The winner of a trick leads to the next trick. Tricks won by the opponents are kept in one pile.

Result of play   The bidder totals the values of the cards in her tricks and in the three buried cards, and adds this total to her meld total (plus 10 points, if she took the last trick). If this count equals or exceeds her bid, her bid is made; if it is less, the bid is defeated and the bidder is said to go *double bete*.

SCORING

The score may be either kept on paper or settled with poker chips after each deal. The payments are based on a schedule which varies with the locality. The most common is:

Bid	Base value
300–340	1
350–390	2
400–440	4
450–490	7
500–540	10
550–590	13

A base value is doubled when spades are trumps. Bids over 450 are extremely rare. The scoring for games over 340 frequently varies from locality to locality. Some localities, in order to create "action," give extra bonuses from the kitty (see page 105) for bids over 340 that are made.

When the bidder concedes single bete, he pays the base value of his bid to each opponent and the kitty. When he suffers double bete, he pays each opponent (including the inactive ones) and the kitty twice the base value—four times the base value if spades are trumps.

When a player makes his bid, he collects its base value (doubled if spades are trumps) from each opponent.

KITTY

It is usual to maintain a *kitty*, a common pool of chips. When a player makes a forced opening bid (300, 250, or 200, as the case may be) and concedes single bete without looking at the widow, she pays the base value of her bid only to the kitty. In other cases the kitty neither collects nor pays out on bids up to 340. On bids over 340, the kitty collects and pays out, just as though it were a player. The kitty is originally formed and subsequently replenished, if necessary, by equal contributions from each player. It is divided equally among the players when play finally ends.

IRREGULARITIES

New deal   There must be a new deal by the same dealer if any card of the widow is exposed in the dealing or any two cards in the players' hands. Or if the pack was not properly shuffled and cut, and attention is called to the fact before the widow is dealt.

Exposure of widow   If, before the bidding ends, a player sees a card in the widow, he may not make another bid. If he exposed a card in the widow, there must be a new deal by the next player. The offender must pay to each other player (including the inactive players and the kitty) the base value of the highest bid prior to his offense.

Wrong number of cards   If a player has too few cards and another player or the widow has too many:

1. If the error is discovered before the bidder has properly exposed the widow, the incorrect hands must be rectified.
2. If the error is discovered at any later time, the bid is made if the bidder's hand and discard, if any, are correct; if either is incorrect, the bidder loses either single or double bete, depending on whether or not he had led.

If the widow is found to have too few cards, there must be a new deal by the same dealer.

Exposed The bidder is not subject to penalty after exposing cards. If a player exposes a card during the bidding and then becomes an opponent, the bidder may require, or forbid, the lead of that card at the offender's first opportunity to play it. If the opponents expose two or more cards after the opening lead, the bid is made.

Bid out of turn A bid out of turn is void without penalty, but it may be accepted by one player or two entitled to bid.

Improper burying If, after the bidder leads, she is found to have buried a card that she had melded or to have buried too many cards, she is double bete.

Revoke A player is said to *revoke* (or to *renege*) if he fails, when able, to follow to a lead, play over a trump lead, trump a plain lead, or play an exposed card when properly required by the dealer.

The bidder may correct a revoke without penalty provided he has not played to the next trick. An opponent may correct a revoke before he or his partner has played to the next trick. However, if the bidder does not make his bid, the deal is void. Cards played after a revoke may be withdrawn if the revoke is corrected.

If a revoke is not corrected in time, play ceases. If the offender was the dealer, he or she is double bete. If the offender was an opponent, the bid is made.

Error in count of meld Correction may be made at any time before settlement is reached if an incorrect value was agreed upon for a bidder's meld.

STRATEGY

In bidding The most costly error is bidding on the hope that the widow contains the cards that you need, as opposed to bidding on cards that you hold. A hand with a suit, such as A-K-Q-J, which needs only one card (the 10) to complete a flush, is known as a one-chance suit. Even if your side-suits are of good quality, you should not bid it. Your chances of improving a one-chance suit are 5 to 1 against you. As another example, a hand with ♠A-♡A-♣A would be known as a one-chance hand. (It needs the ◇A). With a two-chance hand, the odds are 2 to 1 against you. You should bid a three-chance hand if all chances are solid. The odds on improving your hand are about even. Below is an example of a good three-chance hand (using a 64-card deck):

♠ A	♠ K	♠ Q	♠ J	
♡ A	♡ 10	♡ K	♡ J	
◇ A	◇ 10	◇ K	◇ J	◇ 9
♣ A	♣ 10	♣ 9		

This hand is a cinch 300 bid; it is a better 350 bid.

If you can make any flush with the widow's help, you are a cinch. There are, also, numerous two-card chances. Do not count on them; just remember that they are there. By the way, you may wish to know that the odds on a four-chance hand are 3 to 2 in your favor; on a five-chance hand they are 2 to 1 in your favor.

Of course, you bet all four-ace hands and better, unless the rest of your hand is terrible.

In betting it is sometimes advisable to stoss (bid with little chance that you can make your bid). Remember, however, that there is a lot of danger in a *stoss*. You may be left in your bid with a hopeless contract and be forced to pay single bete. On the other hand, if you choose the right opponent, you are in no danger. I used to play in an Auction Pinochle game where one of the players, when he held a hand which would warrant a bid of 350, would always respond to a 360 stoss with a bid of 400. In a game where the first bidder is forced to make a bid of 300, and the next bidder calls 310, it is silly to stoss. There is a good chance that the 310 bidder wanted to tempt the next bidder to make a higher bid.

In bidding you should, naturally, count both your melds and your playing points. In counting playing points, be conservative. An A-10-K in a side-suit should be counted as 15. If you can discard the 10-K, you are sure of 25 points. In making a low bid, estimate the widow as 30 points; in making a high bid, count it as only 20 points.

PLAY

After picking up the widow, you must discard if you plan to play the hand. In general, you should discard from your short suits. If you have six (or more) trumps, you can blank an ace. Of course, you should remember to lead it right away. If you have only five trumps, you should keep a guard for your ace.

With a trump flush, the standard lead is the king. Hopefully this will pick up the 10 and ace of trumps from your opponents. Each player is forced to win a trump lead if he or she can. In leading a nontrump suit, lead an ace to avoid a *shmear*. (A shmear is a play of an ace or 10 by an opponent on his partner's trick.)

Defense The defender's first aim is to win as many 10-point cards as possible. In the game I used to play, the participants would overlook the value of these cards. The experts used to laugh at our defense. However, we might let the bidder win by 30 or 40 points when perfect Pinochle defense would hold him to 10 points. They never realized that our big losses were due to an attempt to find a way to defeat the contract. (Needless to say, my partner and I were the winners in that game.) As an example, toward the end of the hand I hold A-10-9 of a suit to the left of the bidder and my partner leads the ace of that suit. If we need three tricks in the suit, I follow with the nine; if we need only two tricks, I follow with the ten.

♣ ◇ ♡ ♠

PARTNERSHIP AUCTION PINOCHLE

The vogue in four-hand bidding games, starting with Auction Bridge, caused the original four-hand Pinochle game to be abandoned, but it has survived in Partnership Auction Pinochle.

PRELIMINARIES

Players   Four players in two partnerships, sitting opposite each other at the table.

Cards   The 48-card Pinochle deck.

The deal   Each player is dealt 12 cards, three at a time.

BIDDING

Beginning with the player to the left of the dealer, each player in turn, clockwise, has one opportunity to either bid or pass. All bids must be in multiples of 10, with 100 the minimum bid allowed. No suit is mentioned. The player making the highest bid becomes the *bidder;* he or she then names trumps for that deal.

MELDING

All four players may meld. The list of basic melds is the same as in two-hand Pinochle (see page 97). In addition, double melds have extra value as indicated below:

Double Melds	Value
Double flush	1500
All 8 aces	1000
All 8 kings	800
All 8 queens	600
All 8 jacks	400
Double Pinochle	300

Partners must meld separately; they may not pool their cards to build up joint melds. However, for scoring purposes, all their melds are totaled and a memorandum is made of the amount. A side does not receive credit for its melds unless it takes a trick. (The trick need not contain a counting card.)

PLAY

After all the players have picked up their melds, the player to the dealer's left makes the opening lead. A player must follow suit, if able. When a nontrump is led, a player who is void of that suit must trump, if able. When a trump is led, a player must play a higher trump than any already on the trick. (If he cannot play a higher trump, he still must follow suit with a trump, if able.) As in other Pinochle games, a trick is won by the player who played the highest trump; if there is no trump on the trick, it is won by the player who played the highest card of the suit led. When duplicate cards are played on the same trick, the first played is the higher. The winner of a trick leads to the next trick.

The object of the play is to win cards of counting value, as shown in the table on page 96. Winning the last trick counts 10 points.

SCORING

Each side counts the total value of the cards on the tricks which it has taken and (provided that it has won at least one trick) the value of its melds. If the bidder's side won at least the amount of its bid, the number of points bid (not the number made) is added to its running score. If the bidder's side failed to make its bid, the number of points bid is subtracted from that total. The opponents add the total of the points that they made (the value of their melds plus the value of the cards on the tricks they have taken) to their accumulated score.

GAME

The side which first reaches a total of 1000 points at the end of a deal wins the game. It is usual to allow *declaring out*. As in other Pinochle games, play ceases and the total count is verified. If the player's side who declared out has the required number of points, it wins, regardless of the total number of points the opponents have. If the side which declared out does not have enough points to make game, that side loses the game at once.

If both sides reach or exceed a total of 1000 points at the end of a deal, the bidder's side wins. When you are pretty sure that the bidder has exceeded 1000 points, it clearly is to your advantage (assuming that you are an opponent) to declare out as soon as you feel that you have a reasonable chance of having the required total. You cannot do worse than lose, and you have already done that if you permit the deal to go to its conclusion.

IRREGULARITIES

New deal   There must be a new deal by the same dealer if a card is exposed during the deal; or if the pack was not properly shuffled and cut, provided that attention was drawn to the fact before the last card is dealt; or if at any time one hand is found to have too many cards and another hand to have too few.

Bid out of turn   If a player bids out of turn, his bid is void and his side may not bid again. Any previous bid made by his partner still stands.

Insufficient bid   If a player makes an insufficient bid, she must make that bid sufficient and her partner must pass at her next opportunity. (It is not unethical to deliberately make an insufficient bid in order to cut the partner out of his or her turn to bid and, hopefully, to obtain the opportunity to name the trump suit.

Exposed cards   If a card is exposed during the bidding, the offender's partner must pass (unless, of course, he had made a legal bid prior to the exposing of the card). If a player exposes a card during proper play, the card must be left face up on the table and be played at the owner's first legal opportunity. If the card is still not played when it is the turn of the offender's partner to lead, either of their opponents may name the suit to be led.

Play out of turn   If a player leads or plays out of turn, the card is treated as an exposed card.

Revoke As in other Pinochle games, a player revokes when he fails to follow suit, when able; to trump when void in a nontrump suit which was led and which he was able to trump; to play over on a trump lead, when able. A player may correct his revoke up to the time that he or his partner plays to the next trick. If not corrected in time, it is established, and the offending side may not score for points taken in play (but does not lose its melds if it had previously taken a trick).

♣   ◇   ♡   ♠

DOUBLE-PACK PINOCHLE

This game is now the most popular form of Partnership Auction Pinochle and follows its rules except as noted below:

PRELIMINARIES

Cards A pack of 80 cards formed by shuffling together two regular Pinochle decks after first removing the nines. Thus, we have four cards of each rank in each suit; ace (highest), 10, K, Q, J (lowest).

The deal Each player receives 20 cards in batches, usually five at a time.

BIDDING

The minimum bid is 500. In making a bid, the player may also announce that she holds a flush or long trump suit (but she must not name that suit or give any other information).

If a player wishes, she may announce the total value of all or part of her melds before any bid is made. After the bidding has started, such an announcement constitutes an overcall of 10 points for each 100 points, or fraction thereof, announced. For example, announcing a meld of 120 points is an overcall of the previous bid by 20 points; an announcement of a total meld of 240 points is an overcall of 30 points.

MELDS

Besides the basic melds (see page 97), the following melds are allowed with the values indicated:

Double aces	1000	Triple kings	1200
(two of each suit)		Triple queens	900
Double kings	800	Triple jacks	600
Double queens	600	Double Pinochle	300
Double jacks	400	Triple Pinochle	450
Triple aces	1500	Quadruple Pinochle	1000
(three of each suit)			

Quadruple aces, etc., merely count as two double aces. Note that there is no increased value for a double flush. A side's melds do not count unless that side has won a trick.

SCORING

The point values of the cards are 10 for each ace, ten, and king and nothing for the queens and jacks. The last trick counts 20. If the bidding side makes in melds and tricks at least what it has bid, it scores all that it makes. If a bid is defeated, the amount of the bid is deducted from that side's score. The other side scores all that it makes in either case. Game is fixed at various amounts in different circles: 5000 or 4500, or sometimes 3500. If both sides reach game in the same deal, the bidder's side wins.

Poker

GENERAL

The following rules are applicable to all forms of Poker, except where specifically noted otherwise.

Players Two to ten players; best is six to eight. More than eight plays can play only stud poker.

Cards A regular deck of 52 cards; occasionally, the joker is added. The cards rank ace (highest), K, Q, J, 10, 9, 8, 7, 6, 5, 4, 3, 2 (lowest). The ace also ranks low in the sequence 5-4-3-2-A. It also may, with prior agreement rank both high and low in high-low games (see page 125). The joker, when used, is a wild card (see page 125). Suits are ignored except for flushes. Poker is almost invariably played with chips of various colors.

The deal The first deal may be determined by cut, the low card indicating the dealer, or by one of the players taking a deck and dealing the cards, one at a time, until one of the players receives a jack. This player becomes the first dealer. After the first hand the deal rotates clockwise. In all forms of Poker, after the deck has been shuffled and cut by the player on the dealer's right, the cards are dealt, one at a time, beginning with the player on the dealer's left. Each player usually receives five cards, but in some of the poker variations described later more or fewer than five cards may be dealt. Depending upon the game being played, all or only a portion of the cards will be dealt face down.

Poker is a game in which the players bet as to which player holds the best hand. All bets made by the players go into a pile of chips in the center of the table known as the *pot*.

The object of the game is to win the pot. This may be done in either of two ways: first, if two or more of the players have

114

put the same amount of chips in the pot (on the last betting interval of the game), there is a *showdown* in which the hands are shown and the best hand wins; second, if during the regular betting cycle a player makes a bet which none of the other players is willing to match, that player wins the pot without showing his hand. No one is eligible to compete for the pot unless he is willing to match at least the highest bet made by any of his predecessors.

This introduces the factor of *bluffing;* that is, betting on a weak hand in the hope that all other players will fail to match that bet and will drop out.

RANK OF POKER HANDS

The following card combinations have value in poker. They are listed in order of seniority; that is, any given combination is beaten by those listed above it and will, in turn, defeat all of the combinations listed below it.

Straight flush   Five cards in sequence in the same suit constitute a straight flush. If two players have straight flushes, the straight flush headed by the highest card wins. A-K-Q-J-10 (called a royal flush) beats a K-Q-J-10-9, and 6-5-4-3-2 beats a 5-4-3-2-A. The royal flush is the highest hand in a game where there are no wild cards; when there are wild cards in the game, the highest hand is five of a kind.

Four of a kind   This requires any four cards of the same rank. Between two such hands, the higher-ranking four cards win. When there are wild cards in the game, it is possible for two players to hold four of a kind of the same rank. In this case, the player with the higher fifth card wins.

Full house   Three of a kind and a pair make a full house. Between two full houses the one with the higher-ranking threes wins. If there are wild cards in the game and the two players hold threes of the same rank, the player with the higher-ranking pair wins.

Flush   Any hand with five cards in the same suit con-stitutes a flush. Between two flushes the one containing the highest-ranking card wins. If these two cards tie, the one with the next highest card wins, and so on down to the last card. Thus a hand containing A-K-10-9-3 of hearts beats a hand containing the A-K-10-9-2 of spades.

Straight Any five cards in sequence (but not all of the same suit) make a straight. Between two straights the one beginning with the higher-ranking card wins. The highest possible straight is A-K-Q-J-10 and the lowest is 5-4-3-2-A.

Three of a kind This needs three cards of the same rank combined with two unmatching cards. Between two threes the higher ranking three wins. If there are wild cards in the game and the two players hold threes of the same rank, the higher of the remaining two cards determines the winner. If these two cards are identical, the winner is determined by the rank of the fifth card. Thus K-K-2 (deuces wild)-J-9 beats a hand composed of K-K-joker-J-7.

Two pairs This needs two cards of any one rank plus two cards of a different rank plus one unmatched card. Between two such hands the one with the higher-ranking pair is the winner. If these two pairs are the same, the hand with the higher second pair is the winner. If the hands contain two identical pairs, the higher-ranking fifth card determines the winner.

One pair This needs any two cards of the same rank combined with three unmatching cards. (A player is dealt a single pair about two times in five deals.) Between two hands with identical pairs, the hand with the higher of the first-ranking unmatched cards wins. If these cards match, the hand with the higher second ranking unmatched cards wins. Finally, if these two cards match the winner is determined by the higher of the fifth cards. For example, Q-Q-10-7-3 beats Q-Q-10-7-2.

High card About one out of every two hands that a player is dealt will consist merely of five unmatched cards. Between two such hands the winner is determined in the same manner as in the case of one pair.

Identical hands   Hands identical in all respects tie. The suits of which the hands are composed make no difference.

ROTATION

In Poker everything passes from one player to the player on his or her left; that is, clockwise. The deal passes this way, the cards are dealt this way, and the turn to bet rotates this way. No player should do anything until the player to his or her right has acted.

RULES OF BETTING

Betting occurs during periods of the game known as betting intervals. The number of *betting intervals* depends upon what form of Poker is being played. For example, in Draw Poker the first interval occurs when all players have been dealt the original five cards; in Stud Poker it occurs when each player has received his first two cards. In each betting interval some player has the right, or duty, of betting first. Usually there is some maximum or minimum amount, agreed upon in advance, that he may bet. He has to place the number of chips that he wishes to bet into the pot and, at the same time, announce the number of chips that he is betting. When the designated player has made his first bet, each player after him must, in turn, do one of the following:

Pass (drop out)   Drop out of the pot (or *pass*), which means that he discards his hand and has no further interest in that particular pot. A player should not bet or drop out before his proper turn to bet. To do so in advance may affect the action taken by one of the players whose turn to bet would normally occur prior to that of the offender. When a player drops, he forfeits all rights to any of the chips that he may have put into the pot previously. They will eventually belong to the winner of that pot.

Call (see)   This means that the player puts enough chips into the pot to make his total contribution match the greatest number of chips that any previous player has bet.

Raise This means that, in addition to matching the amount that any previous player has put into the pot, she puts in an added amount (not exceeding the amount previously agreed upon for the maximum raise), and now has put more chips into the pot than any other players. The excess amount that she put into the pot is the amount of her raise. All the other active players must now, in turn, either drop, call, or raise. Usually there is a limit in the number of raises that can be made during any one round of betting.

Betting continues until all bets are *equalized*. This occurs when it becomes the turn to bet of the last player who raised, and all succeeding players have either dropped or called.

For example, assume that the first bettor puts in three chips (the limit); the second player to bet called, putting in three chips; the third player raised the limit by putting in six chips; the fourth player, in an effort to limit the amount of the raises during this round of betting, put in seven chips, thus raising the pot one chip; and the fifth player also raised one chip by putting in a total of eight chips. Assume that, by prior agreement, there can be only three raises per betting interval. The last bet, therefore, represents the last allowable raise for this betting interval. There can be no more raises. Hence, each active player must, in turn, either drop or call (by bringing the total number of chips that he has put into the pot up to eight).

In many forms of poker a player is permitted to *check* when no player, whose turn to bet has come before him, has made any actual bet. When a player checks, he is really making a bet of zero chips. Each player after him may also check up to the time that some player makes an actual bet. Thereafter each player must, in turn, either drop, call, or raise. A player who once drops cannot reenter the action on that particular pot. He has forfeited all interest in it. If everyone checks, the cards are dealt for the next round. If everyone checks on the last betting interval, the showdown follows.

LIMITS

Most individuals play with a chip limit, as previously discussed. Other popular ways of determining the limit are:

Pot limit The first player whose turn it is to bet may bet any number of chips up to the number of chips in the pot. Any player betting after him or her in the same betting interval may raise by as many chips as there are in the pot after he calls. That is, he may if he wishes, announce his intention of raising the *size of the pot*. He then puts in enough chips to match the previous raise, then counts the pot and matches the total for his raise! For example, assume that there are 10 chips in the pot and that the first player bets 10 chips. The next player to bet may raise the size of the pot by putting in 40 chips—10 to match the last raise and 30 to match the size of the pot after he has called. This makes the total in the pot 60 chips.

Suppose that another player decides to call. She will put in her matching 40 chips, making the total 100 chips. Now the original bettor may call for 30 chips or raise up to 130 chips— the size of the pot after he calls. Clearly this method of determining the limit for any given bet can result in a very high-stake game. Some limit should be set as a maximum allowable raise, because the player with plenty of capital can frequently freeze out another player, even though the latter has the better hand. Two players, playing in concert, can whipsaw any third player. Never play pot limit with strangers!

Table stakes This is an all-purpose game in which the action on any one deal is limited by the number of chips in front of the player when the deal starts. In standard table stakes he can bet all of his chips at once. Assume that A, B, and C are competing for a particular pot. A has 100 chips in front of her on the table, B has 120 chips, and C has 50 chips. Suppose B bets 60 chips. Then C, who wishes to call, puts in his 50 chips and pushes the entire pot—except for the 10 chips which he did not match—to one side. These 10 chips are used to start a second pot in which only A and B have any interest. It is now A's turn to drop, call, or raise. Suppose A decides to raise 30 chips. She puts 50 chips in the portion of the pot that C has put to one side (thereby equalizing this pot in which A, B, and C all have an equal interest). She also adds 40 chips to the side pot in which only A and B have an interest.

Now it is B's turn to drop (note that, if he does not call A's last raise of 30 chips, he loses not only his interest in the side pot but also his interest in the main pot that C had put to one side), call, or raise. If he decides to raise, he might as well limit his raise to 10 chips because that is all that A has left in front of her on the table. Assume that he decides to call. He then puts 30 more chips in the side pot, thereby matching the total of A's bets. By assuming that this betting interval is the last one in this particular hand, A and B play showdown for the 80 chips in the side pot, and A, B, and C play showdown for the original pot—150 chips plus any chips in the pot at the time that B made his bet of 50 chips. When playing table stakes, no one can add to the chips in front of him on the table after the deal has started, but between deals he may add as many chips as he wishes.

Comment on the need for limits We just commented on the need for a limit to the maximum size of a raise in pot limit. In an ordinary limit game, where there is a limit per raise that is within reason, there is also a need for a limit on the number of raises per betting interval. If you do not, what did happen to my father many, many years ago, is almost certain to occur. Father was playing in a $5 limit stud game (all players could easily stand this limit). Three players were left in the pot; two showed a jack up and the third a ten. The two with a jack started raising back and forth—obviously they each had a pair of jacks—and soon the third man started begging for mercy. They answered him, "We aren't going to stop until you drop!" He appealed to my father, who had dropped earlier, saying, "Counselor, what should we do? I already have $500 in the pot, and these men are taking advantage of me since they are far wealthier than I am." My father replied, "This is a gentleman's game. I suggest that you agree on some limit, such as $250 a person, and then play the hand out."

It was grudgingly agreed to. With a bit of luck the man with the 10 won the pot.

ARRANGING THE GAME

Nothing is needed except a table, chairs, cards, and Poker chips. The chips should be white, red (worth five white chips), and blue (worth 10 white chips). Other commonly used values are white (worth five units), red (worth ten units—two whites), and blue (worth 25 units—five whites). One member of the game is usually selected as banker. At the start all chips are the banker's property. He or she sells or issues them to the players, usually the same amount to each player. When a player runs out of chips, he should buy additional poker chips from the banker. He should not buy or borrow chips from the other players. It is very convenient to have some higher-value chips, usually yellow, in the game.

IRREGULARITIES

Exposed cards If a card is exposed during the original deal, the deal continues and there is no correction. If more than one card is exposed in the same hand, the owner of that hand, provided that he has not looked at any other card in his hand, may demand a new deal. In general, regardless of the irregularity, a player may not ask for a new deal if he looked at any of his cards voluntarily.

After the first betting interval, the exposure of any card is treated as follows: The card is considered a dead card; that is, it is buried. The dealer then proceeds to deal all the other players the cards due them. He or she then deals a replacement to the owner of the exposed card. The affected player may not take the exposed care even if he would like to have it.

Incorrect number of cards If a player determines that she has an incorrect number of cards *prior to looking at any of her cards*, it is a misdeal. If she has looked at her hand and she has too many cards, she forfeits all interest in the pot and her hand is dead. If she has too few cards, the dealer gives her enough cards to complete her hand.

♣ ◇ ♡ ♠

DRAW POKER (JACKPOTS)
(PASS AND OUT)

In Draw Poker the dealer gives each player five cards, face down. The remaining cards are set aside and there is a betting interval. Then each active player (in turn) may discard one card or more, frequently limited to three cards by prior agreement, and the dealer gives him or her replacement cards from the top of the remainder of the deck (which he had previously set aside for this purpose). A player does not have to make any discards. He may, if he so desires, keep his original five cards. In this case, he is said to *stand pat*. Now there is second betting interval followed by a showdown in which the player with the best hand wins the pot.

In the first betting interval the eldest hand (the player to the left of the dealer) has the first turn to bet. He must either drop, check, or bet. If he checks, each of the following players has the same option until a player *opens* by making the first bet. Thereafter each player, in turn, must either drop, call, or raise until the betting interval is over.

In the most popular form of Draw Poker, called Jackpots, a player may not open unless he or she has a pair of jacks (or a better hand). In another popular form called Pass and Out, a player may open on anything, but each player, in turn, must either drop or bet; there is no checking.

In these forms of poker, as in many other games, it is customary for each player to *ante* one chip of lowest value (one white chip) before the deal. If no one opens, the chips from the ante remain in the pot and everyone antes again. Then there is a new deal by the next player to the left. (Frequently the dealer is required to put in the ante amount for all the players, thus eliminating confusion as to who has anted up.)

The draw begins after the first betting interval, that is, when all bets have been equalized. The dealer picks up the remainder of the deck and stands by to deal replacement cards. The first active player to his or her left then discards one card or more, announcing the number as he discards, and the dealer gives him that number of cards from the top of the deck. If a player does not desire to draw any new cards, he announces this fact by knocking on the table or otherwise signifying that he is *standing pat*. The privilege to discard and draw replacement cards passes, clockwise, from one active player to the next active player until all active players have either drawn the cards that they want or indicated that they desire none. Now another betting interval starts. The player who opened has the first opportunity to check or bet. If he or she checks, the next active player to his or her left has the same options. If the opener dropped after the draw, the next active player to his or her left has the first turn to bet. Once a bet is made, each active player, in turn, thereafter must either drop, call, or raise until the bets are again equalized. At this point (or when every player has checked) the second betting interval is ended.

The showdown follows. Every player who has not previously dropped now places all five of his cards face up on the table. Any hand which does not have five cards in it is dead—its owner does not share in the pot. Usually each player announces the value of his hand by saying, "three sixes" or "queens up" (meaning two pairs, the higher of which is queens), but such announcement is not required. If a player does announce her hand and has more—or less—than the values she announced, she need not stick by her announcement. It is a tradition of poker that "the cards speak for themselves."

A player who announces three of a kind when, in fact, he holds a full house may, at any time before the pot is actually gathered in by another player, correct his announcement. However, in some circles the practice is that, once a player calls his hand, he cannot change it. It is important that agreement be reached as to whether or not another player may call attention to the call and whether or not a player may correct his call after his attention has been called to the error. A player who is in the final showdown may not throw away his hand without showing it simply because another player has announced a higher-ranking hand. Every player who is "in on the call" must expose his full hand, face up, on the table in the showdown. In many games a player who is in on the showdown, but does not claim to have the high hand, does not have to show his hand. However, there is one exception to this rule. The opener is usually required to show his hand to prove that he did hold "openers."

When the hands are shown in the showdown, the player having the highest-ranking Poker hand wins the pot. The cards are then assembled and reshuffled. The players ante for the next deal and there is another deal by the next player to the left. Frequently two decks of cards are used. While the dealer is dealing with one of the decks, the player two places to his left reshuffles the other deck.

COMBINATIONS

In some localities combinations other than the standard ones are counted in the showdown. Some of the more popular are as listed below:

Big Tiger   A *Big Tiger* is a hand with five unmatched cards—king high and eight low.

Little Tiger   A *Little Tiger* also is a hand with five unmatched cards—eight high and three low.

Big Dog   A *Big Dog* also is a hand with five unmatched cards—ace high and nine low.

Little Dog   A *Little Dog* also is a hand with five unmatched cards—seven high and deuce low.

Kilter   The *Kilter* is played in some localities. It loses to a straight, but beats three of a kind. It consists of the 9-5-2 plus two cards of different rank between the two and the nine. (Of course, the hand must not contain a pair or be all of the same suit.)

Blaze   The *Blaze* is another special combination played in some localities. It also loses to a straight and beats three of a kind. If you happen to be playing both *Kilter* and *Blaze*, be sure that you reach mutual agreement as to which is the higher rank. It consists of a hand containing five face cards.

The last four combinations are listed in order of seniority; that is, a Big Tiger beats a Little Tiger, which in turn beats a

Big Dog, which in turn beats a Little Dog. All combinations beat a straight and lose to a flush.

When it is necessary to break a tie between any two of these combinations, the rules are the same as for breaking ties between any two hands which do not contain a pair or better.

High-low   Almost any form of Poker may be played high-low. There is no difference in the original betting, but in the showdown the highest-ranking Poker hand and the lowest-ranking Poker hand divide the pot equally, the high hand receiving any odd chip. Players must decide in advance whether the ace will rank only high or will rank high or low at the player's option.

Wild game   A joker added to the pack, or any other card (or cards), may be designated, in advance, to be wild. The holder of a wild card may designate it to stand for any card that he wishes. A wild card ranks exactly the same as the card it represents. Except by special "house rules," it cannot stand for a card that the player already holds. For example, double-ace flushes and five of a kind cannot exist without prior agreement.

The bug   The joker is called the bug when it can be used in only the following ways: to fill a straight flush, a flush, a straight, or—failing one of these uses—as an ace. Thus two aces and the bug are three aces, but two kings and the bug are merely two kings and an ace.

With a repair   Just as many forms of Poker can be played with or without the high-low feature or the wild-card feature, many forms can be played with or without the *with a repair* feature. This feature consists in offering each active player (each player who still holds an interest in the pot)—just before the final showdown—an opportunity to improve his hand by dealing him one additional card, face down. It is known as a *buy repair* when the players desiring a repair pay a fixed amount into the pot, usually the amount of the limit raise. In this case a player may look at his repair card before making a discard to bring his hand back to the proper size. It is known as a *free repair* when the player desiring a repair does not have to pay into the pot to receive one. On the other hand, the player desiring a free repair must make a discard before he looks at his repair card. This requirement can present quite a problem when the game is high-low and the player's hand is such that he will have to decide whether he wishes to go high or low before he makes his choice of discard.

♣   ◇   ♡   ♠

OTHER FORMS OF DRAW POKER

BLIND AND STRADDLE

This game of Poker, also called *Blind Opening, Blind Tiger, Tiger* (and other names, including *English Poker, Australian Poker,* and *South African Poker*), is an early form of Poker that is still played. There is no ante. The first bet, called *blind,* must be made by the eldest hand putting one white chip or more into the pot according to the game custom.

The player on his left must put in two or more chips as a blind *straddle.* Each player in turn thereafter may, but need not, double the last blind bet as an additional straddle. The number of straddles is usually limited to three.

Five cards are then dealt to each player. After everyone has looked at his or her hand, the player to the left of the last straddler must either drop or place a bet equal to the last straddle; there is no checking. Each active player now must in turn either drop, call, or raise. When it becomes the turn of the eldest hand to bet, he may take into consideration the chips that he had bet blind in calculating the number of chips he now has to put into the pot to call or raise. All of the straddlers have the same option. When all bets have been equalized, there is a draw. After the draw is completed, the nearest active player to the left of the dealer must either drop or bet. Subsequently, all active players must, in turn, drop, call, or raise. When the bets are equalized, there is a showdown.

STRAIGHT DRAW POKER

Straight Draw Poker is the game previously described as *Pass and Out*. It is also called *Passout, Bet or Drop,* and other names. Usually checking is not permitted. However, in some localities checking is permitted in the betting interval after the draw.

♣ ◇ ♡ ♠

LOWBALL

Lowball is similar to Draw Poker except that there is no minimum requirement for opening the pot and that, in the showdown, the lowest-ranking Poker hand, as differentiated from the highest-ranking Poker hand, wins the pot.

In addition, the ace ranks only low; flushes and straights have no value. The lowest possible hand—5-4-3-2-A—is called a *bicycle*. (It makes no difference whether the cards are all of one suit or of two or more suits). Since aces are low, a pair of aces beats a pair of deuces.

In some localities Lowball is played in conjunction with Draw Poker. If a deal of Draw Poker is passed out, the hand becomes Lowball. Players may check, and if no one bets, there is still a showdown, the lowest-ranking hand taking the pot. This game is sometimes called *Jacks Laid Back*.

♣ ◇ ♡ ♠

STUD POKER

Stud Poker is one of the best of the variations of Poker where some of the cards are dealt face up. It is sometimes called five-card Stud Poker to distinguish it from seven-card Stud (see page 128), which has become at least as popular.

The dealer deals each player a *hole card* face down and then a card face up. Each player looks at his or her card, but does not show it. The deal is now interrupted by a betting interval. In the first betting interval, the player who was dealt the highest-ranking face-up card must bet or drop. If there is a tie for highest-ranking face-up card, the first player to be dealt his card bets first. The duty of making the first bet passes clockwise if a player drops. After the first bet, the betting interval continues until all bets are equalized, each player dropping, calling, or raising when it is his or her turn to bet.

The dealer now gives each active player a second face-up card. Now there is another betting interval, commencing with the player with the highest-ranking Poker hand showing. This betting interval is similar to the first betting interval except that checking is allowed during it and subsequent intervals. A pair, of course, outranks any combination that does not contain a pair; between two pairs the higher one outranks the lower in the final showdown. If there are no pairs, the highest-ranking card showing determines the preference. A tie is broken by the second-ranking card in the tying hands. If these cards also tie, the final determination is left to proximity in rotation to the dealer, as in the case of the first card.

In a similar manner the dealer deals a third face-up card followed by another betting interval; then the dealer deals a fourth (and final) face-up card. There is then the final betting interval, followed by each remaining active player turning up his or her hole card for a showdown.

During the play of the hand, a player who desires to drop indicates the fact by turning face down all the cards he has been dealt. It is not permitted for a player who drops to show his hole card to any of the active players.

In many places where five-card Stud Poker is played high-low, after the fourth betting interval is completed, any active player is permitted to turn up her hole card and to receive her last card face down.

SEVEN-CARD STUD POKER

Seven-card Stud Poker is similar to five-card Stud Poker with the following exceptions:

Initially each player is dealt, one at a time, two cards face down and one card face up, and then there is a betting interval. Now, as in five-card Stud Poker, the dealer deals three rounds of cards face up, each round being followed by a betting interval. At this point in the play of the hand, each active player has two cards face down and four cards face up, and there have been four betting intervals.

Finally, each active player is dealt one more card face down and there is a final betting interval. Then each active player turns his three hidden cards face up and selects from his seven cards any five cards that he wishes to constitute his final Poker hand. Now there is a showdown to determine the winner of the pot. It is advisable that prior agreement be reached as to whether "cards speak for themselves" or the hand stands as the player calls it. In other words, may a player change the five cards that he had selected and the call that he had made after his attention has been called to the fact that his call could be improved upon?

This game is also called *Down-the-River* and *Seven-Toed Pete*, among other names.

SIX-CARD STUD POKER

Six-card Stud Poker is identical to five-card Stud Poker except that after each player has been dealt his or her fourth face-up card and the betting interval following it has been completed, each player receives a final face-down card, followed by a final betting interval. Each player then turns his six cards face up and proceeds to select five of them to form his hand and makes his call in the final showdown, similar to the procedure after the last betting interval in seven-card Stud Poker.

EIGHT-CARD STUD POKER

Eight-card Stud Poker is identical to seven-card Stud Poker except that after each player has been dealt his or her seventh face-down card and the betting interval following it has been completed, an eighth card is dealt face down to each active player and there is a final betting interval. Each player then turns his eight cards face up and proceeds to select five

of them to form his hand and makes his call in the final
showdown, similar to the procedure after the last betting
interval in seven-card Stud Poker.

SEVEN-CARD HIGH-LOW STUD POKER

Seven-card high-low Stud Poker is played exactly the same
as seven-card Stud Poker up to the end of the last betting
interval. Now the players face their seven cards and select
five of them to form their best high hand and "high-hand
showdown" takes place. After this the players select five
cards from their seven cards to form their best low hand and
"low-hand showdown" takes place. A perfect low is 5-4-3-2-
A, regardless of whether or not all are of the same suit. (But
see later.) Seven-card high-low Stud Poker is a better game
when *declarations* are played. When they are being played,
after the final betting interval and before any of the down
cards are faced, each player in turn (the last raiser calling
first) must call *high, low,* or both *high and low.* A player may
win only that part of the pot for which he or she declares. If
he declares high and low, he must at least tie each way or he
receives nothing. If he is tied, the portion of the pot in which
he is tied is shared with the player(s) who tied him. Frequently this game is played with the requirement that a player
who declares both high and low must win both; that is, if he
is tied for either high or low, he loses everything. A mutual
agreement should be reached on how to play this declaration.
As an alternative way of making declarations, one can have
all players declare simultaneously by concealing a chip in
their hands (white for low, red for high, and blue for both) and
having all active players expose their chips at the same time.

Variation 1   A combination of 5-4-3-2-A is considered a
straight (beating three of a kind) and five cards of the same
suit are considered a flush (beating a straight). In this case
the perfect low is 6-4-3-2-A, not all of the same suit. Here,
again, one should be sure there is a clear understanding of
what a perfect low is before one deals this game.

♣   ◇   ♡   ♠

DEALER'S CHOICE

Most Poker games played casually by social groups are Dealer's Choice games under the following rules:

1. Each dealer, as his or her turn comes to deal, announces the game to be played—five-card Stud Poker, seven-card high-low Stud Poker, etc.
2. If any card is to be wild, the dealer must announce this fact now.
3. No dealer is bound by the previous dealer's game, except by previous consent. In case this is agreed to, when the game is completed, the deal reverts to the player who missed his option to select his game. (See *Burn*, page 135, for an example.)
4. A dealer is not limited to the more common forms of Poker; she may select any of the games to be described later or she may make one up by using her imagination, provided it is simple enough to be described and is understandable to the other players.

♣   ◇   ♡   ♠

SPIT IN THE OCEAN

The dealer places one card face up in the middle of the table and deals each player four cards, face down, as in regular Draw Power. The up-card is wild as well as all others like it. Each player treats the up-card as the fifth card in his hand. There is a betting interval followed by a showdown.

VARIATION 1

After the betting interval, instead of an immediate showdown, each player turns up any one card from his or her hand, followed by a betting interval, then a second card followed by a betting interval, etc., until after the fourth betting interval the last card is turned face up on the table for a showdown.

VARIATION 2

Instead of one card, the dealer places three cards, face up, in the middle of the table. Each player may select any one of these three cards to be the fifth card in his hand. The card that he selects, and all like it, are wild as far as that player's hand is concerned. The betting cycle may follow either that of the basic game or that given in variation 1.

♣   ◇   ♡   ♠

CINCINNATI (CORY SPECIAL)

After dealing each player five cards as in Draw Poker, the dealer places five cards, face down, in a row in the middle of the table. Then there is a betting interval, eldest hand betting first. When the betting is equalized, the dealer turns up one of the cards in the middle of the table and there is another betting interval. The last raiser bets first. If there was no raise in the previous interval, the duty to bet rotates one player, clockwise, from the previous original bettor. The dealer then turns up the second, third, fourth, and fifth, of these cards, with a betting interval following the turning of each card.

Then each active player selects any five of the ten cards available to him (that is, from the five in his hand and the five now face up on the board) to be his hand in the showdown.

CORY SPECIAL

This game is similar to Cincinnati except that it is played high-low with the low card in each player's hand being wild *for high only;* only the natural value of the cards count for low. As in other games, the lowest possible hand is 6-4-3-2-A (of which, of course, not all are the same suit) or 5-4-3-2-A (regardless of suit), depending upon the custom of the locality. Also, it is frequently played *with a repair* feature (see page 125). When this is done, the dealer must be careful to specify whether he or she is playing with a "buy repair" or with a "free repair."

♣   ◇   ♡   ♠

FIERY CROSS

The play of this game differs but little from Cincinnati. The five cards placed in the center of the table are put in the form of a cross. The card in the center of the cross is usually turned up last. It, and all like it, are wild. Each player may select the five cards to form his hand from the five cards in his hand and from either the three horizontal cards or from the three vertical cards. It is also known as *Criss-Cross*.

This game is frequently played high-low with (instead of the center card) the lowest card in each player's hand, and all like it, wild (as far as that player is concerned) for high only. *With a repair* feature adds greatly to the game.

♣   ◇   ♡   ♠

LAMEBRAIN PETE

This game is the same as Cincinnati except that the lowest card in each player's hand and all like it are wild.

♣   ◇   ♡   ♠

OMAHA

This game is similar to Cincinnati except that each player is dealt two cards face down instead of five. After the betting interval each player selects her hand from the two cards dealt to her and the five cards on the table.

HOLD-'EM POKER

This game is the same as Omaha except that after the first betting interval, three of the center cards are turned face up at the same time; then there is a betting interval. Then the fourth and fifth cards are turned up, with a betting interval after each card is turned.

SHOTGUN POKER

The deal is the same as in Draw Poker, except there is a betting interval after the third, fourth, and fifth cards have been dealt. From here on, the game is the same as Draw Poker.

SHOWDOWN POKER

This game is frequently played at the end of a Dealer's Choice session to determine who wins the "odd-change pot." It consists merely of the dealer dealing five cards to each player face up, one at a time. There is no draw and the high hand wins the pot.

♣   ◇   ♡   ♠

BURN

Burn is frequently played in Dealer's Choice sessions. Although it has little connection to Poker, it adds variety and excitement. It starts with an ante, usually the amount of the maximum limit raise. Then each player is dealt three cards face down and a card is dealt face up in the middle of the table to indicate the trump suit. There is now a draw with each player discarding as many cards as he wishes, zero to three, with the dealer giving him an equal number of replacement cards. There is no advantage for a player to hold any cards in his hand other than those in the trump suit.

Play now starts with eldest hand leading to the first trick, and the winner of each trick leading to the next trick. Each player must follow the rules of Bridge: On each trick a player must follow suit if able. If he cannot follow suit, he may play any card remaining in his hand. A trick is won by the player who played the highest trump. If there is no trump on the trick, it is won by the player who played the highest-ranking card in the suit led.

When play is completed, each player who took a trick receives one-third of the pot. Now all players ante the same amount as they did at the start of the game. In addition, the players who failed to take a trick must put into the pot an amount equal to the total in the pot when the first round of play started.

The deal now passes to the player to the left of the original dealer. She must deal the same game, following the same procedure as the original dealer, except that after the draw each player must announce, in turn, either *pass* or *play*. It is very bad etiquette for a player to announce his decision before it is his turn. If he passes, he has no interest in that particular pot; he does, however, retain his interest in the next round, assuming that there is one. If he says "play," he is saying that he wishes to compete for the pot. After all players have declared their intentions, play starts with the first active player—the player who first announced "play"—to the left of the dealer leading.

After the second round is completed, each player takes one-third of the pot for each trick that he took. If each player who said that he wished to "play" takes at least one trick, the game is over and the deal reverts to the player to the left of the one who started Burn.

If any player who said that he desired to "play" failed to take a trick, that player is *burnt* and the third round of the game follows. The next player on the last dealer's left becomes the new dealer. Play continues as in the second round. First, all players (including the players who announced "pass" on the previous round, and those who were burnt) ante. In addition, each player who competed in the previous round and was burnt must put into the pot an amount equal to the total amount that was in the pot at the beginning of the play of that round. Then play in the third round continues as before—the deal, the draw, the declarations ("pass" or "play"), the play to the three tricks by the players who announced "play," the distribution of the pot between the players who said "play" and who took at least one trick.

This cycle continues until a round is played in which no player is burnt. The game then ends and the deal reverts, as before, to the player to the left of the original player to announce and deal Burn.

♣   ◇   ♡   ♠

ANACONDA

Each player is dealt seven cards, face down. Then there is a betting interval (sometimes omitted), after which each player still in the pot passes three cards to the player on his or her right (or left, as agreed). Each player then discards two cards, leaving himself five cards for his final hand. There is now a betting interval. Each remaining player then arranges his five cards in any order that he wishes and places his hand on the table face down.

After each player has placed his or her hand on the table, each turns the top card face up, followed by a round of betting. The second card is then turned face up, followed by another round of betting. This process is continued until a showdown is reached. Note that once the first card is turned face up, a player cannot change the order in which he has arranged his cards.

♣   ◇   ♡   ♠

BUTCHER BOY

The dealer deals all cards face up. When any player is dealt a card of the same rank as one of the cards previously dealt, that card is given to the player holding the first card of that rank. There is a betting interval, with the player to whom the card was transferred making the first call—pass, check, or bet. The deal then continues with the first card being dealt to the player who would have received the transferred card.

Butcher Boy is usually played high-low. Play ceases when any player is dealt four of a kind. The player with the four of a kind receives half the pot for high hand; the remaining players still in the game compete for low hand and the other half of the pot. Since not all players have five cards at this point, low hand is determined as follows: A player with more than five cards may select any five as his or her low hand. A player with fewer than five cards is considered to have the vacant places filled with cards of the lowest rank. For example, a three-card hand with 9-5-4 is treated as though it were 9-5-4-2-2, the lowest-ranking card being a deuce. Note that the two deuces do not count as a pair of deuces. This hand beats a five-card hand of 9-5-4-3-2.

♣   ◇   ♡   ♠

MEXICAN STUD

There is no difference between this game and five-card Stud Poker except that each card is dealt face down, and after each card is dealt, a player turns one of his or her two face-down cards face up, thus keeping whichever card he or she wishes as the hole card.

♣ ◇ ♡ ♠

BASEBALL

Baseball is similar to seven-card Stud Poker, played with all nines and threes down wild, plus the following special rules:

1. Whenever any player is dealt a three face up (remember that there will be three rounds of cards dealt face down and four rounds dealt face up—the order in which these rounds are dealt depends upon the dealer), he must decide whether he wishes to drop out of the pot or to "buy the pot" (pay a forfeit to the pot equal to the number of chips already in the pot) and retain his interest in the pot. If he does buy the pot, that three is also wild. The dealer must wait for a player to make his decision—and the required contribution, if any, to the pot—before another card is dealt. Any card dealt in the meantime is considered dead.

2. If a player is dealt a four face up, he or she may either keep it, or discard it and have it replaced by another card. In some circles, a player who receives a four face up automatically receives an extra card, face down, after all active players have received the card which was owed to them in that round. A four dealt face down is of no significance.

Baseball should always be played high only.

FOOTBALL

This is the same game as baseball, except that all sixes and fours are wild. A four dealt face up requires the player either to drop or to match the pot, and a deuce dealt face up entitles the player to receive an extra card immediately, face down.

♣   ◇   ♡   ♠

CORY BASEBALL

This game is a combination of Cory Special and Baseball. It is played high-low, with low being, as in Cory Special, a natural low. High, however, is determined differently. In Cory Special the low card in each player's hand is wild, but not so in Cory Baseball. In lieu thereof, in Cory Baseball every nine and every three in the players' hands are wild and also every nine exposed in the center of the table is wild. If a three is exposed, it also is wild, but every player must either drop out or pay a penalty to the pot equal to an agreed amount, usually about equal to five maximum raises. If a four is exposed, every player is dealt an extra card, assuming that there are sufficient cards remaining in the deck. Declarations are usually required. (See seven-card high-low Stud Poker, page 130.)

♣   ◇   ♡   ♠

RED AND BLACK

This is another game played in Dealer's Choice which bears little resemblance to Poker. It is a high-low game similar, as far as dealing, betting, and drawing are concerned, to high-low Draw Poker. It is in determining the high and the low hand that the two games differ. Standard Poker combinations are of no significance. The value of a hand is determined by computing the total value of the cards composing it, where all red cards count plus and all black cards count minus. Aces count one each, face cards ten each, and the spot-cards the number showing on their faces. The high hand is the hand with the highest plus or the lowest minus total count; the low hand is the one with the highest minus or the lowest plus total count.

♣ ◇ ♡ ♠

THREE-CARD POKER

Each player is dealt three cards face down with the deal being interrupted after each round for a betting interval.

After the third card is dealt, and the third betting interval is completed, there is a showdown in which three of a kind is the highest-ranking hand. The next highest is a three-card straight flush, followed by a three-card flush, a three-card straight, a pair, and the high card among three unmatched cards.

This game may also be played high-low. In this case the ace ranks high in a high hand and low in a low hand. Usually declarations are required. (See seven-card high-low Stud Poker, page 130.)

♣ ◇ ♡ ♠

TWO-CARD POKER

Each player is dealt two cards, face down, with a betting interval after the first and second round. There is a showdown after the second betting interval in which a pair is the highest hand and high cards determine the rank among hands without a pair.

This game is frequently played with wild cards (usually the deuces, or one-eves—the jacks of spades and hearts, and the king of diamonds). It is also played high-low with the ace ranking high in a high hand and low in a low hand. If playing high-low, the players should declare "high" or "low" before the showdown.

♣ ◇ ♡ ♠

HURRICANE

This is the popular name for two-card Poker when played high-low with deuces wild.

♣ ◇ ♡ ♠

PASS ALONG

In playing this game, the dealer should announce in advance whether it is *six-card* or *seven-card Pass Along*, the number depending upon the number of players in the game, and whether or not there will be a repair. There is a betting interval after the first round of cards is dealt. At the conclusion of this round of betting, the dealer deals a card, face up or face down as she desires, to the player on her left. That player must decide whether to keep all his cards or to pass a card. He may pass any card in his hand—he is not limited to passing the card that he just received—face up to the player on his left and receive another card from the dealer. In determining whether or not a card should be dealt face up or face down, the dealer tries, as far as she can, to give each player the same number of face-down cards. After the first player to the dealer's left has received his replacement card, if any, the dealer moves to the second player to her left and, if that player has not received a passed card, deals him a card.

That player now has the same option that the first player had—he may keep the card that he has received or pass any card in his hand, face up, to the next player on his left and receive a replacement card from the dealer. This process continues around the table until the dealer reaches her own hand. If the dealer decides that she wants a replacement, she buries the card that she does not want on the bottom of the deck rather than pass it on to the player on her left. This completes the dealing of the second round. It is followed by a betting interval, as are all rounds thereafter. The third-to-last round is dealt in a similar fashion. After the last round of betting, there is a repair, followed by a betting interval (if the dealer had announced this fact in advance) and a showdown. If there is no repair, the showdown follows directly after the last betting interval. In each round, of course, the dealer deals a card only to the active players; that is, to those who have not passed.

Normally, just after the last betting interval and before the final showdown, each player declares whether he is going high, low, or both. (See seven-card high-low Stud Poker, page 130.) This game, when played high-low with a repair, is also known as *Dick's Game*.

♣   ◇   ♡   ♠

FIERY CROSS—EXTENDED

This game is quite similar to Fiery Cross. After dealing each player five cards, the dealer puts nine cards on the table in the form of a cross—five cards vertically and five cards horizontally. Here again, depending on the dealer's choice, either the center card and all like it are wild, or the lowest card in each player's hand and all like it are wild. Also, this game may be played high-low and with a repair. It differs from Fiery Cross only in the manner in which the cards are turned face up to form the cross. After each betting interval, the dealer turns two cards face up (rather than the one card turned up in Fiery Cross) until after five betting intervals only the center card remains.

♣   ◇   ♡   ♠

NIGHT BASEBALL

Night Baseball, sometimes called *No Peek*, is played with almost the same rules as Baseball. Each player is dealt seven cards face down (six when there are eight players). The players are not allowed to look at their hands. They may place the cards in any order that they desire. The player to the left of the dealer turns one of his cards face up. If it is a four, he receives from the dealer another card face down. If it is a three, he must, as in Baseball, either match the pot or drop. If it is a wild card (a nine or a three) and he buys the pot, he must turn another card. There then is a round of betting.

It is now the next player's turn. He faces his cards, one at a time, until his hand beats that of the player on his right. He, of course, has the same options as the first player: If a nine turns up, it is wild; if it is a three, he must match the pot or drop; if it is a four, he gets an extra card, face down. When there are seven players, there is no replacement card left for a player who turns up the fourth four.

If the second player or any succeeding player in his turn fails to beat the previous player's hand, he is, of course, out of that game, and the next player to his left starts to turn up cards in an effort to beat the best previous hand. In this case, there is no betting interval. However, there is a betting interval every time a player turns a card which gives him the high hand. He retains the remainder of his cards face down until it is his next turn to play.

This process continues until all players have had an opportunity to turn their cards face up. The high hand at the final showdown wins the pot.

Like regular Baseball, Night Baseball should never be played high-low.

♣ ◇ ♡ ♠

BEECHER'S GAME

This game is five-card Stud Poker played high-low with a free repair. It makes an excellent game for six to eight players.

Rummy

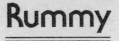

Rummy is one of the most popular games in the United States; perhaps we should say it is also one of the most well-known. This is probably so because it is basically a simple game to describe, and also, once you have mastered it, it becomes a simple matter to understand any of its variations.[1]

The early forerunner of the game, Coon-Can, spread from Mexico to the southwestern United States in the early twentieth century. The object, as in most Rummy games, was to get rid of one's hand by forming it into sets of three or four cards of the same rank or three or more cards in sequence in the same suit.

Since the rules of Coon-Can varied greatly from one locality to another, and since it has been almost completely superseded by other forms of Rummy, no attempt will be made to define its rules. Rather we will start with the rules of basic Rummy.

---

[1] There are no official rules for Rummy. Those given in this chapter are the ones commonly followed. It is, however, a good practice to review the principal rules under which you are to play whenever you start any game of Rummy or similar game. There are many minor variations which creep into these games in different localities.

♣ ◇ ♡ ♠

RUMMY

PRELIMINARIES

Players Two to six players each playing for himself or herself.

Cards A standard 52-card pack with the cards ranking: K (highest), Q, J, 10, 9, 8, 7, 6, 5, 4, 3, 2, A (lowest). The king, queen, and jack count 10 points; the remainder count the number of pips.

The deal Draw or cut for the deal. Any player may shuffle, the dealer having the right to shuffle last. The player to the right of the dealer cuts the cards. The dealer then distributes the cards, one at a time, beginning with the player to his left and moving in a clockwise direction until he has dealt 10 cards to each player when there are two players; seven cards are dealt when there are three or four players; six cards when there are five or six players.

When there are two players, the deal alternates. When there are more than two players, the deal rotates around the table in a clockwise direction.

Stock and discard piles The undealt remainder of the pack (called the *stockpile*) is placed in the center of the table, face down. Next the dealer turns the top card of the stockpile face up and places it alongside the stockpile to form the beginning of the *discard pile*.

OBJECT

The object of the game is to form the hand into sets or *melds*. There are two kinds of melds:

Groups Three or more cards of the same rank, such as
♡8, ◇8, ♣8, or ♠4, ♡4, ◇4, ♣4 form a group.

Sequences Three or more cards of the same suit form a
sequence; one example is ◇J-◇10-◇9. In a sequence, the
ace may count only as one. Such sequences as ◇2-◇A-◇K
or ◇A-◇K-◇Q are not allowed.

PLAY

The player to the left of the dealer plays first. The opportunity to play then passes continuously to the left (clockwise).
Each player at his or her turn must adhere to the following
procedure:

Draw A player begins by drawing one card from the top
of either the stockpile or the discard pile.

Meld A player does not have to *meld* or *lay off* just
because he holds the necessary cards. He may, if he so
chooses, make a discard (see below). On the other hand, he
may place any number of cards from his hand face up on the
table, provided that they form proper groups or sequences, or
proper additions to the groups or sequences already on the
table, regardless of which player originally placed these sets
on the table.

Discard The player then ends his turn by placing one card
face up on the discard pile, except that he need not make a
discard if he has melded and/or laid off all of his cards.[2]

End of play When a player melds and/or lays off all of her
cards, she thereby goes out and wins the deal. Play ceases
and the hand is scored. If no player has gone out by the time
the stockpile is exhausted, the discard pile is turned face
down without shuffling to form a new stockpile and play is
resumed.

------

[2] A frequent variation to this rule is to require a player to make a
discard to complete his play regardless of whether or not he had
melded and/or laid off all of his cards. It is obvious that this change
makes quite a difference in a player's strategy.

SCORING

When a player goes out, thus winning the hand, each of the other players pays the winner for the points corresponding to the cards remaining in his hand: The picture cards each count ten, the ace one, and the other cards count their index value; that is, ♡9 would count nine points, ♣3 three points. All cards still in the hand must be paid for, regardless of whether or not they could have been melded!

IRREGULARITIES

New deal   There must be a new deal by the same dealer if a card is exposed in the dealing; if, *before play begins*, any hand is found to have the wrong number of cards; or if a card is found face up in the stock.

Incorrect hand   If a player is found to have an incorrect number of cards in her hand after play has begun, she must correct it in the course of the play. If she has too many cards, she must correct it by omitting one turn to draw, or more if necessary. If she has too few cards, she must correct it by omitting one discard, or more if necessary. Also, she may not meld at any turn in which she holds an incorrect hand.

Drawing two cards   If a player inadvertently draws two cards from the stockpile and sees them both, he shall put the top card in his hand and place the other card face up near the discard pile. He then continues his play as usual. The next player then has the choice of taking as his card the top of the stockpile, the top of the discard pile, or the card exposed in error. If he does not take the exposed card, it is placed in the middle of the discard pack and is, of course, out of play.

Play out of turn   If a player draws out of turn and then completes his play by discarding, the play stands as made and the player to his left plays next.

If a player draws out of turn and the error is noted before she discards, she must keep the drawn card but the play reverts to the proper player. When it becomes the turn of the offender to play, she must begin her play without drawing a card. If a player melds after drawing out of turn and the error is noted before she discards, she must retract the melded cards until it becomes her turn to complete her play.

Discarding two cards   If a player discards two cards and the error is noted before the next player completes his play, the offender must retract one of the two cards. He may choose either of the two cards unless the next player has already picked up one of them. If the error is first noted at a later time, it must be corrected as prescribed under "Incorrect Hand," page 148.

Incorrect meld   If a player lays down cards which do not, in fact, form a correct group or sequence, or a correct addition to a previously melded group or sequence, he must retract all of the incorrectly melded cards upon demand, provided that the demand is made before the cards are shuffled for the next deal.

Error in scoring   An error in scoring a hand may be corrected at any time before the cards are mixed up in preparation for the next deal. An error in scoring an agreed score may be corrected any time it is noted.

♣   ◇   ♡   ♠

KALUKI

The rules are as in regular Rummy except:

1. A 108-card pack, formed of two regular 52-card packs plus four jokers, is used.
2. Fifteen cards are dealt to each player when there are two, three, or four players; 13 cards when there are five players; and 11 cards when there are six players. Each player plays for himself or herself. Aces may be used either high (◇A-◇K-◇Q) or low (◇3-◇2-◇A), but

one cannot play around the corner (as in ◇2-◇A-◇K).
Also, in scoring, aces count as 15.

3. A player's first meld must count 51 points or more.
4. A player may not take a card from the discard pile or lay
   off on melds exposed face up on the table until he has
   made his initial meld; but he may do so if he first makes
   his initial meld in that turn.
5. The jokers are wild. A joker used in a meld counts the
   same number of points as the card it replaces. After a
   player has drawn her card, and before she melds or
   discards, she may exchange the appropriate natural
   card for the joker in *any* exposed meld.
6. A player who goes out scores all the points left in the
   other hands; the joker counts as 25 points. (In one scoring variation, the winner collects one point from each
   loser for each card in his hand; two points for the joker.)

Caution   Before starting to play, be sure to reach an agreement as to whether or not the cards laid off at the time of a
player's first meld may count toward the 51-point requirement
and whether or not a player may use a joker that he has
exchanged from the board to make his first meld during the
same turn.

♣   ◇   ♡   ♠

BOATHOUSE RUM

The rules are as in regular Rummy except:

1. Each player, in turn, draws the top card of the stockpile,
   or before drawing that card, he may draw the top card of
   the discard pile and then either the next card of the
   discard pile, or the top card of the stockpile. The player
   drawing then completes his play by discarding one card,
   regardless of whether he drew one card or two.
2. Play does not end until a player can lay down her entire
   hand at one time.
3. An ace counts either high or low and a sequence can
   "go around the corner" as in ◇2-◇A-◇K.

4. In scoring, a player pays only for those cards which do not form proper groups or sequences. He pays the winner either one point for each card remaining or the value of all unmatched cards, the ace counting eleven, as agreed to in advance.

♣ ◇ ♡ ♠

CONTINENTAL RUMMY

Until Canasta replaced it about 1950, this was one of the most popular forms of Rummy. As in basic Rummy, the sole object is to form matched sets. It differs from Rummy in several important respects, one of which is that each deal constitutes a complete game.

PRELIMINARIES

Players Two to twelve players, usually four or five.

Cards Two regular packs plus two jokers for two to five players; three packs, plus three jokers for six to eight players, and four jokers for nine to twelve players. The ace ranks high (◇A-◇K-◇Q) or low (◇3-◇2-◇A). The jokers and all deuces are wild.

The deal Each player is dealt 15 cards, usually three at a time. The next card is turned face up to start the discard pile and the remaining cards are placed face down to form the stockpile as in regular Rummy. The winner of each deal becomes the next dealer.

MELDING REQUIREMENTS

To go out, a player must meld his or her entire hand at one time. Only sequences count; groups may not be melded.

Only the following combinations of sequences are acceptable:

1. Five three-card sequences.
2. Three four-card sequences and one three-card sequence.
3. One five-card sequence, one four-card sequence, and two three-card sequences.

Three five-card sequences, although possible, are not allowed.

PLAY

The play is the same as in regular Rummy except that no melding is permitted until a player can meld his entire hand.

SCORING

The winner collects from each of the other players one point for going out plus two points for each joker and one point for each deuce that he melds. At times, various pre-agreed bonuses are collected for special circumstances such as going out on the first round.

IRREGULARITIES

They are the same as in regular Rummy plus: If a player claims to go out when he cannot legally do so, he must turn his hand face up and continue to play until either he or some other player can legally go out. If any other player has exposed his hand, he may pick it up without penalty.

STRATEGY

Draw and hope! Previous discards by your left-hand opponent may give you a clue as to which of your cards may safely be discarded. Usually, however, you must sacrifice safety in discarding to the primary objective of completing your own hand.

♣   ◇   ♡   ♠

CANASTA

Canasta, in its many forms, is the most popular game in the branch of the Rummy family where the main object is to score points by melding as opposed to scoring by "going out." From 1950 to about 1952 it was the biggest fad in the history of card games. Most players follow the rules of one of the modifications of the basic game.

PRELIMINARIES

Players   Four players in two partnerships. The game is also popular in the two-hand form. While there are adaptations for three, five, and six players, these are seldom played.

Cards   There are 108 cards—two regular 52-card packs plus four jokers. Sequences do not count, and except for cutting for partners, seats, and the deal, rank has no part in the game.

The deal   Each player is dealt, one at a time, 11 cards. The stockpile and discard are formed as in regular Rummy.

PLAY

As in regular Rummy each player in turn (clockwise), beginning with the player to the left of the dealer, must draw a card from the top of the stockpile or from the top of the discard pile if he meets the legal qualifications. He may meld if he legally can, provided he wishes to, as he is not required to meld merely because he is legally able to do so. He must discard one card, face up, on the discard pile. In "going out," he may omit the discard.

Wild cards   All jokers and all deuces are wild cards and may be designated to be any rank for the purpose of completing or augmenting a group.

MELDS

A meld comprises three or more cards of the same rank *provided that they include at least two natural cards and not more than three wild cards*. A side may not meld more than one group of the same rank. After a player has melded a group, any additional cards of the same rank melded by her or her partner must be *laid off* on this set; that is, they must be added to it. When it is a player's turn to play, she may (after drawing a card from the stockpile or the discard pile) lay off on any group melded by her side. She may never lay off any of the opponents' melds.

Point value   The cards have the following point values:

Each joker	50
Each 2	20
Each ace	20
Each K, Q, J, 10, 9, 8	10
Each 7, 6, 5, 4, black 3	5

Initial meld   In each deal the initial meld made by a side must meet a specific meld requirement; that is, the total value of all cards melded at that time must meet or exceed a specific minimum. This minimum requirement depends on the side's accumulated score (from previous deals) at the beginning of the present deal.

Previous score	Requirement
Minus	0
0–1495	50
1500–2995	90
3000 or more	120

FROZEN DISCARD PILE

The discard pile is said to be *frozen* against one side before that side has made its initial meld or against both sides when the pile contains a red three or a wild card (having been turned up by the dealer to start the discard pile) or when a wild card has been discarded. Note that, if a player discards a wild card, the following player is required to draw from the stockpile unless he or she can play any two wild cards of the same rank and make a legal meld.

PICKING UP THE DISCARDED PILE

A player may pick up the top card of the discard pile only under the following two conditions:

1. If the discard pile is frozen, a player may take the top card only if he can add to it (from his hand) two or more *natural* cards of the same rank and make a meld. If the discard pile is not frozen, he may, in addition, take the top card of the discard pile if he can add to it (from his hand) one natural card of the same rank, plus a wild card, and make a new meld; or if he can lay it off on a meld previously made by his side.

2. Also whenever a player legally takes the top card of the discard pile, he must pick up the remainder of the discard pile.

To amplify the above, if this is the first meld made by the side (the discard pile is frozen), it must, of course, meet the minimum requirement. The proper procedure is for the player to lay down on the table two or more natural cards of the same rank as the top card of the discard pile plus enough other melds to meet the minimum requirement. After the other players are satisfied that he can make a legal meld by using the top card and meet the minimum requirement, he picks up the top card and adds to it the cards he has exposed. He then must pick up the remainder of the discard pile.

If the player whose turn it is to draw (or his partner) has previously made an initial meld, the pile is frozen for his side. He may (assuming that he wants to) pick up the top card of the discard pile provided he uses it to lay off on one of the melds previously made by his side or to make a new meld using two or more natural cards of the same rank or to make a new meld using one natural card of the same rank plus one wild card. In all cases he picks up the remainder of the discard pile.

RED THREES

When a player draws a red three from the stock, he or she must immediately place it face up on the table and replenish the hand by drawing the top card of the stock.

If the last card of the stock is a red three, the player who draws it places it face up on the table, melds if he can, but may not discard, and the hand ends at that point.

If a player picks up a discard pile containing one red three or more (possible only if they were turned up initially), he places them face up on the table but does not draw stock to replace them.

If a player is dealt any red threes as part of her original hand, she must place them face up on the table at her first turn to play and must replenish her hand from the stockpile either before or after her regular draw.

If a player fails to replenish his hand for a red three and the error is not discovered until the next player has drawn, play continues without correction.

When play ends, a partnership that has melded is credited with 100 points for each of its red threes or with 800 points for all four red threes. The same amounts are deducted if the partnership has not melded.

When a player inadvertently fails to place a red three on the table at his first proper opportunity, he may correct the error without penalty at any subsequent turn to play. If the hand ends before his correction is made, the offender's side is penalized 500 points.

When a player is *dealt* a red three, the replacement of that card by drawing from the stockpile does not count as the beginning of his play but as a preliminary to his play. If such replacement happens to be another red three, the principle continues. When this preliminary replacement has been made, he may choose whether to draw from the stock or the discard pile. If, however, he *draws* a red three from the stock as a normal rather than a preliminary play, he is committed to a draw from the stock. He may not change his mind and take the discard pile.

BLACK THREES

When a player discards a black three, the next player may not take the discard pile at that turn, but subsequent plays are not affected.

A player may meld two black threes and a wild card, three black threes, or four black threes:

1. Only from his hand.
2. Only when melding out at that turn.

A player may not make a Canasta of four black threes and three wild cards.

CANASTA

A melded group of seven or more cards is known as a *Canasta*. It is known as a *natural (or pure) Canasta* when it is formed entirely of natural cards or as a *mixed Canasta* when it contains one wild card or more. The foremost object of play is to form Canastas, since they carry the largest scoring values, and a side is not permitted to go out until it has completed two or more Canastas.

Normally, a Canasta is stacked on the table with a red card on top when it is a natural Canasta and with a black card (if possible) when it is a mixed Canasta. Note that a mixed Canasta may not contain more than three wild cards. Any number of natural cards may be added to a Canasta. When melding a Canasta as part of the initial meld, the bonus for forming a Canasta cannot be counted toward meeting the minimum requirement.

It is not necessary to meld all seven cards at the same time to form a Canasta. The addition of a wild card to a natural Canasta changes it to a mixed Canasta (with its lower bonus value). It is, therefore, usually best to lay off wild cards elsewhere.

GOING OUT

A player *goes out* when he gets rid of the last card in her hand. She may, at this time, meld three or four black threes and she may or may not make a final discard.

THE LAST CARD OF THE STOCK

When a player draws the last card of the stock and then discards without melding out, the next player must take the discard pile if the top card of that pile matches one of his side's melds and if the pack does not contain a wild card or red three. Also, he may if he wishes, take the top card and meld it with a pair of natural cards of the same rank and then pick up the remainder of the discard pile. If he takes it and discards without melding out, the next player has the same rights and obligations, etc., until a player melds out or until some player at his proper turn fails to take the pile.

In this situation, a player who holds only one card must, when possible, take a one-card discard pile and go out.

If no player melds out, the scores are counted, but no one receives the going-out bonus.

Melding out concealed   A player receives an additional bonus of 100 points (200 in all) when he melds out his complete hand at one turn, including at least two Canastas, and without adding any cards to melds made previously by his partner. This is known as melding out *concealed*. When a player melds out concealed, he need not have any minimum count.

A player may take the discard pile and meld out concealed provided he meets all the normal requirements (including the minimum count, if this is the initial meld for his side) for taking it.

ASKING PERMISSION TO GO OUT

At his proper turn to play, before melding or indicating a possible meld, a player may ask, "Partner, may I go out?" It is strongly recommended that only this phrase be used. A player may go out without asking this question. A player who asks this question before drawing retains the right to take the discard pile. Partner must reply either "Yes" or "No" (nothing more), and the answer is binding.

A player must go out if he melds or indicates a meld before asking the question or if he transmits information by the tone of his question.

If a player, after asking the question but before receiving a reply, melds, indicates a meld, withdraws his question, or gives any other information—or if partner, in giving a negative answer, transmits information—either opponent may require the player to go out or not to go out. If a player cannot go out when required (see above) or after receiving an affirmative answer to the question, his side is penalized 100 points.

If a player who receives a negative answer proceeds to meld all of his cards so as to complete the play of going out, he must rearrange those melds so that at least one card will remain unmelded after he has discarded. The card or cards so remaining become penalty cards, which must be melded or discarded at the first opportunity thereafter.

SCORING

Scoring is kept on paper and is cumulative. When play ends, each side reckons its basic count as follows:

Going out unconcealed	100
Going out concealed	200
Each red three	100
All four red threes	800
Each natural Canasta	500
Each mixed Canasta	300
Melded cards	Point value

If a side has no melds at all, its red threes count minus. The total point value of all cards remaining in the hands of both partners is subtracted.

The final net amount is written on the score sheet and added to or subtracted from the previous total. The side which reaches 5000 points wins the game. If both sides reach 5000 points during the play of a hand, the side with the higher score at the end of the hand is the winner. Settlement is made on the basis of the difference of the final totals.

CANASTA VARIATIONS

Canasta is played with many variations. In fact, any group that plays together frequently tends to establish its own "table rules."

For example, the minimum melds may be set at 120, 150, and 180; Canastas consisting of all aces or all sevens receive larger bonuses.

It is wise, when you are playing for the first time with a new group, to inquire about these rules.

TWO-HAND CANASTA

The regular rules of Canasta apply, except:

1. Each player receives 13 cards.
2. When drawing from the stockpile, the player takes *two* cards rather than one. She still discards only one card at the end of her turn.
3. A player must have two Canastas to go out.

CANASTA FOR THREE PLAYERS

The player who cuts highest chooses his seat. The player who cuts lowest sits to his right and deals the first hand. Each player is dealt 13 cards. At the end of the game the highest scorer wins from each opponent and the second highest scorer wins from the low scorer. Players may agree that only the high scorer be the winner and that only 11 cards be dealt instead of 13.

♣   ◇   ♡   ♠

CANASTA FOR FIVE PLAYERS

The two who cut high form a team against the three who cut low. The team of two plays throughout; the team of three alternates. The two players of the second team who cut the higher cards play the first hand; the inactive player of the team of three then takes the place of his partner who had cut the second-highest card for the second hand; the inactive player then replaces his partner who had cut the highest card for the third hand, etc. An inactive partner may not advise his partners and has no rights except to correct an error in scoring at the end of the hand.

♣   ◇   ♡   ♠

CANASTA FOR SIX PLAYERS

There are three forms of six-hand Canasta:

1. The three who cut high form a team against the three who cut low. There are only two active players for each team during any hand. Otherwise the rotation of players and the rules of four-hand and five-hand Canasta apply.
2. The three who cut high play against the three who cut low as two teams of three players. All six play with partners sitting alternately. When a player asks permission to go out, she may ask only one partner.

3. There are three partnerships of two players each. They are seated around the table as follows: A, B, C, A's partner, B's partner, C's partner.

♣   ◇   ♡   ♠

SAMBA[3]

PRELIMINARIES

Cards   Three regular 52-card packs plus six jokers.

The deal   Each player receives 15 cards.

PLAY

In drawing from the stockpile, each player takes two cards but discards only one card.

MELDS

In addition to sets formed of cards of the same rank (*groups*), *sequences* (three or more cards in the same suit of consecutive rank) may be melded. Sequences may range from ace (high) to four (low). A sequence of seven cards is called a *Samba*. No wild cards may be used in a Samba. No more cards may be added to a Samba. Only two wild cards may be used in a group meld. Natural cards from the hand may be added to a Canasta but the top card of the discard pile may not be used for this purpose.

A partnership may meld more than one group of the same rank. Either partner may combine such melds for Canasta building. Likewise, sequence melds in the same suit may be

---

[3] Samba, which was one of the early variations of Canasta, was largely constructed by the late John R. Crawford of Philadelphia.

combined, provided that they adjoin properly and that no more than seven cards are involved.

Initial meld   The initial meld requirement is:

Accumulated score	Minimum requirement
3000 to 6995	120*
7000 and up	150*

*Red threes do not count toward the minimums

The score for game is 10,000.

TAKING THE TOP CARD OF THE DISCARD PILE

The top card of the discard pile may be taken only by melding it with a natural pair or (if unfrozen) by laying off the top card on a group or sequence meld of fewer than seven cards. As in Canasta, the remainder of the discard pile must be picked up whenever the top card is played legally. Note that a wild card cannot be used to help obtain the discard pile and that the top card cannot be added to cards in the hand to form a sequence.

GOING OUT

A side may not *go out* until it has completed two Canastas. For this purpose a Samba is considered to be equivalent to a Canasta. There is no special bonus for going out concealed. Also, there is no special rule relating to a one-card discard pile.

SCORING

The bonus for going out is 200 points. Each Samba counts 1500 points; all six red threes count 1000 points. Game is 10,000 points. All other scoring is as in Canasta.

♣ ◇ ♡ ♠

BOLIVIA

This game is similar to Samba except three or more wild cards may be melded. A Canasta of wild cards, called a *Bolivia*, pays a bonus of 2500 points. Game is 15,000 points. At least one of the two Canastas required to go out must be a Samba.

♣ ◇ ♡ ♠

BRAZILIAN CANASTA

Wild cards and sequences may be melded. A wild-card Canasta pays a bonus of 2000 points and a Samba pays a bonus of 1500. An uncompleted meld toward these Canastas or Sambas costs 1000 points when anyone goes out.

Other differences are:

1. The top card of the discard pile may not be counted to help form the initial meld.
2. At an accumulated score of 7000 to 7995 points the initial meld requires a Samba or a Canasta.
3. At an accumulated score of 8000 to 8995 points the initial meld requires a Samba or a Canasta in a total meld of at least 200 points.
4. At an accumulated score of 9000 and up the initial meld requires a natural Canasta or a Samba.

The same is 15,000 points.

OKLAHOMA OR ARLINGTON

PRELIMINARIES

Cards Two regular 52-card packs plus one joker, 105 cards in all.

Players Two to five players, each playing for himself or herself, may play.

The deal Each player receives 15 cards.

PLAY

As in Canasta, a player may take the top card of the discard pile only to meld it and, after completing his meld, he must take the remainder of the discard pile. Valid melds include both sequences and groups of the same rank, as in regular Rummy. The ace may be used as high or low in a sequence. A player may lay off on his own melds but none may be built above four cards.

The queen of spades The queen of spades may never be discarded unless played as the final discard on going out.

Wild cards The joker and all twos are wild cards. In melding a wild card a player must announce the natural card it represents. She may later retrieve the joker by replacing it with the natural card which she announced. She then restores the joker to her hand. Melded deuces may not be retrieved.

Game Game is 1000 points.

SCORING

When play ends, the player's melds count for him, and cards left in his hand count against him, as follows:

Cards and bonuses	Value
Any ace	20
Queen of spades melded	50
Queen of spaces unmelded	Minus 100
King to 8, inclusive	10
7 to 4, inclusive	5
Joker melded	100
Joker in hand	Minus 200
Deuce melded as king to 8	10
Deuce melded as 7 to 4	5
Deuce in hand	Minus 20
Going-out bonus	100
Winning-game bonus	200

♣　◇　♡　♠

PANGUINGUE OR PAN[4]

PRELIMINARIES

Players　There are six to nine players.

Cards　Eight Spanish decks of 40 cards, each formed by deleting the eights, nines, and tens from standard 52-card deck.

The shuffle　Because of the large number of cards, shuffling is a communal task. After the shuffle, the cards are cut into two parts; the *head* is used in dealing and the *foot* is a reservoir to be used as needed.

---

[4] Pronounced pahn-gheeng-ghee. The rules for Pan vary from one club to another. The rules listed here are those commonly followed.

The deal Ten cards are dealt to each hand, five at a time. Following the tradition of its predecessor Coon-Can, the rotation of the deal and play is to the right rather than to the left as in most other games. The balance of the head is placed face down to form the stockpile and the top card is turned over beside it to start the discard pile.

GOING ON TOP

Since Pan offers less opportunity than most other games of the Rummy family to improve the original hand, every player is first given a chance to drop out of the deal. Each in turn, counterclockwise, either stands or drops. The hands of those who drop are collected and placed under the foot of the pack. In Pan clubs a player who drops has to pay a forfeit, which is placed on the foot of the pack. Dropping is therefore called *going on top*.

PLAY

Each player, in turn, from the left to the right, draws one card—either from the top of the stockpile or from the top of the discard pile—and discards one card. The discard may not be drawn to combine with cards from the player's hand in a new meld (only to be laid off on one of the player's own melds), and the card from the stockpile may not be kept unless it is immediately melded with two cards from the player's hand. Consequently, the card drawn is never put in the player's hand, and if it came from the stockpile, it is immediately exposed for all players to see. The player's original hand thus never changes, except by subtraction—by melding and by discarding after a meld. (In many public gambling clubs the house rule is that no discards may be drawn; the top of the stockpile must be drawn at each turn.)

After drawing and before discarding, a player may meld as many sets as he holds or add to his existing melds.

Game The object of the game is to meld 11 cards. The first player to do so wins the game.

MELDS

Each meld must comprise at least three cards. It may contain as many as 11 cards. The melds are classified for convenience as *sequences* or *sets*. Sequences are colloquially called *stringers* or *ropes*. Only three cards may be melded in any original set. Later, however, a player may add to her own melds (but not to those of her opponents).

Sequence Any three cards or more in sequence in the same suit, such as ◇J, ◇7, and ◇6.

Sets Three cards of the same rank and of different suits, such as ♠3, ◇3, ♣3, or of the same rank and of the same suit, such as ♣3, ♠3, ♠3. In addition any three aces or any three kings form a valid set regardless of suit. Aces and kings are called *noncomoquers*.

Conditions Certain melds are called *conditions*. On melding a condition, the player immediately collects chips from every other player. All threes, fives, and sevens are valle (pronounced "valley") cards; that is, cards of value. Cards of other rank are *nonvalle*. The conditions are as follows:

1. Any set of valle cards not in the same suit—one chip.
2. Any set of valle cards in the same suit—four chips if in spades, two chips in any other suit.
3. Any set of nonvalle cards in the same suit—two chips if in spades, one chip if in any other suit.
4. Any sequence of 3-2-A in the same suit—two chips in spades, one chip in any other suit.
5. Any sequence of A-K-Q in the same suit—two chips if in spades, one chip if in any other suit.

Increasing melds A player may add one card or more to any of his or her own melds provided that the character of the meld is not changed. To a set of different suits any card of the same rank may be added; to a set of cards of one rank in the same suit only cards of the same rank and suit may be added. When cards are so added to a condition, the player collects the value of the original condition for each additional card, except that for addition to a set of three valle cards in the same suit the payment is only two chips if in spades and one chip if in any other suit.

By the addition of cards one meld may be split into two, provided that each comprises a valid meld in itself. For example, the Q-J-7-6 of diamonds may, by adding the king and five of diamonds, be split into the two sequences K-Q-J and 7-6-5 of diamonds. If splitting a meld creates a condition, it is duly collected. Also, a player may take a card from one of his melds to complete a new meld, provided he leaves a valid meld. For example, from the sequence 6-5-4-3 of hearts he may take either the 6 or the 3 of hearts to help form a new meld but not the 5 or 4 of hearts. Toward the end of a game an important, and irritating, rule is that, if the discard fits with a meld of the in-turn player, he must draw it and meld it upon demand of any of the other players. The result of making this demand is to make it harder for the victim to go out when he holds a pair. In this case he must draw the card from the discard pile and then split his pair when he makes his required discard.

GOING OUT

Any player showing 11 cards in melds wins the game, and she collects one chip from every active player. The winner also collects all over again for each of her melds. In addition, the winner collects the forfeits put "on top" by the players who dropped from the deal.

When a player has no card left in her hand, having melded 10 cards and needing only to pick up one card and meld it, to bring her meld up to 11 cards, the player at her left may not discard a card which can be added to any of her melds—thereby putting her out—unless the player at her left holds no safe card.

IRREGULARITIES

Wrong number of cards   If a player, before he has made his first draw, finds that he has more or fewer than 10 cards, the dealer must withdraw the excess cards and put them with the discarded hands of the retired players or he must serve the short hand with cards taken from the center of the pack. If a player's hand is found to be incorrect after his first draw, he must discard his hand and retire from that deal. Also, he must return all collections he has made for conditions and must continue to make due payments to others for conditions and winning.

Foul meld   If a player lays down any spread not conforming to the rules, he must make it valid on demand. If he cannot do so, he must return any collections made in consequence of the improper spread and legally proceed with his turn. If he has already discarded, he must return all collections that he has made on that hand, discard his hand, and retire from play until the next deal. He must continue to make due payments to others for conditions and winning. However, if he has canceled the meld or made the meld valid before he has discarded, there is no penalty.

♣   ◇   ♡   ♠

GIN RUMMY[5]

PRELIMINARIES

Players   There are two players.

Cards   The regular 52-card pack. The cards rank downward: K (highest), Q, J, 10, 9, 8, 7, 6, 5, 4, 3, 2, A (lowest).

---

[5] Although the complete history of Gin Rummy is known (it was introduced in 1910 at the Knickerbocker Whist Club by Elwood Baker who demanded another sort of contest when he was cut out of a bridge game), there is almost no uniformity in Gin Rummy custom. No serious attempt has been made to establish a rigid set of rules to govern the game. On the other hand, laws are necessary and the following are proposed—as is the case for many of the games discussed in this book—in the hopes that they will prove to be a firm foundation upon which players may build to form the game most satisfactory to their group.

Value of cards   The K, Q, J, 10 count 10 points each, the ace one point, and the other cards their pip values. Some players like to play with the ace being used in round-the-corner sequences (such as ◇2-◇A-◇K or ◇A-◇K-◇Q). In this case the ace counts 15. This option, although it may seem a small change, actually makes the strategy of the game quite different—so different that it is really an entirely new game. This point will be discussed later on.

THE DEAL

Players cut for the first deal. Thereafter, the winner of each hand deals first. The winner of a game deals the first hand of the next game.

The dealer deals ten cards to each player and then (depending upon the rule adopted by the players) deals the twenty-first card to his opponent, face down, or he deals it, face up, to start the discard pile. In this case it is known as the *upcard*. He places the remainder of the deck, face down, in a pile (known as the stockpile) in the center of the table. This completes the deal.

New deal   There must be a new deal if one of the following problems arises:

1. The wrong player has dealt and the fact is discovered before the first play.
2. The deck is incomplete.
3. A card is face up in the deck.
4. A card is exposed in the dealing.
5. It is discovered at any time that both players have the wrong number of cards.
6. Only one other player has the wrong number of cards, but it is discovered before the first play.
7. A foreign card is found in a player's hand as one of his proper number of cards.
8. There are other cases which may turn up during the play which will be discussed on the following pages.

PLAY

When the dealer has dealt the twenty-first card face down to his opponent, play starts by his opponent making a discard, if he does not wish to knock (see page 173). This discard starts the discard pile. By custom the discard pile and the stockpile are placed side by side.

If there is an upcard, play starts by the dealer's opponent drawing this card or saying that she does not wish to draw it. In the latter case, the dealer has the choice of taking or refusing the upcard. If the dealer refuses the upcard, play reverts to his opponent, who then draws from the stockpile. In all cases, the player who takes the upcard or draws from the stockpile completes his turn by discarding.

Play ends when a player knocks (see page 173) or when a player draws the fiftieth card (the last card but two in the pack) and discards without knocking. In this case the hand is a draw and nobody scores.

DISCARDS

It shall constitute a discard if a player makes one of the following moves:

1. Places or drops a card on the discard pile.
2. Detaches a card from his hand, with the apparent intention of discarding it, and holds the card so that his opponent can name it.

Should two or more cards be discarded simultaneously, the player may choose her discard and pick up the others without penalty. Except by prior agreement, neither player may look at any discard except the top card of the pile.

Should a player discard without first having drawn a card, he must draw from the stockpile at his next opportunity without discarding. He may not knock at this time.

Should a player incorrectly pick up the wrong discard, he may correct, or be made to correct, the error.

MATCHED CARDS

A matched card is:

1. A card which forms a part of a group of three or four cards of the same rank—for example, three kings or four aces.
2. Part of a sequence of three or more cards of the same suit—for example, ◇10, ◇9, ◇8, or ♣6, ♣5, ♣4, ♣3. A matched card may be used in a group of the same rank or in a sequence, but not in both at the same time.

Except when specifically agreed to, the ace may not be used in a sequence containing the king.

THE KNOCK

After drawing and before discarding, a player may knock if her net total (the total of all unmatched cards in her hand exclusive of her discard) is 10 points or less.

A player knocks by indicating his intention to his opponent in a clear manner, such as:

1. Saying "Gin" or "Down."
2. Announcing a total.
3. Intentionally exposing a part or all of his hand.
4. Discarding face down.

After knocking, a player discards and exposes her hand, indicating clearly the arrangement of her matched cards and the count of her unmatched cards, if any. The actual count of the unmatched cards is taken if the player has miscounted. Once a player has announced her hand, she may not change it except to rearrange it to correct an irregular knock.

After one player has knocked, the other player places his matched cards, face up, on the table. He may then take his unmatched cards and use them to extend melds made by the player who knocked. Also, he may rearrange his own matched sets and layoffs, if any, until he has abandoned his hand.

It shall constitute an irregular knock when the total of the knocker's unmatched cards exceeds 10 points, but can be reduced to 10 points or less by:

1. Rearranging the knocker's matched sets.
2. Changing his discard.
3. By a combination of changing his matched sets and changing his discard.

The offender must correct an irregular knock if he can, and if his opponent sees how, the opponent can compel him to do so. It shall constitute an illegal knock when a player knocks with a total of more than 10 unmatched points which cannot be corrected as indicated above. A player who has made an illegal knock must immediately expose his entire hand and make as many matched sets as he can. If there is more than one way to do so, the offender has his choice. These matched sets must remain face up for the remainder of the hand. The offender may add to them, but he may not rearrange them or otherwise change them. After the offender's opponent continues his play, the offender may pick up his unmatched cards.

IRREGULARITIES

Irregular deck or hands   Except as required in the section on required new deals, when one player is found to have an incorrect number of cards before his opponent has knocked, his opponent may:

1. Demand a new deal.
2. Continue play. In this case, if the offender has too few cards, she corrects it at her next play, or plays by drawing without discarding. If she has too many cards, she corrects it by discarding without drawing. In either case, she may not knock until after her first regular play.

If the error is discovered after a knock, the error may not be corrected. The offender may not claim a Gin or an undercut bonus. He can lose or draw the hand, but he cannot win.

Should a foreign card be found in the stock or in a player's hand in addition to his regular 10 cards, it is removed and play continues.

After the score has been agreed upon and the cards have been abandoned, such score is final and not subject to change by any subsequent discovery.

Exposed cards and premature play   Should the nondealer draw from the stock before the dealer has refused the upcard and the dealer elect to take the upcard, the draw from the stock stands and the nondealer loses his option to take the dealer's discard. Should a player draw from the stockpile before his opponent has discarded, the draw stands.

If a player drawing in turn sees one card or more to which he is not entitled, every such card must be placed, face up, next to the discard pile. The nonoffender at his next turn to play, prior to the time as he draws from the stockpile, has the right to take any one of these cards as his draw. Once the offender draws from the stockpile, the right shifts to the offender until such time as all such cards are picked up or the offender forfeits his rights by drawing from the stock-pile. An alternative rule frequently adopted is that, once the nonoffender draws from the stockpile, the remaining exposed cards are placed in the discard pile—the offender never has an opportunity to select any of them.

Should a card be found face up in the stockpile, it must be placed in the stockpile, the remaining cards must be re-shuffled, and play is resumed.

Should a card, face up or otherwise, be found outside the deck during the course of play and before a knock, it must be shuffled with the stockpile.

Should a card or cards be found on the floor or elsewhere where a player who is short an equivalent number of cards might have lost them, such card or cards shall be considered to belong to her, and her hand is not regarded as irregular.

Should a card become exposed by falling out of a player's hand, there is no penalty except that, if it falls on the discard pile, it is considered to have been discarded.

SCORING

The first player to accumulate 100 points wins the game and receives a 100-point bonus. Each player then adds to his score 25 points for each hand he has won.

Example of scoring

First hand   You knock with 5 and your opponent has 16. You score a net 11 points.

Second hand   You score 25 points for Gin and your opponent has 23. You win a total of 48 points, an accumulated score of 59.

Third hand   Your opponent knocks for 8 points and you have 42 points. He scores a net 34 points.

Fourth hand   Your opponent knocks for 10 points and you undercut with 5 points, giving you 25-points bonus (for the undercut) and 5 points (for the net difference in your total scores). This makes your cumulative score 89 points.

Fifth hand   You knock with 2 points and your opponent has 23 points. You score a net 21 points for a cumulative score of 110 points and the game.

GIN RUMMY	
You	Opponent
11	34
59	
89	
110	34
100	game
75	boxes
285	
34	
251	

You now compute your final score. In addition to your 110 points, you have won four boxes (at 25 points per box), while your opponent has won only one box. This gives you a net 75 points for boxes. You also have won 100 points as a game bonus. This makes your gross score 285 points. From this you subtract your opponent's 34 points, giving you a net final score of 251 points, or a plus 300 if you are rounding off your game scores.

STRATEGY

Gin Rummy is easy to learn and simple to play. It is a fine, exciting combination of skill of the player with luck of the game. There are three times when skill of the player is most likely to come to the forefront, namely:

1. Should you pick up your opponent's discard or draw from the stockpile? The answer is, in general, quite simple. As a general rule it never pays to pick up a discard "on speculation." That is, holding a ♠10 and a ◇9, do not pick up a ◇10. It is a sound play to pick up your opponent's discard when it completes a meld in your hand; that is, when it matches a natural pair that you already hold or when it forms the third card of a sequence. It is also usually a good practice to pick up the discard when it extends a meld that you already hold; that is, when it forms a fourth card of a group or of a sequence. The possible exception to this is when you do not hold a card suitable for discard.

Suppose you hold a four-card sequence, three kings, and ♠9-◇9-◇8. If you pick up a king (to match the three kings that you already hold), what will you discard? Do you wish to hold all three cards and play for a Gin or should you discard one of them and hope to reduce your count to the point where you can knock?

On the other hand, when you are playing with an upcard, it is sometimes a good strategy to pick it up assuming that you hold a card which you can conveniently discard, whether or not you have any use for it, when you are the dealer and your opponent has refused it. It frequently upsets his play to know that this card is in your hand. He has no way of knowing whether or not you have any other cards to go with it.

2. Should you discard so as to reduce the value of your unmatched cards or to improve your chances of Gin? This is a moot point. Early in the play of a hand you

usually take your chances and hold your best combinations. Later, however, it will pay to begin to be defensive and you should discard your higher cards. This is particularly true when the ace counts one! As mentioned earlier, this greatly affects your strategy. When the aces count only one point each, there is a greater likelihood that your opponent will be able to knock, and you do not want to be caught with a huge count merely because your hand has fine possibilities.

When the aces count 15 points each, you can afford to make a more aggressive try for Gin, but when they count only one it is imperative to try and cut the unmatched total of your hand down to reasonable proportions and hope that, while doing so, you can develop a few matched pairs along the way. Keep your losses under control. There is no need to take a whipping just because you have been dealt a poor hand.

3. Should you knock at your first opportunity? In general the answer to this question is, "Yes."

This is particularly the case when aces count only one point each. On the other hand, early in the play of the hand, when your unmatched count is low, it may pay to wait a few draws and hope for either a Gin or an undercut. There is nothing like a few undercuts to make an opponent question whether or not he or she should knock. On the other hand, you always feel foolish when you fail to knock and your opponent Gins on you.

♣   ◇   ♡   ♠

OKLAHOMA GIN[6]

In Oklahoma Gin, the upcard determines the requirement that must be met for a player to knock. If the upcard is a court card (king, queen, or jack) or a ten, the requirement is

---

[6]Oklahoma Gin should not be confused with the variation of Canasta known as "Oklahoma." See page 165.

10 points or less, as in Gin Rummy. If it is a spot card, the number of pips on the card determines the upper limit at which one can knock. For example, if the upcard is the ♡7, a player cannot knock unless the total of her unmatched points is seven or less. If the upcard is an ace, a player may not knock unless she holds a Gin.

In Oklahoma Gin, in addition to the usual 25 points for a Gin or an undercut, a bonus of two *kisses* is awarded for a Gin and a bonus of one *kiss* for an undercut. Each kiss is worth 25 points when the game is being totaled.

When the upcard is a spade, scores for that hand, including any kisses awarded for Gin or undercut, are doubled.

In all other respects Oklahoma Gin is similar to regular Gin Rummy.

♣ ◊ ♡ ♠

HOLLYWOOD GIN

Hollywood Gin is regular Gin Rummy in all respects except that the scoring rules are changed so as, in effect, to permit three games to be played simultaneously. When a player wins his first hand, it is scored in his column in the first game. When he wins his second hand, it is scored in his column in both the first and second games. Similarly, his third and subsequent wins are scored in his column in all three games. After the three games are terminated, they are scored separately. When a game is ended, no further scores are entered in its columns. When the third game ends, a new series is usually started—although some players prefer to start the new series after the completion of the first two games in the current Hollywood.

Frequently additional bonuses, known as *kisses*, are given for Gin and for an undercut (two for Gin and one for an undercut, as in Oklahoma Gin).

Note that from here on, any scores that your opponent makes will score in all three games unless some of them have already been completed.

When playing Hollywood Gin, the total required for the game is usually 150 points. For example, assume that you are playing Oklahoma Gin and that the results of the first 10 hands were as follows:

First hand Opponent scores 18 points in his or her first game.

Second hand You score 15 points in your first game.

Third hand You score 17 points in your first and second games.

Fourth hand You score 13 points.

Fifth hand You score Gin (25 points plus two kisses for Gin) and 10 points for the unmatched cards in your opponent's hand. Note that the kisses are indicated by an asterisk (*). The bonus value for the kisses is not added in the total score until the game is over and the score is being computed.

Sixth hand Opponent scores 22 points in his first and second games.

Note that from here on, any scores that your opponent makes will score in all three games unless some of them have been completed.

Seventh hand You score 25 points for an undercut, plus 5 points for difference in score, plus one kiss.

Eighth hand You score 50 points for a spade Gin, plus 6 points (two times the difference in scores of 3 points), plus four kisses for a spade Gin.

Ninth hand Opponent scores 13 points. Note that this is entered only in the last game. The first two games are over. However, it is a valuable win for your opponent because it saves him from a possible skunk in the last game.

Tenth hand You win 16 points, thus completing all three games in the Hollywood.

GIN RUMMY					
You	Opp	You	Opp	You	Opp
15	18	17	22	13	13
32	40	30		48 **	
45		65 **		78 **	
80 **		95 **		134 **	
110		151 ****	22	150	13
166 ***	40	150	game	150	game
150	game	100	boxes	100	boxes
100	boxes	175	kisses	175	kisses
175	kisses	576	22	575	13
591	40	22		13	
40		554		562	
551		1667	Final Score		

♣ ◇ ♡ ♠

THREE-HAND GIN RUMMY

FIRST METHOD

Each player cuts. The player who gets the lowest card stays out the first hand. The player with the next lowest card deals. At the end of each hand the loser goes out and the idle player takes his or her place. Each player plays for himself, hands he wins being credited to his individual score. The game ends when a player's accumulated score reaches 100 points or more. After the game and box bonuses have been added, each player pays the differences in scores to each player having a higher score. If one player is shut out, he or she pays the 100 point bonus to the winner only.

SECOND METHOD

Each player draws a card; the player with the high card is "in the box." The other two players are partners and play against him or her throughout the game. The partner cutting the highest card deals the first hand, and the other partner sits out but may consult on the play. The active partner has the final decision. When the active partner loses a hand, the idle partner takes his place. One score is kept for the player in the box, another for the two partners. If the player in the box wins the game, he collects the full amount from both of the partners. If he loses, he pays each partner the full amount. In other words, the player in the box plays for twice the amount that the partners play for.

♣   ◇   ♡   ♠

FOUR-HAND PARTNERSHIP GIN RUMMY

First comes the draw for partners and seats. The partners sit opposite each other at the table. One member of each side cuts for deal. Each member of the side cutting the low card deals the first hand to his right-hand opponent. Thereafter the players alternate opponents. After the first hand, the winners of the last hand deal the next hand.

Only one score is kept for each side. For example, if one member of a side wins by 12 points and the other member of that side loses by 8 points, that side wins the hand by 4 points and will eventually win the box bonus for that hand.

Drawn hands are not replayed. Game ends when one side wins 125 points or more. All other scoring is as in two-hand Gin Rummy.

Seven Up

From the old English game of High, Low, Jack, and the Game, a large number of American games have developed. From Colonial days to the time of the Civil War when Poker developed, it was the favorite of the American gamester. The basic game, Seven up, derived its name from the fact that seven points were required to win.

PRELIMINARIES

Players Two to four players. Four players may play, each for himself or herself or as partners.

Cards A standard pack of 52 cards ranking as follows: ace (highest), K, Q, J, 10, 9, 8, 7, 6, 5, 4, 3, 2 (lowest).

The deal Each player receives six cards, dealt three at a time. The dealer turns the next card face up; this card proposes the trump suit. If it is a jack, the dealer scores one point.

THE TRUMP

The player to the left of the dealer, after looking at his hand, says, "I take it" or "I beg." If he says, "I take it," the suit of the turnup card becomes trump and play begins. If he says, "I beg," he passes the decision to the dealer. The latter may then say, "I take it" or "I refuse." If the dealer says, "I take it," the suit of the turnup card becomes trump and play begins. If the dealer says, "I refuse," this second refusal rejects the turnup card as the trump suit. It is then discarded. The dealer then *runs the cards;* that is, she deals three cards to each player and makes a new turnup. If this card is of the same suit as the previous turnup, it must be discarded and the cards must be run again, and so on, until a new suit is turned. This suit becomes trumps.

If a jack is turned up by the dealer for the new suit, the dealer scores one point. If all cards are exhausted before a new trump is determined, all cards are picked up, reshuffled, and there is a new deal by the same dealer.

PLAY

Once the trump is decided, each player reduces his or her hand, if necessary, to six cards by discarding the excess cards face down.

The player to the left of the dealer makes the opening lead. The remaining players play in rotation. On nontrump leads they must follow suit or trump; that is, on nontrump leads a player may, if he so desires, play a trump even if he has a card of the suit led in his hand. If a player is unable to follow suit, he may play any card that he wishes including a trump. Each trick played is kept separate in front of the player who takes it.

A trick is won by the highest trump on it. If there is no trump on the trick, it is won by the highest card of the suit led. The winner of a trick leads to the next trick.

SCORING

The object of the play is to score points. There are at most four points which may be won on each hand, namely:

High—scored by the player playing the highest trump.
Low—scored by the player playing the lowest trump.
Jack—scored by the player winning it in a trick.
Game—scored by the player winning the highest number
  of points, where each card counts as follows:

Each ten	10 points
Each ace	4 points
Each king	3 points
Each queen	2 points
Each jack	1 point

If there is only one trump in play, it counts two points (one point for high and one point for low). If it is the jack, it counts three points (one point for high, one point for low, and one point for jack).

GAME

The player, or side, first to reach seven points wins the game. If more than one player reaches game on the same deal, the points count in the order high, low, jack, and finally, game. The first player to reach seven wins the game.

IRREGULARITIES

New deal   There must be a new deal by the same dealer if there is a card exposed during the deal or if the pack was not properly shuffled and cut, provided attention was called to the fact before the deal was completed.

Exposed card   If a card is exposed through no fault of his or her own (as when the pack is run), its owner may have it replaced from the top of the pack after all other players have received their cards. In partnership play only, a card exposed (except in legal play) must be left face up on the table and must be played on demand of either opponent (provided that its play is legal).

Revoke   Failure to follow or trump a nontrump lead or to follow a trump lead when able constitutes a *revoke*. A player may correct a revoke provided that he does so before he or his partner plays to the next trick. Cards played to the trick after the revoke may be withdrawn if the revoke is corrected. If not corrected in time, the revoke stands. The offender may not score for jack or game. Each opponent scores two points if the jack is in play—one point, if the jack is not in play— plus any points that they may have earned for high or low.

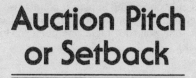

Auction Pitch
or Setback

Seven up grew into Pitch, where the maker of the trump suit led first and was required to "pitch" or lead a trump. This game, in turn, became Auction Pitch when bidding was added. Now the early game has vanished and it is simply called "Pitch."

PRELIMINARIES

Players   Two to seven players, best for four. There are no partners.

Cards   A regular pack of 52 cards with each suit ranking ace (highest), K, Q, J, 10, 9, 8, 7, 6, 5, 4, 3, 2 (lowest).

The deal   Each player receives six cards, dealt three at a time.

BIDDING

Each player, in turn, beginning with the player to the left of the dealer, has one chance to bid or pass. In the bidding, no suit is mentioned; the only possible bids are one, two, three, or four. A player may indicate that he or she bids four by *pitching* (making an opening lead) in the suit he or she selects as trumps.

PLAY

The highest bidder, the *pitcher*, makes the first lead, and the suit he leads becomes trumps for that deal. (If he names one suit but leads another, the lead governs.) As in Seven Up, a player able to do so must follow suit or he may, if he so desires, play a trump (even though he holds a card in the suit led) when the suit led is a nontrump suit. In all other respects the play follows that of Seven Up.

SCORING

The rules for scoring are also the same as in Seven Up except that, if two or more players tie for game, no one wins it. Also, some players play that the one who takes the trick with low on it wins low (just as in the case of the jack). If the pitcher wins as many points as he had bid (or more), he scores them all. If he fails to make as many points as he had bid, he is *set back* and his bid is deducted from his score. Each opponent of the pitcher scores the points which he himself made. The pitcher scores first and the other players score in the order of high, low, jack, and game. The first player to score seven points (some play 11 or 15 points) wins the game.

IRREGULARITIES

Misdeal If a player exposes a card or misdeals in any respect, she loses the deal. There must be a new deal by the next player.

Exposed card A card exposed during the bidding is not penalized. A card exposed during the play must be put face up on the table and played at the first legal opportunity.

Pitch out of turn If a player pitches out of turn, the correct leader may:

1. Let the lead stand and immediately name the trump suit; he then must lead a trump at his first opportunity.
2. Require the incorrect pitch to be withdrawn and, furthermore, may require the offender, at his next turn to play, to trump (or not to trump) or to follow suit with his lowest (highest) card.

Revoke   As in Seven Up, failure to follow suit or to trump a nontrump lead, or to follow a trump lead, when able, constitutes a *revoke*. A revoke may not be corrected and play continues. The offender is set back the amount of the bid. Each of the other players scores the number of points he or she wins.

STRATEGY

The dealer, bidding last, has a great advantage and should press it when able by taking risks to win the bid. The first two hands to the left of the dealer should be conservative.

A holding of three points warrants a gamble on making game. The jack, once guarded, is worth one point. In bidding it is reasonable to hope that the king will be high or the three to be low. Side aces and tens strengthen the hand but cannot be relied upon to ensure game.

♣   ◇   ♡   ♠

SMUDGE

The rules of Pitch are followed except that, provided a player is not in the hole, he or she can make game in one hand by bidding four and making it. The bid of four is called *Smudge*. For a player with a minus score, a bid of four, if made, counts only four points.

Spades

PRELIMINARIES

Players   Four players in two partnerships.

Cards   The standard deck of 52 cards. They rank ace (highest), K, Q, J, 10, 9, 8, 7, 6, 5, 4, 3, 2, (lowest). Spades are always trumps.

The deal   Each player receives 13 cards.

BIDDING

Starting with the dealer, each player in turn (clockwise) bids the number of tricks he expects to win. His bid plus his partner's constitute the contract of the partnership. Note that the sum of the bids does not have to equal 13.

A player may choose to bid *nil*, indicating his intention not to take any tricks. After a player has bid nil, he discards three cards from his hand (face down) and puts them in the middle of the table. If his partner has already bid, his partner then gives him three cards from this hand and picks up the three discards; otherwise, partner must wait until after he has bid to make the exchange.

Before he looks at his hand, a player may bid *double nil*, thereby doubling bonuses and penalties, and exchange three cards with his partner just as in bidding nil. If both partners bid nil (or double nil), there is no exchange.

PLAY

Eldest hand (the hand to the left of the dealer) leads first. She may lead any suit except spades, a suit which may not be led until the suit has been "broken" by a spade discard on another suit (unless the player on lead has no suit other than spades). All players must follow suit if possible. As usual, a trick is won by the player who played the highest trump or, if there was no trump on it, by the player who played the highest card in the suit led. If a player is void in the suit led, she may either trump or discard, as she sees fit. Each trick is kept by the player winning it.

SCORING

The object of the game is to fulfill the contract made by the partnership. If one partner has bid nil or double nil, his contract and his partner's are scored separately; then the scores are combined. Tricks count 10 points each for the partnership if the contract is made and 10 points each against it if set. (Negative scores are possible.) Tricks won in excess of the contract count one point each. A bid of nil scores 100 points if made and scores a penalty of that amount if set. Double nil scores a 200-point bonus or penalty. If both partners bid nil or double nil, the partnership receives 200 points if both make the contract, no score if either is set.

GAME

Game consists of 500 points. If both sides score over 500 points on the same deal, the partnership with the higher total wins.

♣ ◇ ♡ ♠

SPADES FOR TWO

There is no deal. The cards are shuffled and cut and placed face down in the center of the table to form a *stockpile*. (Turn to start alternates between the two players.) The player starting the hand takes one card from the top of the *stockpile*. If he wants to keep that card, he looks at the next card of the stockpile and discards it, face down, to start the discard pile;

if not, he discards his first card to start the discard pile. He then picks up the second card on the stockpile and must keep this card. Note that a player may not look at the second card before he decides whether he wants to keep the first card.

Thereafter, each player, in turn, discards one card and keeps one card until the stockpile has been exhausted. At this point each player should hold 13 cards. The discard pile is then put aside. It plays no part in the subsequent play of the hand.

Double nil must be bid before a player has drawn any cards. In all other respects, the bidding, play, and scoring are as in four-hand Spades.

Spite and Malice

PRELIMINARIES

Players   Two to five players.

Cards   For two or three players, two standard 52-card packs are used plus four jokers; for four or five players, three packs plus six jokers. Jokers are wild and may be used as any desired rank except aces.

Rank of cards   The cards rank in their normal fashion: K (highest), Q, J, 10, 9, 8, 7, 6, 5, 4, 3, 2, A (lowest).

The deal   The jokers are removed from the deck and the cards are shuffled. The cards are then dealt into piles of 13 cards each—one such pile for each player. Each player places his pile, known as the *payoff pile*, in front of his place at the table and turns the top card of the pile face up. Each player is then dealt four cards face up. These cards form the start of his *side stacks*. The dealer then adds the jokers to the remaining cards and, after shuffling them, deals five cards, face down, to each player (known as his or her *hand*). The remainder of the cards are placed, face down, in a pile (known as the *stockpile*) in the center of the table.

Object of the game   To get rid of one's payoff pile.

PLAY

Each player plays in turn, beginning with the player to the left of the dealer and then proceeding clockwise around the table. When it is a player's turn to play, he must first play any aces in his hand, in his side stacks, or on the top of his payoff pile. These aces form the beginning of the center stacks. Note that there cannot be more than four *center stacks*. The player then makes any other legal plays that he desires. He is not required to make a play merely because it would be legal to do so. A legal play consists in playing the top card of his payoff pile, the top card of one of his side stacks, or a card from his hand on one of the center stacks, provided that it is of the next *higher* rank than the top card of that pile. He will almost always make the play from the top of his payoff pile first whenever he can.

After playing the top card from his payoff pile, he turns the next card face up. Note that there is no requirement as to suit; all that is necessary is that the card played to the center stack pile be one rank higher than the one already there. The player will, of course, continue playing off his payoff pile as long as he can.

Also, the player may play any card in her hand to her own side stacks provided that it is one rank lower than the card on the top of that stack.

If the player plays the last card of any of his side stack piles, he may replace it with any card in his hand. If he plays all five cards in his hand, he draws a new five-card hand from the top of the stockpile in the center of the table. He then continues to play as long as he wishes—or, what is more likely, as long as he is able—drawing a new hand every time that he exhausts his old one. He may play any joker in his hand upon one of his own side stacks (for later play to the center stacks) or he may play it on one of the center stacks in preparation for a later play upon that same stack (or possibly to block the next player from making a play from his payoff pile).

When a player has made all of the plays that she wishes, she completes her turn by discarding a card upon one of her own side stacks. Note that there is no requirement that this card be of the next descending rank. It may be any of the cards left in her hand at the time.

Each succeeding player starts by playing any aces that he may have, provided that he does not exceed the limit of four center stack piles. In this case he may play his ace upon any of his own side stacks provided he happens to have one headed by a deuce. He then, after he has made all of the legal plays that he desires, completes his turn by playing a card from his hand upon one of his own side stacks.

When it is a player's second, or later, turn to play, he proceeds as above except that, before making any play, he draws enough cards from the stockpile to bring the total number of cards in his hand up to five.

When any center stack is built up to the king, it is set aside and a new stack is started with an ace. Note that a joker cannot be used as an ace. When the stockpile needs replenishing, these stacks are reshuffled and added to the stockpile.

SCORING

A player who first reduces her payoff pile to zero is the winner. She then collects from each of the other players the number of points corresponding to the number of cards remaining in their payoff pile.

STRATEGY

This game is well named. Frequently you find yourself playing "with malice" in an attempt to "spite" your opponents. It is most important that you do not play only to maximize your chances of playing off a card from your payoff pile but that you are also careful not to play a card that enables your opponent—particularly your left-hand opponent—to make a play off from his or her own payoff pile. Also, whenever possible, you should build up a dangerous center stack pile to the point that it is no longer of any value to your opponents. In other words, you not only need to watch your own cards, but also must keep a close watch upon your opponents' cards in relation to the present status of the center stack piles.

Solitaire with One Deck

The best way to learn a new Solitaire game is to provide yourself with the deck(s) of cards that will enable you to follow descriptions exactly.

The rules of Solitaire are there to make the game interesting. After all, you are playing to amuse yourself. Do not take shortcuts to help achieve the desired results. If the game does not want to come out for you, and you tire of it, try another. The first game described below, Devil's Despair, I have never been able to do!

♣   ◇   ♡   ♠

DEVIL'S DESPAIR OR ACCORDION

Start laying the cards down in a row, one at a time. Look at each card as you face it. If it is of the same suit or the same rank as either the card adjacent to it or the card three piles before it, you may place that card (and all under it, if any) on top of the card it matches (in suit or rank). When doing so changes the suit of a previous pile, you may find that further moves are available to you.

For example, suppose you have placed, in succession, the following cards:

♠A   ◇K   ♡10   ♣3   ♠6   ◇7   ♡J   ◇3   ♠9   ♡3

Note that you have not had any opportunity to make a play until you turned up the 3 of hearts. You cannot play the spade

9 on the spade 6, since there are three intervening piles. Neither can you play the diamond 3 on the diamond 7, for there is only one intervening pile. However, you can make quite a few moves.

♡3 on ♡J gives ♠A ◇K ♡10 ♣3 ♠6 ◇7 ♡3 ◇3 ♠9;
♡3 on ♣3 gives ♠A ◇K ♡10 ♡3 ♠6 ◇7 ♡3 ♠9;
♠9 on ♠6 gives ♠A ◇K ♡10 ♡3 ♠9 ◇7 ♡3;
◇3 on ◇7 gives ♠A ◇K ♡10 ♡3 ♠9 ◇3;
♡3 on ♡10 gives ♠A ◇K ♡3 ♠9 ◇3;
♠9 on ♠A gives ♠9 ◇K ♡3 ◇3;
◇3 on ♡3 gives ♠9 ◇K ◇3;
◇3 on ◇K gives ♠9 ◇3.

You have been lucky enough to compress ten piles into two piles! Clearly you can go no further at the moment, so you return to turning up cards from the deck one at a time.

This process continues until you reach the end of the deck. If you end up with only one pile, you have won; if not, try again!

♣   ◇   ♡   ♠
_____

CANFIELD

Place 13 cards, face down, in a pile on the table. This pile is known as the *reserve*. Turn the top card of the reserve face up. (Whenever this card is played, the next card in the reserve should be turned face up.) The next card on top of the pack is turned face up and placed upon the table in the row above, and slightly to the right of, the reserve pile. This card is your first *foundation card*. Now deal four cards, face up, in a row to the right of the reserve pile, to form your *tableau*. The cards remaining are known as your hand.

EXAMPLE OF CANFIELD LAYOUT

The seven of clubs is the first foundation card. Other sevens, when available, will go to its right. The ten of clubs tops the reserve pile. The four tableau cards are in a row to the right of the reserve pile. Note that the jack of spades may be played on the queen of diamonds. Then the ten of clubs may be played from the reserve pile to the blank left by the jack of spades, and the card now on the top of the reserve pile is turned face up.

SAMPLE CANFIELD LAYOUT

Whatever the rank of the first foundation card, the other three cards of the same rank are also foundation cards. When any of them become available, place them in the same row as the first foundation card.

PLAY

Play now begins. If you are lucky, you may find one of your foundation cards in the tableau; if so, move it immediately up to the foundation row. Also, you may add to the foundation cards in ascending sequence in the same suit. The ace follows the king. The last card in any foundation pile will be one rank lower than that of your original foundation card. The object of the game is to build up all four foundation piles to 13 cards. For example, if the first foundation card was ♠J, you would play on it the ♠Q, ♠K, ♠A, ♠2, and so on, up to ♠10.

You are entitled to have four tableau files. Any blank file created in your tableau during the play should be replaced from the top of the reserve. As you play this card, you should immediately turn the next card in that pile face up. Once the reserve pile is exhausted, any blank file may be replaced from the top of the *waste pile* (see below). Usually, if you can exhaust the reserve pile, you will win the game.

On your tableau you build down in sequence—red suit on black suit and black suit on red suit—as opposed to the foundation, where you build up in sequence in the same suit. The top card of a tableau pile may be played on a foundation pile but never in open tableau spaces. Also, all cards in a pile may be moved to the top of another pile provided the bottom card of the tableau pile being moved is of the opposite color and one rank lower than the top card of the tableau pile on which it is being placed.

When all plays have been made that are available to you, pick up the remaining 34 cards in your hand and, being careful not to disturb the order of the cards, turn them in batches of three cards, face up, thus forming a *waste pile*. At any stage in this process the top card of the waste pile may be played onto either the foundation or the tableau. This exposes a new card on the top of the waste pile. It, in turn, may be played onto either the foundation or the tableau. Remember, the top of the reserve may be played at any time on either the foundation or on the tableau.

When you have exhausted your hand, pick up the waste pile without shuffling, turn it over, and it becomes your new hand. You may continue the process of going through the hand by threes until you win or until play comes to a standstill.

VARIATIONS

Variation 1 Instead of taking the three-card packet directly off the top of your hand, count the cards off the top. This will result in exposing a different set of cards as you go through the hand the next time and, in effect, this almost doubles your chance of winning.

Variation 2 Instead of taking the cards from your hand in packets of three, take them off one at a time, but go through your hand once only.

Variation 3   This is similar to variation 2 except that you go through your hand twice. It is known as Rainbow.

♣   ◇   ♡   ♠

JOKER CANFIELD

This is similar to Canfield except that it is played with a 53-card deck. (The joker is added to a regular 52-card deck.) Whenever the joker, which is a wild card, comes up in natural play, it must be placed on the top of one of the foundation piles. It is treated exactly the same as if it were the card it represents. For example, if you have ♡4 (the foundation card), ♡5, ♡6, joker, the next card to be played on this pile is the ♡8. If later in the play the ♡7 becomes available, it should be substituted for the joker, and the joker should again be placed as a wild card upon one of the foundation piles. If the joker is turned up as the first foundation card, call it what you please, naming both the suit and rank.

♣   ◇   ♡   ♠

POUNCE

This is Canfield played by two to six players, each using a deck with a different back design. When each player has dealt his or her reserve and four tableau cards, play begins by all players simultaneously. All aces are foundation cards and must be played as soon as they become available. Any player may play on any of the foundation cards exposed face up in the center of the table. The winner of the game is the first player to exhaust his or her reserve. As an alternative, one may play until the game comes to a standstill, and the winner is determined by the number of cards each player has played on the foundation piles.

♣   ◊   ♡   ♠

KLONDIKE

LAYOUT

The normal method of dealing the layout is to place one card, face up, on the table and follow it by six cards, face down, in a row going to the right. Next, place one card, face up, on the first downcard and follow it by five cards, face down, one each on top of each pile previously established. This process is continued with rows of four cards, three cards, two cards, and finally, one card, face up, on top of the right-hand pile.

As a check you should now have one card in the left-hand pile, two cards in the next pile, three in the next, etc., until you find seven cards in the right-hand pile. Also, the top card of each pile should be face up and the remaining cards face down. These face-up cards are known as the *tableau*.

FOUNDATION PILES

The aces are used to start the foundation piles. As soon as any ace becomes available, it should be placed in the row above the tableau. Build up on these piles, in sequence, in the same suit.

OBJECT OF GAME

The object of the game is to put all of the cards in the pack on the foundation piles, each of the four piles running from the ace up to the king. There remain, of course, no cards in the hand or in the tableau.

TABLEAU

Build down—in alternating colors—on the face-up cards in the tableau. The top card of any tableau pile is always available for play on a foundation pile. Except for the ace, you have the choice of building on the foundation or leaving the cards in the tableau to help in future play. All the face-up cards in a tableau pile may be moved on top of another pile when its bottom card is one rank lower than the top card of the other pile and is of opposite color. (Some players permit a single card to be moved even when there are other face-up cards below it.)

SAMPLE KLONDIKE LAYOUT

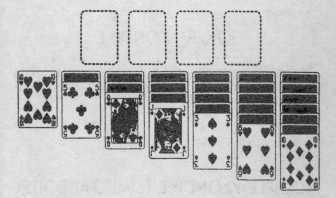

Whenever all the face-up cards have been played off a tableau pile, turn the next card face up. It now becomes available for play. A space becomes available if no face-down cards remain to be turned up. Such spaces may be filled only by a king (plus, of course, any cards which have been played upon the king).

PLAY

Turn up cards from the *stockpile* (cards remaining after you have dealt the original layout of 28 cards) one at a time and play them, assuming that they are playable, upon either the foundation piles or the tableau piles. Put unplayable cards face up in a *waste pile* in front of you on the table. The top of the waste pile is always available for play on either the foundation piles or the tableau piles. As in Canfield (variation 2), you go through the stockpile once.

VARIATIONS

One can go through the stockpile three cards at a time as in Canfield or can play as in variation 1 of Canfield.

♣   ◇   ♡   ♠

JOKER KLONDIKE

This form of Klondike differs from regular Klondike in exactly the same manner as Joker Canfield (described previously) differs from Canfield.

♣   ◇   ♡   ♠

MULTIPLE KLONDIKE (SIMULTANEOUS)

This game is for two or more players, all playing on the same foundation cards. It is desirable to have the backs of each deck of cards a different design so as to facilitate the sorting of the cards after each game. Prior agreement should be reached as to whether or not a player must play an ace as soon as it becomes available. If two or more players try to play identical cards upon a foundation pile, the player who put it on the pile first makes the play; any other player must restore his card to where it came from before he can resume play.

Play continues until the game is blocked or one player plays all of her cards on the foundation piles. The winner is the player who has played the largest number of his or her cards on the foundation piles.

♣ ◇ ♡ ♠

MULTIPLE KLONDIKE (ALTERNATIVE)

Play as in simultaneous Klondike, but each player plays in turn. Each player manipulates his or her own tableau, but the foundation piles are common property and either player may play on them. When the layouts are dealt, the lowest-ranking one-card pile determines which player plays first. If these cards are of the same rank, the lowest of the two face-up cards on the two-card piles determines who goes first, and so on. A player's turn ends when he plays a card face up on his waste pile. If a player fails to play an ace when able to do so (and the players have agreed that aces must be played as soon as available), his turn ends there unless he has completed a subsequent play before his opponent stops him.

Play ends when the game is blocked or when one of the players has played all of his or her cards on the foundation piles. The winner is the player who has played the higher number of cards on the foundation piles.

♣ ◇ ♡ ♠

AGNES

Follow all the rules of Klondike except for the following modifications:

1. After having dealt the 28-card layout, place the top card on the stock pile to designate the rank of the foundation cards. Build the foundation up, in sequence, in the same suit (the ace ranking between the king and the deuce), as in Canfield.
2. Below the tableau, deal a row of seven cards to form the *reserve*. These cards are available for play on either the

foundation piles or the tableau piles. Whenever play comes to a standstill, deal another row of seven cards on the reserve, forming piles. Do not fill in spaces in the reserve except by subsequent deals.

3. Only the top card of a reserve pile is available for play. After the third round of seven cards has been dealt, turn the last two cards face up; they are available for play.

4. A space in the tableau may be filled only by a card of the next lower rank of the card that you turned up to start the foundation piles.

♣   ◇   ♡   ♠

THUMB AND POUCH

This game is similar to Klondike in all respects except, in building upon the tableau, a card may be built upon any card of the next higher rank of any suit but its own instead of building in alternating colors. Either the top card of a tableau pile or all the face-up cards may be moved as a unit. A space may be filled by any available card.

♣   ◇   ♡   ♠

SPIDERETTE

LAYOUT

Deal 28 cards in tableau as in Klondike.

PLAY

There are no foundations; all building is on the tableau piles. Build down in sequence, ending with the ace, regardless of suit (but prefer to build in suit when a choice is available). The top card of any pile is always available for moving. Cards at the top of a pile that are in correct sequence in the same suit may be shifted as a unit to build elsewhere. When a face-down card is bared, turn it face up; it is now available for play. A space made by playing all the cards in a pile may be filled by any available card or *build* (a set of cards in the same suit and in proper sequence).

Whenever play comes to a standstill, deal a row of seven cards, one on top of each of the seven tableau piles. Any blank file in the tableau should be filled before dealing these seven cards. Put the last three cards on the first three piles when blocked after the third round.

The object of the play is to get all 13 cards of the same suit in correct sequence on top of a pile. Whenever you are able to assemble such a suit, discard it from the tableau and continue in your efforts to assemble another suit. The game is won if you assemble all four suits.

♣ ◇ ♡ ♠

WILL-O'-THE-WISP

The same as Spiderette except that the layout consists of 21 cards in seven piles of three each, with the top card of each pile face up.

♣ ◇ ♡ ♠

MOTHER'S KLONDIKE

LAYOUT

First deal a regular 28-card layout as in regular Klondike. Then deal the remainder of the deck, face up, in four rows of six each upon the right-hand six piles of the tableau.

PLAY

Similar to Klondike in that the aces are the foundation cards and they are played upon, as usual, in ascending rank in the same suit. However, the play of the tableau is quite different.

Examine the 24 face-up cards (the tableau piles should be spread out so that all face-up cards may be seen). If you find a card of the same suit and one rank lower than the top card of a different tableau pile, that card, and all of the cards on top of it, may—if you so desire—be moved as a unit and placed upon the top of the second pile.

If a face-down card is bared, it is turned face up. If a blank file is created, it is filled by transferring any king along with the cards on top of it to fill that space.

COMMENTS

There is room for much more skill in this game than in most Solitaire games because you can analyze all possible plays before you decide on the order in which you wish to make them. Whenever possible, you must avoid a move which will result in the top card of a pile covering up a card of the same suit that is one rank higher or one rank lower. There is also a chance to use your judgment when you have more than one king face up and a blank space which you can fill.

It should be mentioned that this is a hard game to win, and the amount of time that you will have to spend in shuffling and dealing can be quite frustrating. On the other hand, it does, as mentioned above, present an opportunity to use your skill.

♣   ◇   ♡   ♠

WHITEHEAD

Follow all the rules of Klondike except as follows: Deal the entire tableau face up, overlapping the cards downward in a column so that all may be seen. On the tableau build down in color (red on red and black on black). A space may be filled by any available card or *build* (a set of cards of the same suit in a normal sequence). Any cards on the top of a tableau pile that are in sequence in the same suit may be lifted off as a unit for transfer to another pile.

VARIATION

Similar to Whitehead except that, when blocked, rather than playing the stockpile as in Klondike, you deal one card upon each of the seven piles, again face up. After the third such round the remaining three cards are turned face up and are also available for play.

PYRAMID

LAYOUT

Deal 28 cards in the shape of a pyramid—one card in the top row, two in the second row, and so on down to seven cards in the seventh row. Have the rows overlap slightly but not so much that they are not in plain view. At the beginning of the game seven cards are available for play. This number decreases as the game progresses. Only cards which are wholly uncovered (i.e., cards which do not have any card in the next row covering them) are available for play.

PLAY

Initially play is limited to the pyramid itself. From cards available for play discard any two cards that add to 13. The jack counts 11 and pairs with a deuce; the queen counts 12, and pairs with an ace; the king counts 13 and does not need to be paired with any other card. Hence kings may be discarded as soon as they become uncovered.

SAMPLE PYRAMID LAYOUT

Having made all the plays you can, start turning the cards left in your hand, one at a time. If you cannot play the first card, put it face up in front of you to form a *waste pile*. As you continue to turn the cards in your hand, the top card of the waste pile is always playable. If the card you turn up from your hand adds up to 13 with any of the exposed cards in the pyramid or with the top card on the waste pile, discard the pair and check to see if any of the cards just uncovered are playable. Continue this process until the cards in your hand are exhausted. At this stage of the game, if you have exhausted the pyramid and all of the cards in your hand and in the waste pile, you have won.

As a word of warning, this game very rarely comes out. Even if you allow yourself two or even three passages through the cards (by turning the waste pile over without shuffling), you will find that you rarely exhaust the pyramid, your hand, and the waste pile. At times you will find that you have a choice of plays. When this occurs, you will find that there is some element of skill involved.

♣   ◇   ♡   ♠

WESTCLIFF

LAYOUT

Form the tableau by dealing ten cards in a row face down, followed by another row face down, and then by one row face up. Place the remaining cards, face down, in a pile known as the *stockpile*.

FOUNDATION

As the aces become available move them to the row above the tableau. Build up upon them in ascending order in the same suit. The object of the game is to build all four foundation piles up from ace to king, each in its own suit.

TABLEAU BUILDING

On the tableau, build down in alternating colors. Suits play no part in tableau play. The top of a tableau pile, if the color and rank are suitable, may be shifted to the top of any other tableau pile. In addition, all the face-up cards on a tableau pile may be shifted as a unit, if the color and rank of the bottom face-up card are suitable, to the top of any other tableau pile. Also, the top card and all face-up cards of any given tableau pile are available to fill a space made by the removal of an entire tableau pile.

The top cards of the tableau piles are always available for building on the foundation piles.

When a face-down card of the tableau is bared, turn it face up; it now becomes available for play just as the top card of any other tableau pile is available.

STOCKPILE

After you have completed all plays available with the tableau cards, play of the stockpile begins. Turn these cards up, one at a time, and play them up on either the foundation piles or the tableau piles, as appropriate. Put unplayable cards in a single *waste pile*, face up. The top card of the waste pile is always available for play to the tableau or foundation. Kings may be played in a vacant space in the tableau. There is no redeal.

♣   ◇   ♡   ♠

EASTHAVEN

Easthaven is similar to Westcliff with the exception of the following modifications:

1. Deal only seven piles for the tableau, 21 cards in all.
2. A space may be filled only by a king or a *build* (all of the face-up cards on a tableau pile), with a king at the bottom.
3. Whenever play comes to a standstill, deal another row of seven cards on the tableau. All spaces in the tableau should be filled, if possible, before this row is dealt.
4. After play has come to a standstill, and 49 cards have been dealt, place the last three cards on top of the first three tableau piles.

♣   ◇   ♡   ♠

BELEAGUERED CASTLE

FOUNDATION PILES

Remove the four aces from the deck and put them face up on the table in a vertical column. Build up upon these aces in a suit. The object is to build all four foundation piles up from ace to king, each pile in one suit.

SAMPLE BELEAGUERED CASTLE LAYOUT

| Tableau | Foundation | Tableau |

TABLEAU

Deal the remainder of the pack, face up, in two wings, one on each side of the aces. Each wing consists of four rows (one opposite each ace) of six cards each. Overlap the cards in each row so that each card is visible but only the top card is playable. The normal way of dealing is a column at a time, alternating to the right and left sides of the aces.

THE PLAY

On the tableau build downward, regardless of suit. The top card of any tableau rows may be played at any time upon one of the foundation piles, provided it is of the same suit and one rank higher than the top card of that pile. It also may be played upon the top of one of the tableau rows provided it is one rank lower than the top card of that row (suit makes no difference here). A space made by moving an entire row may be filled by any available card.

STRATEGY

Do not be in a hurry to move. Examine your options carefully. If you cannot find a way to get an open space, you probably will not be able to win the game. Keep the foundation piles balanced at all times. If you let one of them get too far ahead, you will probably find that you have blocked yourself and will be unable to get at a critical card.

VARIATION

The following variation is applicable, not only to Beleaguered Castle but also to all the other variations of it: Any cards on the top of a tableau pile that are in sequence in the same suit may be lifted off as a unit for transfer to another pile.

♣   ◇   ♡   ♠

BELEAGUERED CASTLE PLUS

This game is similar to Beleaguered Castle except that the aces are not removed from the deck. The entire deck is shuffled and dealt face up into two columns, with a space between the columns to allow room for the aces as they become available in regular play. It is obvious that the tableau rows will contain a different number of cards—the top two rows containing seven cards each and the bottom two rows six cards each.

SAMPLE BELEAGUERED CASTLE PLUS LAYOUT

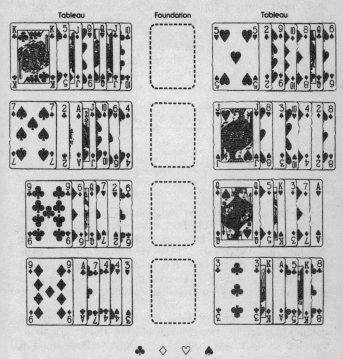

UNDER SIEGE

This game is similar to Beleaguered Castle after the deal, but differs during the deal as follows:

Do not remove the aces from the deck, but start dealing as in Beleaguered Castle Plus. Whenever you come to an ace, place it in the foundation column instead of on the tableau. Also, whenever you come to a card that will play upon a foundation pile while dealing, place that card in its proper place upon the foundation pile to which it belongs. Note that only newly turned cards may be placed upon foundation piles; the tops of tableau piles may not be placed there during the dealing.

Whenever you place a card upon a foundation pile, including the aces, skip the row where it would have gone on the tableau. This will, of course, result in some of the tableau rows being of a different length from other rows.

♣ ◇ ♡ ♠

FORTRESS

This game is still another variation of Beleaguered Castle. As in Beleaguered Castle Plus and Under Siege, the entire deck is shuffled. The layout is then dealt face up in two columns (again with a space between them) of five rows each. The upper row on each side has six cards and the remaining rows have five cards each. Overlap the cards, as in the other games of this series, so that all are visible but only the top card is playable.

As the aces become available, move them to the foundation column between the two columns of rows. Build these foundation piles up, in suit, to the kings. On the tableau build in suit, either up or down, as seems best. Just because you happen to build up on one row, there is no reason why you should not build down on another row.

As in other games, one card at a time may be moved from the top of any tableau pile to any foundation pile.

In addition, any series of cards in sequence in the same suit may be moved as a unit to the top of any tableau pile, provided the bottom card of the sequence being moved is of the same suit and of correct rank to fit on the top card of the tableau pile to which the sequence is being moved.

♣ ◇ ♡ ♠

FORTRESS PLUS

This game is identical to Fortress in all respects except that, instead of having to use the aces as the foundation cards, you may, after looking the layout over, select any card that you wish to be the foundation card. Here, of course, as you build upward on the foundation piles, the ace fits between the king and the deuce.

♣   ◇   ♡   ♠

TEN, TWENTY, OR THIRTY

Deal the entire deck face up, one card at a time, in a single row. As you turn the cards up, discard any two or more adjacent cards which total 10, 20, or 30. Count the kings, queens, and jacks as 10 each. Count the remaining cards as having the same value as the number of pips.

♣   ◇   ♡   ♠

KING ALBERT

Deal nine cards in a row. Follow by eight cards, starting with the second card of the first row. Then deal six cards, starting with the third card, etc. You will end up with nine piles containing one card in the lowest pile, two in the second, three in the third, and so on, up to nine, in the ninth (uppermost) pile. All cards are dealt face up. Spread the cards downward in each pile so that all are visible. Spread the remaining seven cards face up in a fan below the layout. This is called the *reserve*.

As the aces become available, move them to the foundation row above the tableau. Build up upon them, in suit, until you reach the kings.

Build down on the tableau piles in alternate colors. The top card of the tableau pile, if of the proper rank and color, may be played at any time upon a foundation pile or upon one of the other tableau piles. The space created by playing all of the cards in a file may be filled by any available card. All cards in the reserve are available for play on any foundation or tableau pile.

♣ ◇ ♡ ♠

PRINCE ALBERT

King Albert is a comparatively easy game to win. This variation of it, Prince Albert, although it may seem to be only a slight change, is actually considerably harder.

Deal the layout exactly the same as in King Albert, but deal all cards face down except the top card of each tableau pile and the seven cards in the reserve spread. The play is exactly the same as in King Albert.

♣ ◇ ♡ ♠

YUKON

The layout and the foundation piles are exactly the same as in Mother's Klondike (page 205).

Also, the play of the tableau is quite similar except that, instead of the card (and all cards on top of it) to be transferred to the top of a tableau pile being of the same suit and one rank lower, it is only necessary that this card be of the opposite color and one rank lower than the card on the top of the tableau pile to which it is to be transferred.

♣ ◇ ♡ ♠

PATIENCE

LAYOUT

Remove the four aces from the deck and place them in a row to form the foundations. Build up on these foundations, regardless of suit, until you reach a king.

PLAY

Deal the stock, face up, into four reserve piles (in a row under the foundation row), one row of four cards at a time. After dealing each batch of four cards, play what you can from the top of the reserve piles onto the tops of the foundation piles. Cards in the reserve piles become available when they are uncovered, but may not be used to fill spaces. There is no redeal.

♣   ◇   ♡   ♠

OLD PATIENCE

As would be expected, this game is similar to Patience. Start with a full deck including the aces and, after shuffling, lay down four cards face up to start the reserve piles. As soon as any aces become available, they must be placed in the center of the table to start a foundation pile. After placing the aces and other playable cards, if any, on the foundation piles, deal another four cards to the reserve pile. In dealing these cards, look at each one and place it on whatever reserve pile you wish. After each batch of four cards pause and play upward in suit from the reserve piles to the foundation piles. Only the top card of each reserve pile is available for play to the foundation piles.

STRATEGY

When placing a card on a reserve pile, prefer to place it on a higher card rather than on a lower card. When this policy is not feasible, place a card on a pile that does not contain another card of the same rank. Most vital of all is to avoid burying all four cards of the same rank under higher-ranking cards. There is no redeal.

♣   ◇   ♡   ♠

PUSS IN CORNER

This game is similar to Patience in that you start off with the aces in the center.

It is similar to Old Patience in that you play cards to the reserve piles in batches of four, placing each card, after looking at it, on whichever reserve pile you wish.

It differs from both of them in that you build up on the foundation piles red on red and black on black regardless of suits. It also differs from both of them in that one redeal is allowed. Pick up the reserve piles in order, beginning with the left-hand pile, and continue the play as before.

♣   ◇   ♡   ♠

THE CROSS

LAYOUT

Deal the tableau consisting of five cards, face up, in the form of a cross. Then deal a sixth card and place it, face up, beside one of the corners of the cross to establish the foundation card.

FOUNDATION PILES

When they become available, place the other three cards of the same rank as the first foundation card beside the remaining corners of the cross. Build the foundations upward in suit (with the ace ranking above the king) until each pile contains 13 cards.

TABLEAU BUILDING

Build down, regardless of suit; a king ranks under an ace (unless the aces happen to be the foundation cards). One card at a time may be played from the top of any tableau pile. Fill any spaces with any available card from tableau, waste pile or stockpile.

SAMPLE CROSS LAYOUT

Foundation Card

Stockpile

Waste Pile

PLAY

Turn cards up from the stockpile, one at a time, playing them on the foundation piles or on the tableau piles. Put the unplayable cards face up, in a single waste pile. The top of this pile is always available.

SIMPLICITY

The same as The Cross except that the tableau consists of two rows of six cards each, and the thirteenth card establishes the foundation card. On the tableau build down in alternating colors.

ROYAL MARRIAGE[1]

LAYOUT

Remove the king and queen of hearts from the pack and shuffle it. Place the king of hearts on the bottom of the pack and the queen of hearts on the table to your left.

PLAY

Deal the entire deck in a row with the queen, turning one card at a time and, as you do so, discard any one card, or any pair of cards, enclosed by any two cards of the same suit or rank.

---

[1] This game is a variation of Devil's Despair. (page 195).

THE GAME

The game is won if you end up with the Royal Couple—the king of hearts and the queen of hearts—side by side.

♣ ◇ ♡ ♠

OSMOSIS

LAYOUT

Deal four cards face down in a column to your left. Continue dealing two more cards face down, and one card face up on the first four cards. You now have four reserve piles, each consisting of three cards face down and the top card face up.

FOUNDATION PILES

Deal the next card, face up, in the same row and to the right of the top reserve pile. This card establishes the rank of the foundation card. Place the other three cards of the same rank in a column below the first, as they become available.

Build on the top foundation in suit, regardless of rank. The other three foundation piles may also be built upon in suit, but only if the rank of the card being considered for play is identical to that of the rank of a card previously played upon the foundation pile directly above it. That is, with the exception of the first row of the foundation, a card may be played only if it is of the same suit as the foundation card in that row and of the same rank as that of a card in the foundation row next above it.

For example, suppose the first foundation card is the jack of clubs and that you have played upon it the ace of clubs, the five of clubs and the two of clubs. Suppose that you next turn up the jack of diamonds and place it in the foundation below the jack of clubs. At this stage of the game the only cards that you may legally play upon the foundation are the jack of hearts, the jack of spades, the ace of diamonds, the five of diamonds, the two of diamonds, and any club.

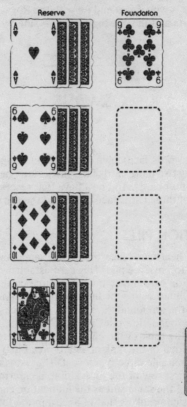

PLAY

The top cards of the reserve piles are available for play on the foundation piles at any time, and when a top card is played, the card beneath it is faced. Turn up the cards in the *stockpile* (the cards remaining after completion of the layout) in batches of three, being careful not to disturb their order.

The top card of any batch is available for play and, if it is played, so is the next card below it (and so on). Put each residue of unplayable cards face up in a single *waste pile*. The top card of the waste pile is always available for play. If any one of the face-down cards in a reserve pile is bared, turn it face up. Spaces left by blanking a reserve pile are not replaced. Redeal without limit until you win or are blocked. The object is to get the entire deck upon the foundation piles.

♣ ◇ ♡ ♠

PEEK

Follow the rules of Osmosis with the exception that all of the cards in the reserve piles are dealt face up and the piles are spread out so that all cards are visible.

STRATEGY

Sight of the entire reserve often shows a hopeless block. On the other hand, it frequently enables a block to be avoided by withholding one foundation card until another becomes available.

♣ ◇ ♡ ♠

SCORPION

LAYOUT

Deal seven cards in a row, the first four cards face down and the last three cards face up. Deal two more rows the same way and then four rows with all seven cards face up. Spread the column downward so that the face-up cards are visible. Place the remaining three cards face down as a reserve.

SAMPLE SCORPION LAYOUT

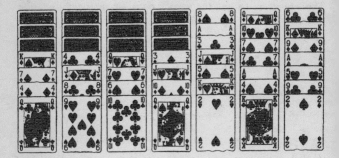

Reserve Pile

OBJECT

All building is confined to the tableau, there being no separate foundation piles. The object of play is to reduce the tableau to four piles, one of each suit, with the cards in sequence from king (at the bottom) to ace (at the top).

PLAY

The play is similar to that in Mother's Klondike. On the top card of any tableau pile may be played the next lower card of the same suit, with the exception that no card may be played upon an ace. Any card in the tableau, no matter where it is located, may be played upon the top card of a tableau pile, provided that it is of the same suit and one rank lower. However, when such a card is played, all the cards on top of it must be moved with it as a unit.

On clearing a face-down card, it is turned face up, and thus becomes available for play. A space that becomes available by playing an entire tableau pile elsewhere may be filled only by a king. Any king in sight may be used for this purpose. As in other moves, when a king is so moved, all cards covering it are moved with it as a unit.

When the game is blocked, deal the three cards in the reserve, face up, upon the left-hand three columns and resume play. If the game again becomes blocked, it is lost.

STRATEGY

As in Mother's Klondike, there is considerable room for skill in this game. One of your first objectives should be to clear the face-down cards. Look at the face-up card covering the first face-down card. Assume that it is the three of clubs. Look to see where the four of clubs is located and find what card covers it—say the eight of hearts. Look for the nine of hearts and see what covers it. Continue this process until either you reach a block or you find a sequence of moves which will uncover the card you are interested in. Check on all piles containing down cards, and attack the one with the simplest sequence of moves which will clear it and let you turn up the down card.

Similarly, when you have created a space, examine the result of transferring each of the kings available. It is quite possible that one may be much more attractive than another.

You do not have to fill a space before you play the reserve cards. It is a good policy to shift your space, if possible, to one of the four right-hand piles before dealing these three cards. After seeing them, you are in a much better position to utilize the space available to you.

The game will become blocked if you permit—assuming that you have some control over it—a reversed sequence such as the ten of hearts over the nine of hearts to be over the jack of hearts; or a *criss-cross*, such as the six of clubs to be directly over the ten of diamonds, and the nine of diamonds to be directly over the seven of clubs.

Suppose that one tableau pile has (reading down) the six of hearts on the eight of hearts and that another tableau pile has the seven of hearts on the five of hearts. To build the five on the six will create a block; the seven on the five, on the six, on the eight. On the other hand, if you place the six on the seven, you will clear the eight, and you will be able to place the six and the seven on the eight, and finally the five on the six.

♣   ◇   ♡   ♠

CALL ELEVEN

LAYOUT

Deal 12 cards, face up, in three rows of four cards each. Pick up the court cards (kings, queens, and jacks) and place them on the bottom of the pack. Replace the missing cards from the pack. Continue this process until the 12 cards in the tableau do not contain any court cards. If there were no court cards in the original layout, place the first court card which turns up during the play on the bottom of the pack. It is not possible to win the game without at least one court card on the bottom of the pack.

PLAY

Deal cards from the *stockpile* (the cards remaining in the pack after completing the layout) on each pair of cards that total 11. When a court card is dealt, it blocks further play on that pile.

THE GAME

The game is won if you succeed in running through the pack and end up with 12 court cards covering the 12 tableau piles.

COMMENT

A little reflection will show that you have no chance whatsoever to win unless the last two cards in the pack are court cards.

♣   ◇   ♡   ♠

GAPS

LAYOUT

Deal the entire deck, face up and not overlapping, in four rows of 13 cards each. Discard the aces, thereby creating four gaps in the layout.

PLAY

Into each gap move the next card higher (in the same suit) than the card to the left of the gap. The sequence ends with the king. There is no card that can be moved into a gap that follows a king. Fill the gap at the extreme left-hand end of a row with a two. The object of the game is to fill each row from deuce to king with cards of the same suit.

REDEAL

When all gaps are blocked, gather all cards that are not in proper sequence with deuces at the left-hand and shuffle them. Do not put the aces back into the pack at this time. Now redeal, filling out each row to 13 after leaving a gap at the right of the cards already in a correct position. Two such redeals are possible.

♣   ◇   ♡   ♠

FIVE PILES

This game is a variation of Pyramid. Deal a row of five cards. Discard any two cards that add to 13, such as nine and four, queen and ace, jack and deuce (the king counts 13 and is discarded by itself). Continue to deal from the deck in batches of five cards, one card to each pile. Discard the pairs adding to 13 whenever they show up at the end of each batch of five cards. Only the top cards of each pile are available for play. The last two cards are spread face up; both are available for play.

The game is won if you can discard the entire deck in pairs, each totaling 13.

Solitaire
with Two Decks

SPIDER

From a pack consisting of two decks, deal 54 cards in ten columns, six cards in each of the first four columns and five cards in each of the last six columns. Deal the last card of each pile face up: the rest are face down.

TABLEAU BUILDING

The ten piles serve as a tableau. There are no foundation piles. The top card of each pile is always available for play upon another pile, provided it is one rank lower than the top card of the pile being built upon. The card being moved may be of any suit (but see below). If you have a choice, in general choose to play upon a card of the same suit. Note that a king cannot be built upon an ace; it may only be moved to a blank space left by playing all of the cards in a pile.

Any or all of the cards, if they are in the same suit and in the proper sequence (downward), may be moved as a unit provided that the highest card of the sequence being moved is one rank lower than the top card of the pile to which it is being moved. If a face-down card is exposed during the play, turn it face up; it then becomes available for play the same as any other top card of a tableau pile. A space made by clearing away an entire pile may be filled by any available card or sequence of cards as long as those cards are of the same suit and in proper sequence (downward).

DISCARD

The object of the game is to assemble 13 cards of the same suit in a proper sequence. Whenever a suit is so assembled, you may lift it off and discard it. The game is won if you discard the whole double pack in eight batches of 13 cards each.

PLAY

Whenever the building comes to a standstill, deal another row of ten cards, one to each pile, face up. All spaces must be filled prior to such a deal.

STRATEGY

As mentioned above, prefer "naturals" (builds in the same suit) when you have a choice. Even ahead of this general principle is the following rule: First make the builds that you can shift later if it seems desirable to do so. For example, if the layout shows two nines and an eight, play the eight to one of the nines; it can be moved later to the other nine if so desired. Among builds that are not natural, start with those of the highest rank.

Try to generate spaces. Sometimes doing so will mean that, having generated a space, you will make the next move from that space rather than making a "natural" move. Use spaces to reshuffle sequences into naturals in so far as possible.

♣   ◇   ♡   ♠

COLORADO

LAYOUT

From a pack consisting of two 52-card decks deal a tableau of 20 cards, two rows of ten each, all face up.

FOUNDATION PILES

As they become available, place one ace and one king of each suit in the row above that tableau. Build the aces up in suit to the kings and from the kings down in suit to the aces.

PLAY

Turn up cards from the stock, one at a time, putting each on a foundation pile or on a tableau pile. In playing to the tableau, you may lay the card on any pile without regard to suit or rank. The tableau, in effect, comprises 20 waste piles. Each card must be placed before the next is turned.

The top card of each tableau pile may be moved to a foundation pile and to no other place. A place in the tableau must be filled at once from the stockpile. It is not permissible to look at the top card of the stockpile before deciding whether or not to make a space. There is no redeal.

♣ ◇ ♡ ♠

CONSTITUTION

Remove from the 104-card pack all aces, kings, and queens. Discard the kings and queens. Place the eight aces in a row to form the foundation piles. Below them deal a tableau of 32 cards, four rows of eight cards each, all face up.

FOUNDATION PILES

Build the aces up, in suit, to the kings.

TABLEAU

Cards may be removed from the tableau to the foundation piles only from the top row of the tableau. On the cards in the top row you may build down in alternate colors. Available for such building are the top cards in the top and second rows. The top card of any build in the top row is available for play upon a foundation pile but not to fill a space.

A space can only be filled by moving up a card from the row below it; it can be any card from that row, not necessarily the one immediately below it. The remaining cards in that column, if any, are pushed upward until a space reaches the bottom row where it is immediately filled by playing a card from the stockpile.

PLAY

Note that stock cards get into play only through the bottom row. They cannot be played directly to a foundation pile. It follows that, if no more spaces can be made at a time when there are more cards left in the stockpile, the game is lost.

STRATEGY

If the tableau is notably deficient in twos or other low cards, plan at once to accommodate a large number of cards in builds on the top row. Play a jack or ten into the top row and play up "feeders" from the lower rows to build on it. In any case, be wary of building on middling low cards—say fours to sevens—for such cards do not "carry their own weight" in the struggle to make space for new cards from the stockpile.

Generally speaking, move up the lowest-ranking cards from each column; certainly twos, threes, and fours must be moved up as fast as possible. Remember there are two ways to get a card from the second row to a foundation pile. One way is to make a space in the top row and move the card up. The other is to build the card on a tableau pile in the top row and go from there to the foundation pile. This second way makes a space in the second row but not in the first row. It has some advantages when your prime aim is to bring more cards into a tableau that is deficient in low cards.

♣ ◇ ♡ ♠

NAPOLEON AT ST. HELENA

LAYOUT

From a 104-card pack, made of two 52-card decks, deal a tableau of 40 cards—four rows of ten each, face up—with the cards spread downwards so that all cards are visible but only the bottom cards are playable.

FOUNDATION PILES

Move the eight aces, as they become available, to the row above the tableau. Build up on the aces, in suit, to the kings.

PLAY

The lowermost cards of each tableau pile are available for play on either the foundation piles or on each other, provided the card being moved is one rank lower than the bottom card of the tableau pile to which it is being moved. If it is being moved to a foundation pile, it must, of course, be of the same suit and one rank higher than the top card of the foundation pile to which it is being moved. A space made by clearing away any tableau column may be filled by playing any available card from the bottom of a tableau pile or from the top of the waste pile.

Turn up cards from the stockpile, one at a time, and put unplayable cards in a single waste pile. The top card of this pile is always available for play to the tableau or foundation piles.

You are entitled to see the next card from the stockpile before making a decision as to your next play. Take advantage of this privilege.

STRATEGY

Drive for a space as soon as possible. This usually involves picking out a pile that has the best chance and being careful not to make plays that would fill a place earmarked for cards from this pile.

♣ ◇ ♡ ♠

LIMITED

Follow all of the rules of Napoleon at St. Helena, except deal the tableau in 12 rows of three cards each to form 12 spread piles. This makes a better game than Napoleon at St. Helena as fewer cards are out of play.

LUCAS

Follow all of the rules of Napoleon at St. Helena, except remove the eight aces from the deck and put them in the foundation row. For the tableau, deal three rows of 13 cards each to form 13 spread piles.

♣ ◇ ♡ ♠

NUMBER 10

Follow all of the rules of Napoleon at St. Helena, except deal the first two rows face down and the remaining two rows face up. On the bottom cards of the tableau piles build down in alternate colors. All the cards on the bottom of a tableau pile that are in correct sequence may be shifted as a unit for transfer to another pile, provided the high card of the sequence is one rank lower than the top card of the pile to which it is being moved.

♣ ◇ ♡ ♠

RANK AND FILE

Follow all of the rules of Napoleon at St. Helena, except deal the first three rows of the tableau face down and the last row face up. On the tops of the tableau piles play down in alternate colors. All the cards on the bottom of a tableau pile that are in correct sequence may be lifted as a unit for transfer to another tableau pile.

♣   ◇   ♡   ♠

INDIAN

Follow all of the rules of Napoleon at St. Helena, except deal only 30 cards in the tableau, one row of ten, face down, and then two rows, face up, making ten spread columns of three each. In tableau building, a card may be placed upon any other card of the next higher rank provided it is not of the suit.

♣   ◇   ♡   ♠

RUSSIAN BANK

Russian Bank is a double Solitaire in which the two players play alternately. The moves are governed by strict rules of order and the penalty for violating is to lose one's turn.

PRELIMINARIES

Players   There are two players.

Cards   Each player uses a regular pack of 52 cards. They should have backs of different color or design so as to facilitate the sorting of the two packs after each game.

Sample layout

Tableau

Player B

Center

Player A

A's hand

A's stockpile

Rank of cards In each suit the cards rank as follows: K (highest), Q, J, 10, 9, 8, 7, 6, 5, 4, 3, 2, A (lowest).

The draw One pack is spread face down on the table and each player draws a card. The player drawing the lower card has his or her choice of seats, and cards, and has the first turn to play. Each player then shuffles his or her opponent's pack and the game is started. It is suggested that, in games after the first one, the loser should have the opportunity to play first.

LAYOUT

Each player counts off 12 cards from the top of his pack and places them, face down, in a pile (known as the *stockpile*) to his right.

He then places four cards, face up, in a column running from his stockpile up toward his opponent. The two columns should be separated enough to allow two additional columns to be placed between them. These eight face-up cards (four from each player) constitute the *tableau*. They are common property. The space between the two columns in the tableau is known as the *center*.

Each player places the undealt portion of the pack, known as his hand, face down on the table to his left.

PLAY

The rules of precedence are:

Rule I *Any ace must be moved to the center as soon as it becomes available* (after which cards of the same suit may be built upon it in sequence from two up to king).

Available card Only one card at a time may be moved. The cards available to be transferred elsewhere are:

1. Top cards of tableau piles.
2. Top card of the stockpile.
3. The card turned up from the hand.

Note that in rules on Stops (see page 242), a card is not deemed available merely because it can be made available by the transfer of covering cards.

Rule II *If an available card can be moved upon a center pile, this move must be made before any other move* (except for moving an ace to the center as prescribed in rule I or for a move prescribed by rules III and IV).

After the first player has made all the possible plays from the tableau to the center, the player must next turn the top card of his or her stockpile face up.

Rule III *After his first turn a player must begin every turn with at least one card face up on his stockpile.*

Assuming no irregularities, when a player ends his turn there is always a card face up on top of his stockpile. However, if he had committed an irregularity, it is possible that he will be stopped at a time when he has no card face up on his stockpile. In that event he must begin his next turn by exposing a stock card.

Rule IV *On moving the last face-up card from her stock pile elsewhere the player must immediately turn another card face up.* Rules III and IV are the only exceptions to rules I and II.

Rule V *If the top stockpile card is playable upon a center pile, tableau pile, or tableau space, it must be so played before a card is turned from the hand.* If a space in the tableau exists, a card from the stockpile must eventually be moved into it. But it is not a violation of rule V to refrain from making a space when possible. It is legal (and some players consider it good tactics) to spread the tableau cards to fill all spaces, so as to get to see the card on the top of the hand before deciding about the stock card.

For example, consider the layout given above, assuming it is player A's first play:

Since there is an ace in the tableau, A's first move must be to move it to the center. Having made all the moves that he can from the tableau to the center, he then turns the top card of his stockpile face up. Let us assume that it is the ◊8. This card is playable in the tableau space vacated by the diamond ace. Assume that the player makes this play. He then must, in accordance with rule IV, immediately turn the next card on the stockpile face up. Assume that it is the diamond deuce. The player must immediately play it to the center pile on top of the diamond ace. Note that, if he plays it on the tableau club three, he will have violated rule II. He must now, again in accordance with rule IV, immediately turn the top card of his stockpile face up. Assume that it is the heart queen.

TABLEAU BUILDING

Cards may be built upon the tableau piles in descending sequence and alternating color: black on red and red on black; a ten on the jack, a five on the six, and so on. Available for building are cards from the stock, the hand, and other tableau piles. Only one card at a time may be moved off a tableau pile. The whole pile cannot be moved as a unit.

When any one of the tableau piles is cleared away, a *space* exists. The space may be filled with any available card, subject to the rules of precedence, including the top card of any tableau pile.

The chief object of building on the tableau is to create spaces upon which the player may play cards from her stockpile. She should make sure to keep rule I and rule II in mind. If she turns up a card which is playable to the center, she should play it immediately. It may not be kept in the tableau to facilitate building.

Rule VI *When moves to the center are possible from both the stockpile and a tableau pile, the move from the stockpile must be made first.*

HAND

When the top card of the stockpile is unplayable (meaning, among other things, that all eight tableau spaces are filled), the player may turn up the top card from his hand. If this card

B's stockpile

B's hand

Player B

Tableau

Center

Player A

A's hand

A's stockpile

proves to be unplayable, it is placed, face up, in a waste pile between the hand and the stockpile, and the player's turn ends. Should he inadvertently place it on the waste pile when it is, in fact, playable, his turn nevertheless ends the moment his hand quits the card.

Examination will show that player A has two choices. He can turn up the top card in his hand (note that there are no blank spaces in the tableau and that there are no moves that can be made to the center) or he can move the three of clubs upon the four of diamonds, thereby creating a blank space in the tableau which can be filled by the queen of hearts from his stockpile. As stated previously, a player may believe it is advantageous to look at the top card in his hand before playing another card from the stockpile, but he takes the risk of being unable to play the card from his hand, in which case his turn is over and he presents his opponent with the opportunity of playing the three of clubs on the four of diamonds, and then playing off one of the cards from *his* stockpile.

If a player turns the top card of his hand face up (either from choice or because he has no other legal move), and the card from his hand can be played, the player must then attend to any other plays now possible. After these have been exhausted, he then turns up another card from his hand.

At this point let us look again at our example. It now appears as shown on the facing page.

After his stockpile is exhausted, a player may move the card from his hand into a tableau space. The top card of the waste pile is not available—it can never be moved anywhere. After the hand is exhausted, the player turns his waste pile over, without shuffling, to form a new hand.

LOADING

At any time that tableau building is legal, a player may get rid of available cards from stock, hand, and tableau by *loading her opponent*. This means building on the opponent's stock and waste piles. Such building must be in suit and in sequence, but the sequence may go up or down or both ways. For example, the ♡5 can be played on the ♡4, and then the other ♡4 can be played on the ♡5.

STOPS

A player may call "Stop!" if he thinks that his opponent has violated a rule of order. The players should then discuss the situation, and if the charge is true, the offender's turn ends. In some circles a rule is considered violated if a player touches a card when he is bound to move another card. The usual practice in social play is to permit the "Stop" only after the offender has actually picked up a wrong card.

SCORING

Play continues until one player gets rid of her whole pack—stockpile, hand, and waste pile—by playing into the center and tableau (and by loading). The winner scores two points for each card left in her opponent's stockpile plus one point for each card left in her opponent's waste pile and hand plus a bonus of 30 points for winning.

IRREGULARITIES

Incorrect builds or plays   These may be corrected only if attention is drawn to them before the offender has made his or her next play. After that, the error—such as an incorrect sequence on a tableau pile—stands.

Improperly exposed cards   If a player turns up a card and sees two or more cards from his stockpile or hand, he restores any card(s) improperly seen and his turn ends.

Stops   When a player violates a rule of order and her opponent calls "Stop," as stated above, the offender's turn ends. Her opponent may let the incorrect play stand or may require its retraction. If it was a play from the stockpile and was allowed to stand, the offender must immediately turn up another card on the top of her stockpile (unless by chance the top card remaining on her stockpile was already face up). A "Stop" may not be called if the offender has been permitted to complete her next play.

STRATEGY

Though Russian Bank requires little more skill than mastery of the rules and close attention to play, it must be classed as a game of skill since a superior player will almost always defeat an inferior player. The correct play is not always obvious.

♣ ◇ ♡ ♠

WINDMILL

LAYOUT

Remove any one ace from the double deck and place it in the center of the table for the first foundation. Deal four "sails" of two cards each, face up—two in the column above the ace, two in the column below the ace, two in a row to the right of the ace, and two in a row to the left of the ace. The layout at this time looks like a cross.

FOUNDATION PILES

Build up on the ace, regardless of suits, until the pile contains 52 cards. Sequence is continuous, the ace going above the king and below the deuce.

Move the first four kings (regardless of suits) that become available into the spaces between the sails. Build these foundation piles downward, regardless of suits, to the ace. The top card of a king-foundation pile may be transferred to the top of the ace-foundation pile provided that it is of proper rank. After such a transfer the next card played on the ace foundation must come from elsewhere.

PLAY

The eight cards of the sails are always available for play to the foundations. A space in the sails must be filled at once

from the waste pile or, if there is no waste pile, from the
stockpile.

Turn up cards from the stockpile, one at a time, putting
unplayable cards in a single waste pile, the top card of which
is always available for play on the foundations or to fill a
space in the sails. There is no redeal.

STRATEGY

Build up the center pile at every opportunity. Do not move
cards from the sails to the king-foundation piles until the
waste pile shows a card that you want to save. The idea is to
have a wide assortment of ranks in the sails and on the king-
foundation piles for wholesale feeding of the hungry center
pile. Do not make spaces in such a hurry that you load the
sails down with three or four cards of the same rank.

The usual rule is that the foundation kings may not be
played upon the ace-foundation pile. Possibly you will want
to reverse this rule after you find out that the game is not as
easy as it seems.

♣ ◇ ♡ ♠

SALIC LAW

LAYOUT

Remove any one king from the double deck and put it to
the left. Deal cards upon it, face up and overlapping to form a
tableau spread downward, until another king turns up. Place
this card in a row next to the first king and then start dealing a
new tableau pile upon it. Continue in this way until you have
eight tableau piles, of whatever lengths, headed by kings.

During the deal place any aces in the row above the kings
and discard all queens.

FOUNDATION PILES

The aces form the foundation piles. Play up on them to jacks regardless of suit.

PLAY

The up-cards of the tableau are available for play on the foundation piles during the deal as well as after it. A bare king, all cards having been played off it, is considered the equivalent of a space. Any available card may be moved upon a king, but spaces may not be utilized until after the deal is completed.

STRATEGY

Use the opportunity of building upon the foundation piles during the deal to make sure that you have at least one space. Except for this purpose do not build foundation piles too high, say above four or five.

♣   ◇   ♡   ♠

FAERIE QUEEN

Similar to Salic Law, except do not discard the queens from the deck. Build up on the foundation piles from ace to queen. After the deal is complete, cards may be built down on the tableau piles, regardless of suit. Only one card may be moved at a time.

♣   ◇   ♡   ♠

CONGRESS

LAYOUT

From the 104-card pack deal eight cards, face up, in two columns of four cards each. Leave a space between these two columns for two foundation columns. These cards form the tableau.

FOUNDATION PILES

Move the eight aces, as they become available, into the two columns in the center between the tableau columns. Build up on them, in suit, to the kings.

PLAY

On the tableau piles build down regardless of suit. Only one card at a time may be moved from the bottom of a tableau pile to the bottom of a foundation pile or to the bottom of another tableau pile. A space in the tableau must be filled at once from either the top of the waste pile or from the stockpile. Custom allows the player to peek at the next card from the stockpile before filling an empty space. But the space must be filled before the next card is placed upon the waste pile. Turn up the cards from the stockpile one card at a time. The unplayable cards are placed face up in a single waste pile. The top card of the waste pile is always available for play. There is no redeal.

STRATEGY

Do not make spaces by tableau building merely because you can. Wait until you have a card on the top of the waste pile worth saving before you make a space. Do not clutter up the tableau with court cards, except as such cards permit you to make spaces.

Also, before moving a card from a tableau pile to a foundation pile, consider whether it will be more useful in the tableau to save lower cards from burial in the waste pile.

♣ ◇ ♡ ♠

RED AND BLACK

FOUNDATION PILES

Remove the eight aces from the double-deck pack and put them in a row to form the foundation piles. Build up on them in alternate colors to the kings.

TABLEAU

Below the aces, deal a row of eight cards, face up, thus forming the tableau. In the tableau build down in alternate colors. The bottom card of a tableau pile is available at any time for transfer to the top card of any foundation pile or to the top card of another tableau pile. Spaces in the tableau must be filled at once from the waste pile or, if there is no waste pile, from the stockpile.

PLAY

Turn up cards from the stockpile, one card at a time. Put unplayable cards in a single waste pile, the top card of which is always available for play on either a foundation pile or a tableau pile.

REDEAL

One redeal is allowed. As an alternative, no redeal is allowed, but tableau piles may be lifted as units in building upon another tableau pile.

Index

The Death Factory

The Death Factory

A PENN CAGE NOVELLA

GREG ILES

𝒲𝓂

WILLIAM MORROW IMPULSE

An Imprint of HarperCollins*Publishers*

Excerpt from *Natchez Burning* copyright © 2014 by Greg Iles.

EPub Edition MARCH 2014 ISBN 9780062336682

Print Edition ISBN: 9780062336699

The Death Factory

WHEN YOU'RE TOLD that your dying father has something important to say to you before he passes, two feelings flash through you: first, the sense that you're in an Alexandre Dumas novel, that some momentous family secret is about to be revealed—the lost inheritance, your true paternity, something like that. But once that passes, you realize that such a conversation is only natural. Because death is the end, and if a man doesn't speak before it silences him, then the things he holds closest die with him.

In a way, I'd been expecting my father to die since I was a senior in high school, when he had his first heart attack. By age fifty he'd had a triple bypass, when the operation was far riskier than it is now. But Tom Cage was nothing if not stubborn. No matter what setbacks he endured after that operation (and there were many), he just kept practicing medicine. Even with diabetes and severe arthritis, he outlived my wife, who was born thirty years after him. And when I moved back to my Mississippi hometown with my daughter, who'd become so paralyzed by grief that she couldn't leave my side, it was Dad and Mom who accomplished the miracle that no therapist in Houston had been able to manage: returning a grieving child to normalcy. Seven years after that, when Hurricane Katrina struck the Gulf Coast and when, as mayor, I began fighting to get basic services like electricity restored to Natchez, my father—by then seventy-three—was still beside me, helping coordinate the effort to get critical drugs to displaced storm victims who had fled north to my hometown.

But this morning, as my fiancée, Caitlin Masters, and I stood in a boat on the Mississippi River, spreading the ashes of a young woman who had died for helping a friend of mine expose a ruinous evil in our midst, I got the call I'd been dreading for years. Dad had collapsed at his office. Only swift CPR by his chief nurse and defibrillation by his partner had stabilized him sufficiently to reach the ER. When Mom called me off the river, she told me Dad was sure he was going to die and needed speak to me—and only me—before the end. I needed to get there as fast as I could.

After Caitlin and I raced back to shore and docked the boat, I floored my Audi all the way to the hospital. For the twenty-five minutes that took, I was certain I would arrive too late. For twenty minutes, my father was dead to me. Yet when Caitlin and I sprinted into the intensive care unit, I was informed that despite suffering a serious myocardial infarction, Dad was alive and had a chance to survive. Natchez's sole cardiologist had just taken off from the local airport to fly his family to Walt Disney World when the ER called his cell phone and told him my father was being brought in with a heart attack. Peter Bruen had immediately landed his plane and raced to the hospital. Within minutes he'd placed a new stent in one of Dad's major vessels—a procedure almost never performed in Natchez, only in nearby cities like Brookhaven or Jackson—and that made the difference between life and death.

Bruen was completing that procedure when I reached the hospital. A whispering crowd had already gathered outside the cardiac cath lab, as doctors and nurses waited to hear the fate of one of their own, a man who had practiced medicine in Natchez for more than four decades and in the army before that. Everyone fell silent as they wheeled Dad out on a gurney and transferred him to the ICU; then restrained applause broke out as he passed from view and Dr. Bruen appeared.

During my first visit to Dad's bedside, I was shocked. His white beard was always well trimmed, but now it looked oddly unkempt, his skin white and waxy. I took his cold hand, whispered that I was there, and asked what he needed to tell me. He opened his eyes and blinked several times, then pointed at his throat. I placed an ice chip in his mouth and repeated the question. He looked at my mother beside me, then croaked, "What are you talking about?"

I looked back at my mother, then after some hesitation asked her to leave me alone with him. Reluctantly, she agreed. After I assured Dad that we were alone, I asked once more what he'd needed to tell me. He said he had no memory of saying anything like that to my mother. I decided to let it go for the moment, and he was obviously relieved.

That was five hours ago.

The first two passed like a death watch, as a solemn parade of hospital workers visited the ICU, quietly paying their respects. But as time slipped by and more lab tests came in, Dr. Bruen came to believe that yet again—against the odds—my father would live to fight another day. During my second visit to the bedside, Caitlin and I told Dad and my mother that only hours earlier we had decided to get married. After a seven-year relationship, that news should have seemed anticlimactic, but somehow it didn't. It actually brought a weak smile to my father's face, and my mother cried, knowing how badly my eleven-year-old daughter has been wanting that. We decided to wait to tell Annie about both the engagement and Dad's heart attack. For the time being, Caitlin would pick her up from school and take her back to work with her.

I've spent much of the time since making the necessary phone calls of a family crisis; various relatives are now arranging to fly in from around the country. Getting to Natchez in a hurry can be difficult. My older sister, who teaches American literature in England, boarded a Virgin Airways flight in London an hour ago, but that's only the beginning of the logistical legerdemain it will take to bring her here by tomorrow afternoon. My dad's two brothers should make it sooner, but probably not until ten or eleven tonight.

My mother hasn't left Dad's bedside. The hospital administrators have suspended their visitation rules for her, if for no one else. Had they not, they probably would have had to arrest her. Seventy-one herself, Peggy Cage has already taken on a ghostly appearance, her skin almost transparent, her eyes alternately hyperalert with fear and clouded by fatigue. Caitlin and I have tried to get Mom to yield her place, but she will not be moved. At 2:45 P.M. Caitlin left to pick up Annie and return to her newspaper, the *Natchez Examiner,* to manage the story that broke five days before Dad's heart attack, one in which she herself played a part, and as a result almost died.

I, too, played a central role in that case, but while I've been besieged by interview requests, I've declined them all. Hardly enough time has passed for me to process the enormity of what took place within the bounds of our little city, the oldest continuous settlement on the Mississippi River. From inside the *Magnolia Queen*—a riverboat gambling casino docked at Natchez—an international crime ring secretly ran a high-end dogfighting and prostitution operation that attracted high-stakes gamblers of all kinds: high-rollers from Las Vegas, NFL players, rap artists, and dogfighters from around the world. The smashing of that ring has led to the exposure of a Chinese connection: a money-laundering, human-smuggling kingpin from Macao named Edward Po, whom the Justice Department and the CIA have been pursuing for years. With the help of her father's media group, Caitlin has pushed this story as hard as she can, earning the enmity of the U.S. intelligence establishment in the process.

Both Caitlin and I lost friends during that case, and partly as a result of that, I changed my earlier decision to resign as mayor. Even my father urged me to stay the course and serve out the remaining two years of my term, despite his initial advice that I not seek the job in the first place. To my surprise, I've learned that the passion of a crusade to save one's hometown can be a contagious thing.

My present dilemma is how to persuade my mother to leave Dad's bedside long enough for me to ask him again what he needed to tell me. Perhaps the passage of time has improved his short-term memory, or eased whatever anxiety is keeping him quiet. Mom has scarcely taken a bite off the trays the nurses have brought, nor has she tasted the fare Caitlin brought in from a local restaurant. For now, I'm working in an uncomfortable chair in the single vacant patient cubicle in the ICU, which has become our informal command center for coordinating this crisis.

My PowerBook lies on the bed, along with my Black-Berry, a Martin Cruz Smith paperback, today's *Examiner*, and work papers from City Hall. An hour ago, unable to deal with the constant barrage of calls from around the state and country, I switched my phone to silent and tried to focus on the novel. My effort was in vain. Again and again I found myself reading the same page while my mind wandered, filling with violent, rushing images from the past ten days. At one time or another during that period, all my family members were put under threat of death, two close friends of mine were killed, and I ultimately had to kill a man. For the first couple of days after that event, I felt I was dealing with it pretty well. But my father's unexpected heart attack coming on the heels of all that seems to have triggered a delayed shock reaction. Since I arrived at the hospital, doctors and nurses have shaken or squeezed my arm to bring me out of a kind of fugue state. One doctor even suggested that I have a neurological exam, given the savage fight I endured only days ago. But the odd trances I'm slipping into feel more like the result of emotional shock than physical trauma.

Rubbing my eyes hard, I focus on the novel again. For a couple of minutes Smith's poetic descriptions of modern Russia draw me out of myself. But then the muted pulses and beeps of the medical gear outside the cubicle lull me into a kind of half sleep. When the glass door to my left slides open, I'm expecting a nurse or administrator to tell me they need the cubicle for a critical patient. Instead I find my father's youngest brother, Jack Cage, looking down at me with concern.

"My God," I say, glancing at my watch, afraid that I've slept away six or seven hours. But I haven't. "How the hell . . . ?"

Uncle Jack smiles. "You know I was never much for waiting."

Jack Cage is seventeen years younger than my father—effectively from a different generation altogether. While

Dad lived through the Depression as a boy, Jack was a classic baby boomer. He sported long hair, rode a motorcycle, and barely escaped serving in Vietnam, thanks to a congenital hearing problem. Though I seldom saw Jack when I was a boy, I idolized him. Unlike Dad's other brothers, who spent their lives in one branch or another of the military, Jack moved to the West Coast and worked in the aerospace industry. By the mid-1980s, he'd switched to the computer business, and now he lives in comfortable semiretirement in Mountain View, California. Jack still has longer hair than most men his age (though it's silver-white now), and his eyes have not lost their youthful twinkle.

"Why didn't you call ahead?" I ask, getting to my feet and hugging him.

"I've been calling you for the past half hour. Your cell kept kicking me to voice mail."

"But why didn't you call from California?"

He draws back, still squeezing my arm as though to hold me up. "We talked, didn't we? I just didn't want to give you guys any false hope that I could get here this fast."

"How *did* you get here?"

A familiar, enigmatic smile tugs at his mouth. "A friend of a friend has a plane."

I glance at my watch again, doing the math. "Must be some plane."

"Hey, I wasn't going to let my big brother go down without saying good-bye, just because the airlines have lousy route tables."

Jack's buoying presence feels semimiraculous, as though I've surfaced from a dark maelstrom. "Has Mom seen you?"

"Not yet. I saw her through the glass, hunched over the bed with her arm on Tom's legs. I didn't know if I should just bust in there."

"Come on."

WHEN MY MOTHER sees Jack, tears fill her eyes. She hugs him for a full ten seconds, pulls back and looks at him as though she can't believe her eyes, then hugs him again. After convincing herself that he's really here, she gently takes my father's hand and squeezes it.

"Tom?" she says near his ear. "Tom? Look who's come to see you."

Dad's eyes flutter, then open and slowly focus as he turns his head toward us. A faint smile touches his lips. "I'll be damned. It's Tonto."

Mom is softly rubbing Dad's arm, as though he might fade into nothingness at any moment. "You're the first to make it in," she tells Jack. "Phil might be in late tonight."

"I cheated," Jack says with a smile. "But don't tell Phil that." He steps forward and takes Dad by the hand. "How you doing, Kemosabe? Not so great, huh?"

"Better than the friends I read about in the obituaries this morning."

"That's the spirit. Do you remember anything of what happened?"

Dad slowly moves his head from side to side. "Just a hell of a pain in my back. Nothing after that."

"Well, you've got nothing to do now but loaf around and let people tell you how glad they are you made it."

"That's right," Dad says, after a ten-second delay.

He closes his eyes, takes a few labored breaths, then opens them enough to locate his baby brother again. "I thought I was taking my last ride this time, Jack."

"You've got a lot of trail left yet," my uncle says with assurance.

Mom smiles, but I see her chin quivering.

"Peg," Jack says softly. "Why don't you let me spell you for a little while?"

"Oh, no. I have to stay here."

"Go, Peggy," Dad whispers. "Take a break."

"I'm not going anywhere. Not yet."

Jack gives her a chiding glance. "You don't want to hog all the quality time, do you? What do you think I came out here for?"

This was a good try, since Mom has a highly developed sense of guilt, but after a couple seconds, she sees through Jack's ploy. "No, you've had a long trip. You go with Penn." She takes my hand. "Drive Jack over to our house and get him settled."

"No," Jack says. "I've got a hotel room right up the road."

"That's ridiculous! Why waste good money on a hotel?"

Jack smiles and shakes his head. "Don't worry about it, Peg."

"I'll put him up with me, Mom," I interject, knowing it's the quickest way out of this pointless discussion.

"You two go on," she insists. "Get Jack settled. I'll take a break later on, after Tom's had some rest and those enzyme tests come back."

Jack hesitates, then hugs my mom once more and says, "All right, Peg. I'll see you in a couple of hours."

Leaning down over my father, Jack squeezes his hand once more, until Dad opens his eyes and nods as if to say *I'm still here.*

"I'll take care of everything," Jack says. "You get some rest."

After Dad nods, Jack straightens up and quickly walks to the door of the cubicle, wiping his eyes on his shirt-sleeve. Mom and I follow him with our eyes, and then I go after him. At the nurses' station, Jack picks up a week-end bag, and we start toward the hospital lobby.

"Did you fly right into Natchez?" I ask.

"Hell, yes. They didn't have any rental cars, but when the guy who runs the airport found out why I'd come, he offered to drive me into town himself. I knew then that I was back in the South."

In the lobby, a nurse stops me and asks how Dad is doing. I give her a brief update, and then Jack and I head for the parking lot, where the late afternoon sun has come from behind the clouds.

"So," my uncle says in a man-to-man voice. "You think Tom's going to make it?"

"For a while," I reply. "If Dr. Bruen hadn't come back and placed that stent, we'd have been picking out a casket today. But Dad doesn't have that long, regardless of this outcome. His heart's about worn out, Jack. He's going to be in failure before long. If he'd quit the cigars and ease back on self-prescribing pain medication, he might stretch that out for two or three years, but . . ."

"I know. He can't keep practicing medicine without the pain meds, because of his arthritis, right?"

"Right."

"Then forget that."

"Mom's pushing him hard to retire."

Jack chuckles. "Never happen. The Lone Ranger dies in the saddle. Might as well chisel that on his tombstone now."

"Let's take Dad's car," I suggest, pointing to a five-year-old black BMW 740, which I bought my father with the proceeds of my second book.

Jack nods, then makes his way around to the passenger side.

"He really thought this was the end," I say.

As Jack looks at me across the roof of the car, I tell him about Dad's urgent request to see me before he died, then his later denial.

"You have no idea what it might have been about?" Jack asks.

"No."

"Something about money, maybe?"

"Could have been. But Dad never cared much about money. And I think all that's pretty well settled."

"Tell you to take care of your mother, maybe?"

"He already knows I'd do that. I think it's something else. But now that he thinks he has a good chance of surviving, he doesn't want to tell me."

"Did he know his chances of survival had improved by the time you asked him the question?"

I think about this. "He knew that Bruen had placed a new stent. He couldn't know how badly his heart had been damaged, because it was far too early for diagnostic enzyme tests. But I think he sensed that he was going to make it."

Jack purses his lips with a speculative cast to his eyes. "Some dark secret? That's what you're thinking?"

I shrug. "Maybe."

"Well . . . maybe together we can get it out of him before I go back home."

With the push of a button on Dad's key ring, I unlock the car and we get inside.

"Smells like cigars," Jack says with a smile. "Every car he ever had smelled like this."

"I hope this one always does."

The heavy doors close with a satisfying *thunk*.

"Tom loves this car," Jack says. "He says it reminds him of his time serving in Germany."

I back out of the parking space and pull up to Jefferson Davis Boulevard. "Where do you want to go?"

"Why don't we go to a drive-through and get some coffee, then take a drive? I haven't been to Natchez in six years, and that was just for Christmas. I must have seen a hundred downed trees during my ride in from the airport. Big oaks."

"Katrina hit us pretty hard, even up here. Some families were without power for a week."

"I'd like to see that gambling boat that nearly sank. Or that *you* nearly sank. Is it still down under the bluff?"

"No. They've towed it to a refitting yard in New Orleans for repairs. I hear the company's going to sell it, and the new owners may reopen in three or four months. Can't let a cash cow sit idle."

"I'd like to see the river, anyway," Jack says. "Being near something of that scale has a way of putting problems into perspective."

"The river it is."

St. Catherine's Hospital stands on high ground about two miles inland from the Mississippi River. I turn north on Highway 61, then pull into a McDonald's drive-through lane and order two coffees, and a chicken sandwich for Jack.

"What's happening in California?" I ask, making conversation.

"Same as it ever was, ever was, ever was."

"And Frances?" This question carries some weight; Jack's wife was diagnosed with lupus eight years ago.

"She's doing as well as can be expected. Up and down, you know. She lives for the grandkids now. Jack Junior just extended his fellowship at Stanford, so we see him a lot. And Julia just moved from Sun to a start-up you haven't heard of yet."

"But will soon, I suppose?"

Jack laughs. "From your lips to God's ears."

As the line of cars inches forward in fits and starts, Jack taps his fingers on the dash. "You know," he says, "there's something I've always wanted to ask you."

"What's that?"

"Why have you stayed in Natchez? I mean, I understand why you came back. Your wife's death, right? And your daughter having trouble with it?"

"That was most of it. More than half." I hesitate, wondering whether today is the day to delve into darker chapters of the past. But the idea that my father might be hiding something makes me think of another mentor who threw my lifelong opinion of him into doubt. "But there was more to leaving Houston than that."

"More than Sarah's death? And your daughter?"

I hesitate a final moment, then plunge ahead. "Yes. Something strange happened just before Sarah died. She only lived four months after the diagnosis, you know. And right near the end, this other thing came out of nowhere. It knocked the cork out of something that had been building in me for a long time, while I was working as a prosecutor. I just didn't know it. After I resigned from the office to focus on writing, I repressed it. I thought I'd put all that behind me. But I hadn't."

"Does this have to do with you shooting that skinhead guy? Arthur Lee Hanratty?"

That name triggers a silent explosion of images behind my eyes: a pale face leering in the dark, a bundled baby blanket clutched in one arm below it, the other reaching for the handle of our French doors in the moonlight shining through them—

"It was *Joe* Lee Hanratty I shot," I say softly. "Arthur Lee was executed in 1998."

"Oh."

"No. This was something else."

Jack nods thoughtfully. "Your death penalty cases?"

"How did you know?"

"I sensed a change in you over the years you worked that job. I could tell you were glad to get out of it. I've been surprised that you haven't written about it, though. Not as a central focus, anyway."

"Not honestly, you mean."

Jack shrugs. "It's your life, man. I'd like to hear about it, but I understand if you'd rather not go there."

An awkward silence fills the car. Thankfully, the SUV ahead of us moves, and the McDonald's server passes me the coffee and a white bag. One minute later I'm turning off Highway 61 onto 84, heading west toward the river while Jack munches on his chicken sandwich.

The road that leads toward downtown Natchez cuts through old plantation lands still verdant with foliage in late October. Where slaves once walked, a foursome of black golfers in bright caps and polo shirts putt white balls across a manicured green. Behind them the sun falls on oak and elm trees hardly dotted with autumn browns, but heavy with Spanish moss. When we reach the intersection with Homochitto Street, I turn right, into town, and soon we're passing Dunleith, the antebellum mansion that I always say makes Tara from *Gone with the Wind* look like a woodshed.

"Why haven't you bought that yet?" Jack asks, elbowing me in the side.

"You couldn't pay me to take on that kind of headache. Besides, a friend owns it, and even he spends most of his time out of town. It's tough living in a house people fly to every weekend to get married." As I brake for the red light at Martin Luther King, I say, "I've actually been thinking about writing about what happened in Houston. But that would upset a lot of people. Maybe damage some careers. It's erupted into a major scandal over the past year, and it's going to get worse."

"Now I'm really interested. You said this happened near the time of Sarah's death? How long before she got sick had you resigned from the DA's office? A while, right?"

"Three years. I left shortly after I killed Hanratty. That experience scared Sarah so bad that she simply couldn't handle me staying in the job."

"So whatever it was took three years to come to a head?"

"If it had been left to me, I probably would have buried it for life. But then someone came walking out of the past, almost like a messenger. And he was bearing in his hands the very thing I thought I'd escaped."

"That sounds ominous."

"It was."

The light changes, and I head into the center of old Natchez, where the doors of the police cars once proclaimed WHERE THE OLD SOUTH STILL LIVES—and not so long ago. I turn left on Washington Street, where my town house stands, then drive slowly toward the river between the lines of crape myrtles drooping over parked cars.

"When I took the assistant DA job in Houston, I was one year out of UT law school. Sarah and I had gotten married my senior year. I was pro–capital punishment, always had been. And in a world of perfect cops, lawyers, crime labs, and juries, I still would be. But Harris County tries more capital cases than any other in the nation. It also sends more people to death row, and they don't linger there for decades. They get executed. I saw that sausage grinder from the inside, Jack. Unlike in the rest of America, the death penalty system in Houston pretty much works as the law intended. Mainly because it's adequately funded. We had enough courts and judges to handle the caseload—or a good part of it—and we could afford to pay visiting judges, experts to testify, and order complex forensic analyses. That streamlined the process, made it practicable. Then you have the Texas ethos that's persisted from the frontier days. 'West of the Pecos justice,' they call it. If somebody stole a horse or shot somebody in the back, they hung him. You can bet the gangbangers who evacuated New Orleans during Katrina aren't finding Texas to their liking."

Jack says, "I've heard Harris County called 'the Death Factory' on talk radio in California."

"They call it that all over the country, and not without reason. Harris County sends more people to death row than the other forty-nine states combined."

"Jesus, Penn."

"I know. I spent most of my time working for the Special Crimes Unit, prosecuting complex cases like criminal conspiracies, serving on joint task forces, that kind of thing. But I also handled a certain number of capital murder cases. It's like a rite of passage in that office, and I did my share. And I don't mind telling you, I had no problem with it. Because when you deal with the victims, as we did, it's hard to see any flaw in capital punishment. I studied the brutalized corpses, examined crime scenes, hugged distraught parents and siblings—some of whom never recovered from losing their loved ones in that way. I heard audio and saw video recordings that killers had made of their crimes. And in every death case I prosecuted, I realized that there was a moment in which the killer had coldly made a decision to take his victim's life. The rapist who strangled a girl after raping her, then stomped on her throat to be sure she was dead. The robber who shot terrified cashiers and clerks who had obeyed every order given to them. The skinheads who chained a guy to a bumper and dragged him over gravel until he was in pieces. When you see that . . . it's hard to see justice in any sentence *but* death."

"But . . . ?" Jack says softly, his eyes knowing.

I sigh heavily. "But over time, certain things began to bother me."

"Such as?"

"Well, for one thing, Houston has no public defender's office."

"Isn't that in the Constitution or something? Or the Bill of Rights?"

"Most people think so, but it's not. And while defendants often received excellent representation from appointed counsel, other times . . . not so much. As time went on, I also realized that most of the judges handling those cases—even the appeals—were former prosecutors, some of them from Harris County itself. I started to feel that the deck was stacked in the state's favor. That bias was so entrenched in the system that even the defense bar sort of accepted it as the reality of Texas. Don't get me wrong, the defendants were guilty. And we were following the law. Joe Cantor always said, 'If the people don't want me to enforce the law, they should change the law or elect another DA. Because not enforcing the law only breeds contempt for it.' And as simplistic as that may sound, he was right."

"Sounds like the worst nightmare of my California neighbors."

A dry laugh escapes my throat. "It is. Another thing: death penalty law in Texas contains almost no subtleties, which you have in other jurisdictions. The end result was, our office took capital cases to trial that never would have seen a courtroom in other jurisdictions, even in other parts of Texas. They would have been pled down to lesser sentences, or even lesser charges. So, I'd had doubts building up for a while. I think Joe Cantor kept me around as a sort of foil—the loyal opposition. Not that I was anti–capital punishment, but I held every case to a very high standard. That's partly what kept me there, feeling like I was working as a check to that 'hang 'em high' bias, keeping the system in balance."

"A seductive lure for a budding crusader like you."

This makes me chuckle. "I guess so. But when Joe Lee Hanratty tried to kidnap Annie, and I shot him, life spun out of control. Overnight, I became a hero in Texas.

I'd sent a skinhead cop-killer to death row, and when his brother tried to kidnap my daughter from her crib in revenge, I gunned him down like it was Dodge City. When some *Chronicle* reporter actually compared me to Wyatt Earp, half the lawyers in the office started calling me 'Marshal.' Joe Cantor loved the notoriety. I truly was his fair-haired boy, then. But Sarah nearly lost her mind. The what-ifs were killing her. What if I hadn't heard the noise that night? What if I'd walked into that hallway just three seconds later? Annie would have been gone. Dead. Sarah wanted me out of the criminal justice business for good."

"So that's when you started writing your novel?"

One block from the river, I turn right on Canal Street and head for Natchez's Garden District.

"No. I'd been writing what became *False Witness* off and on since 1987, when Scott Turow published *Presumed Innocent*. I'd submitted a few chapters to several literary agents under a pseudonym, and one had taken me on after *The Firm* exploded in 1991. By the time I shot Hanratty in 1994, I had a couple of offers on the table. Nothing big. But when the story of the shooting broke, my agent told me if I'd publish under my own name, she could get me two or three hundred thousand dollars for a two-book deal. I swallowed my pride, put a muzzle on my conscience, and took the money. In the end, there was an auction among the major publishers, and I got half a million bucks."

Jack shakes his head. "And the book went to number three?"

"Number four. But that was high enough. That's what allowed me to resign from the DA's office. I just slip-streamed behind Grisham after that, and life got a lot better very quickly—at least in the material sense."

"That's when you moved into that neighborhood where President Bush the elder lived?"

"Tanglewood?" I laugh at Jack's memory. "Yeah. That was the era when Enron yuppies were buying old lots, razing the houses, and building McMansions. But Sarah decided to restore the original house on our lot. It was a midcentury modern, and she wanted a project. We got Annie onto the waiting list at the Kinkaid School, and it looked like we'd landed in the middle of the American Dream. I wrote three more novels in quick succession, and each sold better than the last. Sarah kept working on the house, wouldn't let me help her at all. She also kept my nose to the grindstone on the novels. Like my mom, she didn't trust something as unreliable as publishing."

"And then she got cancer," Jack says in a flat voice.

"Naturally."

To our right appears a low building with a sign that reads THE NATCHEZ EXAMINER. Caitlin's Acura is parked out front, and through the back windshield I can see my daughter's backpack sticking up.

"That's Caitlin's paper," I tell him, trying to delay the conversation. "Annie's with her now. We're hoping to have some better news before we tell her about Dad."

"Good thinking," Jack says. "So, how are you guys doing? Are you ever going to make an honest woman of her?"

This, at least, brings a smile to my face. "Actually, we decided just this morning to get married. Right about the time Dad was having his heart attack."

"Seriously?" Jack gives me a sidelong glance. "Let's hope that's not an omen."

I laugh off his comment, although the juxtaposition of those events is a little disconcerting.

Looking forward again, Jack says, "Is this the way down to the river?"

"It can be. I thought I'd take you up to the city cemetery, where you can see ten miles of the Mississippi from one spot."

"Let's get down to the riverbank first. I want to put my hand in that water. The Mississippi gives me that feeling Don McLean sang about in 'American Pie.' Driving your Chevy to the levee and all that. I know that song was about the loss of innocence, but it makes me feel nostalgia for mine."

This is the Jack I remember. "One nostalgia trip, coming up."

I turn left and drive to where the road ends at a two-hundred-foot drop to the river. Here the roller-coaster-steep Pierce's Mill Road leads down to where the *Magnolia Queen* floated like a nineteenth-century paddlewheel palace only five days ago. I make the dogleg turn slowly, and seconds later a hundred miles of space opens up to the west of us. Five miles of the broad river is rolling toward us from Vicksburg, and Jack's breath catches at the sight of it.

"I'll be damned," he says. "I see the Pacific all the time, but this sight never ceases to amaze me. It just comes out of nowhere."

"I know what you mean. You can see the Rockies for miles, but this divide is like a buried vessel. The aorta of the whole continent."

As we slowly descend the precipitous slope, Jack says, "Tell me something. How did Sarah progress to stage-four breast cancer without noticing anything?"

"It's an old story, I'm told. She was so busy that she simply ignored the signs. She wrote her symptoms off to fatigue and hard physical work, told herself she didn't have time to get things checked out. She was only thirty-six, remember. The last pure joy I remember is a trip we squeezed in to Disney World. Annie was three, and she wore her Snow White costume the whole time. The whole trip was magical. But late that week, I noticed how tired Sarah looked, and how badly she was hurting. She'd been blaming it on tiling floors, stripping furniture, that kind of thing. But the day we got home, she reached down to pick up a box from UPS and felt excruciating pain in her back. That time I made her go to the doctor. When he shot the first X-ray, there it was. Her spine was collapsing, due to bone metastases. They did full-body scans. She had bone mets all over. One of her hips was half eaten away. It was in her liver, too, and soon the brain."

"Jesus. I never knew it was that bad."

I wave my hand as if that could banish the memories. "That was the background of what I'm going to tell you about. Sarah went downhill fast. I was doing everything humanly possible to find a last-ditch miracle. I knew a doctor who was a big deal over at MD Anderson, and *he* knew a guy who was helping to develop a new drug out at UCLA, which turned out to be Herceptin. We actually got hold of some, after phenomenal effort and expense, and Sarah got to take a regimen. But it didn't do any good. It was like trying to stop the *Titanic* from sinking. We were fighting a mathematical certainty."

Jack closes his eyes and sighs like a man who knows all about time and biological entropy.

"Sarah's parents came to stay with us, meaning to help. That didn't work so well. Her dad couldn't stand seeing his baby in that condition. Sarah was down to eighty-five pounds, and the pain was becoming unbearable. Bill had to move to a nearby motel. Eventually, the docs couldn't keep her both lucid and comfortable. But that's what she wanted. Sarah wanted to be home, and she wanted every second she could get with her daughter. Her goal was to reassure Annie until the very end. I never felt so helpless in all my life, Jack. I'd have given every dollar I had to have gone to medical school instead of law school."

"Where was Tom in all this?"

"Natchez, mostly. But he'd been talking to the oncologists all along. He knew what was coming. He was waiting for his moment. And when it came, he rode in like the real Lone Ranger, if there ever was one. He loaded up his car with drugs, drove out to Houston with Mom, and informed the docs he was taking over the case. Mom politely asked the nurses to leave, and she and Sarah's mother started caring for her around the clock. I don't think Dad slept more than three hours out of twenty-four for a week. He lived at Sarah's bedside, administering drugs like some kind of alchemist. I remember him calculating dosages of five different drugs on a legal pad, several times a day. But it worked. He kept her lucid and mostly pain-free until the absolute end."

"That's Tom, right down to the ground."

I nod, thinking of my father lying helpless in his own hospital bed. "You know how people joke about doctors' handwriting? Well, Dad's prescriptions always looked like chicken-scratch, sure enough. But I still have a page of those drug calculations. And they look like they were written by a seventeenth-century mathematician, they're so precise."

"He loved Sarah like his own daughter," Jack says. "He's told me that."

"Well . . . it was near the very end of that struggle that the other thing happened."

"Which was?"

Even now, a shudder of dread goes through me at the memory. "A Hispanic guy knocked on our front door. He looked familiar, but I couldn't place him. He was about thirty, tall, light-skinned, nerdy-looking. Turned out he was a serology technician from the Houston PD crime lab. Felix Vargas. I'd dealt with him on a few cases. Vargas was a chain-smoker, but I could smell alcohol on him the second I answered the door."

"What did he want?"

We've reached the flat riverbank at the bottom of the mill road. Where the *Magnolia Queen* once floated in its movie-prop majesty, now only broken mooring cables trail into the river. The Mississippi is still wearing its summer colors, the muddy brown tide rolling through sandy banks thick with green willow oak and kudzu, and white fields of cotton stretching away over the flat Louisiana delta. I pull to the edge of the asphalt and park at the edge of the gray anti-erosion rocks that slope down to the water.

"You want to get out and dip your foot in the water?" I ask. "You'll have to climb down the riprap."

"I can still manage that," Jack says, gazing out at the slowly falling sun. "But the river can wait. Tell me about the Hispanic guy, Vargas. What did he want from you?"

"Help. He started apologizing as soon as he saw me. He knew the shape Sarah was in. I could hardly get him to stop apologizing long enough to find out what he was doing there. He hadn't called ahead, because he thought I'd refuse to see him, which I would have. But by then, of course, he was there. I was politely asking him to go home and sober up when he grabbed my arm and said, 'A rapist nearly killed a girl, Mr. Cage, and he's about to walk free because of a lab screwup. I think you're the only one who can stop it.'

"That got my attention. I didn't invite him in, but we had a porch swing outside, and I sat on that while Vargas paced around and smoked and told me his story."

"Which was?"

"A Latina girl had been raped and beaten half to death the previous week. Raped with a beer bottle. Her name was Maribel. She was twenty-one years old, fresh out of junior college, a bookkeeper at a trucking company. The alleged perp was the son of the owner. A couple of months before, this Maribel had gone on a few dates with the kid, but she'd ended it after a couple of weeks because she sensed there was something off about him. He had anger problems, and some sexual issues, apparently. Difficulty getting it up, for one thing. And he was only twenty-four."

"Was this guy Latino?"

I shake my head. "Anglo. Last name Conley. And his family had money. Within an hour of his arrest, Wes Conley Jr. had one of the top criminal defense attorneys in the city representing him."

"Go on."

"The girl's story was straightforward. She would have stopped dating Conley much sooner than she did, but she was afraid she'd lose her job, since Conley's dad owned the company. But when she finally got up the nerve to end it, that didn't happen. The kid stalked her a little, called her fifty or so times, but then he seemed to resign himself to it.

"Everything seemed fine. Then Maribel goes to a company party. The Conley kid is there, and he starts talking to her. He's drunk, and hitting on her pretty heavy. Lots of people see it. Later on, though—after the assault—their memories get hazy on that point."

"Employment anxiety?"

"You got it. So, Maribel goes home from the party around eleven, alone. She lives with her mother, but her mother's staying across the complex with a sick friend.

Fifteen minutes after Maribel gets home, Wes Conley shows up at her door."

Jack is shaking his head in what looks like dread.

"She talks to him through the door, tells him to leave. He won't. She's reluctant to call the police because of her job situation. She decides to answer her cell phone, talks to him while looking through the peephole. Conley's got a half-empty bottle of Corona in his hand. He seems calm enough, and he says he needs to give her something. A present he bought her before they broke up. Hoping to avoid a big scene, she opens the door."

"Oh, no."

"Well . . . so far, so good. The kid gives her some gold pin he claims to have bought months before. Then he wants to come in, make out, you know the drill. But Maribel actually talks him out of it and gets him to leave. Jumpy as hell, she calls her sister in Miami and tells her what happened, but she decides not to call the police, even though her sister told her she should."

"I don't think I want to hear this."

"It could be worse. But it was bad enough. Maribel finally goes to bed. Close to an hour later, a loud noise wakes her up. When she gets to her den, there's a guy standing there in a black ski mask and gloves. Before she can even scream, he coldcocks her. Then he picks up Conley's beer bottle from the counter. Maribel had brought it in after he left it on the porch. The masked man beats her with the bottle, which doesn't break, thank God. But then he rips off her panties and rapes her with it. Both holes. Serious trauma, but mostly in the back."

Jack closes his eyes. "I think I'd have quit your job long before you did."

"The guy never penetrates her with his penis, but while she's lying half conscious on the floor, he masturbates over her."

"Leaving DNA?"

"Yes. Most of it hits her nightie, but some hits the floor. Carpeted."

"Okay."

"Once the guy finishes getting off, he stares at her for half a minute, breathing hard. She believes he's getting ready to kill her. But instead, he pulls a camera out of his pocket and shoots a flash picture of her. He leans over her and hisses that if she calls the police, he'll paste the photo all over 'Spick Town.' Then he vanishes, leaving her alive but seriously injured. Once he leaves, she manages to call 911, and the paramedics and cops show up."

"It was the Conley kid wearing a mask?"

"Maribel has zero doubt. First, his size was right. Second, he talked to her while he was raping her—mostly a furious, guttural whisper—but she recognized his voice. Third, the guy smelled like Conley. And that's something we all know, what a lover smells like. Fourth, she recognized his dick. He was uncircumcised, which is rare among white males in Texas. So was our masked perp."

"Goddamn. What happened?"

"The cops listened to her story, then arrested Conley."

"But he told a different story."

"Oh, yeah. He admitted coming on to her at the party, even to going to her apartment. He wanted to get laid, he told the detectives. Who doesn't, right? Maribel didn't want sex, Conley said, but he'd given her the gold pin, and she seemed to feel bad for him, so he laid a guilt trip on her. Probably to get him to go away, he claimed, she gave him a hand job on the porch."

Jack groans. "Which explains the semen."

"On her nightie, anyway. Maribel denied that, of course."

"What about the carpet?"

"The carpet became all-important. Because Conley claimed he never went inside the apartment. He told detectives that after the hand job, he was satisfied, so he split, then went to get stoned with some friends and watch the jets land and take off at the end of the runway out at Hobby Airport."

"The friends backed him up?"

"To the hilt. Five guys, all from affluent families. And because they admitted getting stoned, the cops gave them credibility points for candor."

"What about the camera? The flash photo? The cops never found those?"

"Nope. Maribel identified the camera from pictures as a Sony Mavica, an expensive digital camera, which was unusual for the time. She'd never seen Conley with one before, and she admitted that."

"The cops searched all his computers at home and work for the image?"

"Yes. They found nothing."

Jack shakes his head thoughtfully. "So this crime lab tech, Vargas, must have come to see you about the carpet."

"Exactly. Maribel had showed them the spot where Conley had raped her. The tech at the scene had looked at the carpet under a special light and seen no signs of semen. So they cut out the patch where the girl said the perp ejaculated, bagged and tagged it, and took it down to the crime lab."

"Okay."

"Here's where the problem starts. The head of the DNA section of the crime lab, Dr. Daman Kirmani, decided to handle the carpet analysis himself. He went over the swatch with a light and saw nothing. Then he did a microscopic exam of a random sample of the fibers. Finding nothing, he declared there was no semen on the carpet and reported that to the DA's office. That report became the key factor in what would be the plea agreement. Because the lack of semen on the carpet seriously damaged the credibility of Maribel's story. Forensics had 'proved' there was no semen inside the apartment, other than that on Maribel's nightie. The semen on the nightie *did* belong to Conley, but he'd already covered his ass in his original statement."

"But the medical exam of the girl—"

"Definitely proved a rape occurred. Serious trauma from the bottle. Maribel also had a shattered orbit beneath the eye, a concussion, a broken jaw, two broken teeth, defensive injuries of the hands."

"Christ!" said Jack. "So somebody had obviously beat the living shit out of her."

"Right. And nobody disputed that a violent rape had occurred. But as regards Wes Conley, it was a he-said/she-said deal. As a result, once the cops sifted through all the evidence, the assistant DA saw a fairly weak case against the kid for aggravated rape, which is what the charge should have been. Conley's prints were on the beer bottle, but he'd admitted bringing that with him, and Maribel had admitted bringing it inside the apartment herself. Another tenant of the complex, a Brazilian man, had seen a pickup truck like Conley's parked near her apartment during the time of the attack, but when the cops went back to that guy, he decided he'd been wrong about the time."

"Conley's old man got to him?"

"Probably. But you can almost never prove that kind of thing. Did they buy him off or scare him off? It doesn't matter. His testimony wasn't going to help the state."

"Hey, look," Jack says, pointing upriver.

A long string of barges is rounding a bend in the distance, the deep rumble of the pushboat's engines only a faint hum as yet.

"How long until he reaches us?" Jack asks.

I hear myself answer "He'll be here before you know it," but my mind is already operating on two planes. Speaking about the Avila case is like opening a door, or more like lifting a lid off a sealed well, dark and dank and filled with forgotten things. Jack apologizes for interrupting and asks me to continue my story. I do, speaking on autopilot, droning probably, but my voice is only incidental, for at bottom I am reliving this transformative event in my mind, the very thoughts I had during that time rising from the newly opened well, while my mouth relates some abbreviated version to my uncle, in the way that my hands and eyes often drive while my mind focuses on some deeper thought.

In a Jack Webb monotone I say, "Maribel Avila would have made a compelling witness, but given all the facts, the ADA was reluctant to charge Conley with aggravated rape. The kid had no priors other than a DUI, and he had a top-flight criminal lawyer. Without DNA evidence proving Maribel's story of the post-rape masturbation inside the apartment—*by his client*—that lawyer would have torn the state to shreds in front of a jury. But there was another side to the coin. The kid was scared. He didn't know what evidence the cops had from inside the apartment, and his father didn't want the family name dragged through the mud. The ADA on the case was a tough son of a bitch named Mitch Gaines. Former JAG Corps in the army. I never liked him, but Gaines could get the job done in court. So ultimately Conley's lawyer agreed that the kid would plead guilty to a stalking charge. The sentence was two years, suspended, and he didn't have to register as a sex offender."

"That doesn't sound like a deal a tough son of a bitch would cut," Jack says.

"Yeah . . . well. Mitch was getting pretty senior by then, and he had his mind on bigger cases. As the lab tech put it, 'Since you left, Mr. Cage, Mr. Gaines is the alpha dog over there. He's got his eye on the headlines, and he's got some big cases coming up.' A Latina girl raped in Gulfton wasn't exactly CNN headline material. Plus, Conley's dad had some political stroke. Joe Cantor wouldn't have cared about that, but Gaines might've."

Jack murmurs as he processes my summary, but it's not enough to hold me in the present. The memory of Vargas's visit, and my resulting confrontation with Joe Cantor, finally tips me over the edge of the well and pulls me down into the dark water of the past like lead weights strapped around my waist.

"Why have you come to me, Felix?" I asked, watching him pace from the porch swing.

He lit another cigarette and said, "I was out sick when they brought the carpet in. But when I got back to the office the next day, a colleague told me she didn't think Dr. Kirmani had done a chemical test on the carpet sample. He just looked at it through the microscope and reported it clean."

"Is a chemical test required in that situation?"

"I sure as hell would have done one."

"That's not what I asked."

"Legally required? I don't know. But by common standards and protocols, any reputable crime lab in the country would have done it. And I'll tell you something else. Another case almost exactly like this happened three years ago. Again with a semen stain, and Kirmani saying the cloth was clean. By the time anybody figured out what had happened, a plea had already been cut and signed."

I was still with the DA's office three years ago, at least for a few months. With guilty relief I thank my stars that I was probably gone by the time this happened, or at least never heard about it. "Okay. Did you confront Dr. Kirmani?"

Vargas looked at the ground. "Not then, no."

"Why not?"

"Dr. Kirmani doesn't respond well to having his decisions questioned," *Vargas said.* "Especially by underlings. Kirmani has a Ph.D. in biology, but not molecular chemistry. He's twenty years older than me, but I have more forensic experience than he did when he took that job. So do half the other techs."

"So what did you do?" *I asked, though I suspected I knew the answer already.*

Vargas shrugged. "I waited till that bastard was gone, then did the chemical test myself."

"And?"

"Positive for semen. And I had a colleague observe all this, to preserve the chain of evidence."

"Did you get a DNA match with Conley?" *I asked, though I didn't think I wanted to hear the answer.*

"Only basic serology, so far," *he said.* "But everything matches for the defendant on that level. I should have the DNA finished tomorrow morning. But I'm telling you, Mr. Cage, Wes Conley is the guy. He raped that girl."

"You don't know that yet."

"Yes, I do," *he said.* "I know."

"How?"

"The same way you knew things when you were a prosecutor. Sometimes, you just get an intuition. No, more than that—a certainty. Like you know before you know—before the facts back it up. Like knowing the basketball is going in the hoop the second it leaves your hands."

Like knowing the X-ray is going to come back with a death sentence, I thought. "All right. What did you do next?"

"I got up my nerve and asked Dr. Kirmani about it. Shouldn't he have done a chemical test?"

"And?"

"The question caught him off guard, so he did his patronizing-uncle routine. Assured me everything was fine. No sign whatsoever of semen on the carpet. Chemical test unnecessary."

"Did you tell him you'd done the chemical test yourself?"

Vargas lit another cigarette and nodded.

"And?"

"He blew up. I mean, he went totally ballistic. Threatened to fire me on the spot. He told me my test had to be wrong, because he'd already proved there was no semen on the carpet. He accused me of being drunk on the job, and drunk right then."

I gave Felix a hard look. "Were you?"

He looked away. "I'd had a couple of beers. I was scared to death, man. He was threatening my whole career!"

At this point I was wondering what the hell I'd taken on by even hearing Vargas's story. "Did you go over his head, talk to the director of the crime lab?"

Vargas shook his head. "No point. Those two guys hate each other, but Kirmani has the director cowed because of his Ph.D. Besides, the director doesn't want anyone poking their nose into his quality control. Because it's a fucking mess down there."

"Christ. Did you talk to Mitch Gaines?"

"I thought about it. But in the end, I didn't." Felix shook his head helplessly. "You know that guy."

I nodded. I didn't blame him for not going to Gaines.

"I did talk to a cop I trusted," he said warily, "a junior detective. I told him what had happened. He told me to let it go. He said nobody wanted to know if the crime lab had problems. That would screw up too much for too many people, and there was no money to fix them anyway. He also said Mitch Gaines would be the last guy to do anything to help me."

I wasn't so sure of this.

"So that's when I thought of you." Vargas looked like a troubled boy coming to an adult for help with some problem beyond his ability to handle.

"Felix . . . what do you want me to do?"

"All I know is that I can't handle being the only one to know this stuff. I finally told my wife about it. At first she told me I had to go to the FBI or the state police. But then I made her see that I'd probably lose my job over that. Like a lot of the techs, my credentials aren't exactly up to date in every area. When I brought up the idea of coming to you, she jumped on it. So . . . here I am. Do we let a guy we know raped and nearly killed an innocent girl walk because Daman Kirmani is arrogant, lazy, and stupid?"

There it was, the choice I'd confronted so often in life: the path of least resistance, or the walk over hot coals. I *thought about Sarah lying inside, floating on a carpet of Dilaudid, my mother tending her constantly. It was hard to summon the motivation to help someone else. Vargas was talking again, more about his wife and son and his miserable pay.*

"We're straddling the poverty line, actually," he said.

"Whereas I—"

"You were the boss's mano derecha *at that office, Mr. Cage. Two hundred attorneys up there, and everybody knows Cantor listened to you like nobody else. Wyatt Earp, right? Most of the cops say you could have run against Cantor and beaten him in the last election, or at least been his handpicked successor. And I know you never let that* culero *Gaines intimidate you."*

"Felix . . . you said the plea deal's been signed. The perp's already gone before the judge."

"Yes, this morning." He sucked on his cigarette. "But I heard sometimes they vacate those plea deals."

I shook my head firmly. "Only for material breach by the defendant, almost exclusively. That's as rare as snow in Houston."

"But not impossible?"

"The next thing to it. A plea bargain is like a contract between the state and the felon. You can't simply break it."

Vargas looked desperate. "But we must do something, no? That bastard is guilty."

The more I thought about what Vargas had told me, the more hopeless I realized the case was. Joe Cantor wasn't going to undercut one of his top prosecutors on a plea deal that had already been made. He wouldn't want to create that kind of ill will in his office, and he damn sure wouldn't want to bring down that kind of scrutiny on the crime lab. He would address the crime lab problems if I raised them—privately. But he wouldn't want TV crews hounding him while he was doing it, or legions of convicts filing appeals.

"I don't think there's anything we can do," I told Vargas. "Unless maybe you could find that photo the rapist shot. I know it sucks, but sometimes cases slip through the cracks. I'll push Cantor to check out the crime lab. But reversing a completed plea deal isn't going to happen."

Vargas stared at me for several seconds, then turned as if to go. I wanted to say something more, but before I could, he looked back and said, "There's one more thing, Mr. Cage."

"What's that?"

"You know this girl."

I couldn't believe him at first. It didn't seem possible. "What are you talking about?" I asked.

"The victim. You know her. Maribel Avila."

The name took me a minute. Because the people he was referring to, I hadn't seen since 1988. Then it was like a grenade went off in my brain. "You mean—"

"Dominic Avila," said the tech. "A brick mason. One of your first capital cases, I heard. An Anglo contractor killed him on a construction site. You sent the killer to death row."

In a flash, I saw three pretty little girls in a row sitting in the courtroom watching a murder trial. "And Maribel was . . ."

"The youngest daughter," said Vargas. "She was eleven years old at that time."

"That's who got raped with a bottle?"

Vargas gave me the slow nod. "She's twenty-one now. She just got released from the hospital. She's hurt bad."

"She had two sisters," I said in a monotone. "The mother was named Rosabel."

"Sí. Rosa, she goes by now."

It all came back to me then. Dominic was a talented bricklayer, not some poor schlub fresh over the border who barely knew his trade. A white contractor had been paying him peanuts to do jobs in River Oaks and Tanglewood. Nobody liked the contractor much, but everybody loved Dominic. So the next time they had a job, they tracked him down, not the contractor. Dom resisted at first, but the money was too good, so he started taking the jobs. This contractor was a mean son of a bitch named Cole. Cole told Dominic he was taking food out of his kids' mouths, and threatened to hurt him if Dom didn't stop taking jobs in those neighborhoods. Dominic tried to keep his head down, but he needed that high-end work. So one day Cole showed up drunk at a job site and went after Dom with a hammer. Dom defended himself. Cole went back to his truck, got a .45 from under the seat, and blew Dom's brains out in front of five Mexican workers.

Two miracles made that case different from so many I'd seen before. The first was that the homeowner's wife had walked outside right before the shooting. She'd heard the yelling, and she saw the murder. That wiped out any wiggle room the jury might have had to take the word of a *white shooter over the testimony of some illegals who could barely speak English. The second miracle was that Dominic Avila had been an American citizen for eleven months at the time he was shot.*

"How do you know all this detail?" I asked Vargas. "You didn't hear that in the crime lab."

"I reached out to one of the cops who worked the rape scene," he said. "Then I visited the Avila family."

"Christ, Felix. You're trying hard to get fired, aren't you?"

"I couldn't help it. I knew Dr. Kirmani had screwed up bad, and not for the first time. I had to put a face on the victim to get up the courage to do something about it."

"That's what put me in your mind, isn't it? When you found out about my connection to the Avilas."

Vargas shrugged, but any sense of guilt had left him. He'd already transferred much of the burden of his knowledge onto my back. "Señora Avila wanted to come to you herself, but when she heard how sick your wife was, she said she couldn't bother you at a time like this. 'We must all bear our misfortunes,' she said. 'The Lord tests us all.' "

"Goddamn it," I said, angry that he'd told me. I'm a sucker for nobility, humility, stoicism. And Rosabel Avila had it all, in spades. "There couldn't possibly be a worse time for this, Felix."

At last a little guilt showed in his eyes. "I know." He looked back at his car as though he couldn't wait to leave. "Was I wrong to tell you?"

I got up from the swing, walked up and down the porch, still thinking of Sarah and my duty to her. "No."

"Gracias, *Mr. Cage. So . . . what are you gonna do?"*

"Talk to Mitch Gaines, I guess."

"Shit. Is there any way you can leave my name out of that?"

"I can try. But in the end . . ."

Vargas sighed. "Si. I know. Fuck."

I made Felix give me his cell number, and then he got out of there like he wished he'd never come. And he was right to wish it.

"I've got the distinct feeling this story doesn't end well," Jack says from his seat beside me. "And I want to hear the rest of it. But I need a quick intermission. That coffee's hit my bladder. I'm going to take a leak in the river."

"Jack, that might be danger—"

Before I can finish, he's out of the BMW and making his way down the tumble of gray rocks with surprising agility. At the water's edge, he unzips his fly, takes a stance, and starts urinating into the Mississippi like Patton pissing into the Rhine. When the proud arc finally diminishes to nothing, he zips up, then shields his eyes with the flat of his hand and looks north, then south, as if making some momentous decision. Apparently satisfied, he squats on his haunches and dips his hands into the brown water. Lifting them carefully, he studies the water running through his fingers.

Inside the car, insulated from the wind and sun, I'm suddenly conscious that I'm sitting in the seat my father has occupied almost every day for the past five years. And someday soon—perhaps very soon—I will be taking his place as head of the family. My mother is strong in will, if not in body, but she has always observed the code of southern patriarchy, not out of submission, but out of a sense of tradition that probably predates the Bible. Traditional southern women never yielded all power to men—quite the opposite, in fact—but in formal social intercourse, an eldest son is expected to take up the mantle of his father.

My father did it when his father passed, and Jack, as the youngest son, accepted that as the natural order of things. What does he see, squatting by the river with water running through his fingers? Forty yards beyond him, in the main current of the river, a half-submerged log floats past. That tree might have been lifted off the bank only a few miles upstream, or eight hundred miles north, in Minnesota, but Jack is oblivious.

Fifteen hundred miles to the west, his wife is locked in a battle with her own immune system, which is relentlessly trying to kill her. Someday he will go through the agony I endured with Sarah; yet my greatest fear, losing my father, he endured years ago. How long, I wonder, until we exchange each other's grief? How long before I drop the last spadeful of earth on my father's grave in the cemetery up the hill?

"Now that I've marked my territory," Jack says, nearly startling me out of my skin, "let's ride up to the cemetery. We can watch the sun go down the way the birds do, while you finish your story."

As I turn the BMW in a 180, he says, "So you called Gaines, the ADA who'd pled down the rape case?"

"Yeah. I didn't want to do it—first because I'd been out of the office three years, and it was none of my business. Second, even if I'd still been in, it was considered bad form to interfere in another prosecutor's case. And third, I'd never liked the son of a bitch."

"Why not?"

I shift the BMW into low gear and start climbing the steep incline of Pierce's Mill Road, wondering how log trucks ever made it up and down this slope in the winter. "Huge chip on his shoulder. Gaines went to the University of South Houston Law School, then served in the JAG Corps in the army. I'd gone to Rice, and then UT in Austin, like Joe Cantor. Gaines was four years older, and he resented my rapid rise in the office. To him I was still a Mississippi boy, while he was Texas right down to the Colt he carried in his briefcase. Gaines was a hard-ass, right-wing, Bible-thumping, law-and-order ex-soldier, and he'd never doubted he was right. Not once. The day I resigned from that office was a blue-ribbon day on his calendar."

"And he just loved you sticking your nose into a case he'd just closed."

I share Jack's ironic laugh. "The first thing he said was 'You researching a new book? You wanna make me the hero?'

"I said, 'You're not going to like this, Mitch.'

"I told him somebody had called me about the Avila case. I could feel his asshole pucker through the telephone. He got aggressive from the first second. The plea was signed and already ancient history, he said, not worth talking about. When I mentioned the crime lab, he shut me down right away. But I couldn't figure out why. Gaines had always been a fairly straight shooter. 'If the crime lab has problems,' I said, 'it's going to bite you on the ass eventually. Why not deal with it now?'

"That's when I heard a cagey tone come into his voice. 'Why do you care?' he asked. 'You're a celebrity lawyer now, hobnobbing with the Hollywood crowd. We're still fighting down in the street. We don't need your help, and we don't want it.'

"'Come on, Mitch. I know you don't want a guilty man going free. What are you so afraid of?'

"'Okay, screw it,' he said. 'We've got a big case coming up. Huge. A conspiracy case. We're going to nail one of the biggest traffickers bringing weight over the border.'

"'Who?'

"'Victor Luna.'

"That stopped me. Luna was a cartel lieutenant. He owned a house in Houston, and he was seriously bad news. 'What do you have on Luna?' I asked.

"'We've got him for killing an informant. He pulled the trigger himself. There's DNA evidence critical to that case. So the last thing we need is somebody calling the integrity of the HPD lab into question, especially the serology section.'

"'I get that,' I told him, 'but the Avila case was just a simple fuckup. Dr. Kirmani should have done a chemical test and didn't. That's easy to explain.'

"Gaines only grunted. I felt like I was missing something. 'I don't get it,' I told him. 'Is this like the tip of an iceberg over there?'

"'Wake up, Opie!' he snapped. 'There were problems in that lab when you were trying cases here. Anybody who didn't see that was wearing blinders. We all know they operate on a shoestring. And like everything else, you get what you pay for.'

"'That lab work is deciding whether or not people go to the injection chamber,' I said.

"But Gaines had heard all he wanted to hear. 'I don't have time for your holier-than-thou bullshit,' he said. 'I still work for a living. You want to stick your nose in this, go ahead. But the boss is liable to break it for you. You might have been his heir apparent back in the day, but you quit the team. Joe's got his priorities, and he wants Luna locked in the Walls Unit, waiting for the needle. See how far you get trying to screw that up.' And then he slammed down the phone."

At the top of the hill, I turn left, then left again a block later onto Linton Avenue, the heart of Natchez's Garden District. On both sides of the broad street, three-story Victorians sited on steep hills peer down at us like mansions in a child's fairy tale. "Clearly I was going to be swimming against the current," I say to Jack.

"Did you kick it up the chain to your old boss, the DA?"

"No. I decided to go down and see the Avila family—at least the mother—and to talk to Maribel if I could. I felt I owed them that much."

"Even with Sarah as sick as she was?"

"The whole thing only took an hour. The Avilas lived down in Gulfton, which was just a few miles south of

Tanglewood. Gulfton was one of the original areas of Hispanic settlement in Houston. By the late seventies, it was wall-to-wall apartment complexes, built for young singles who'd moved in during the oil boom. When the oil industry crashed, those complexes emptied out. The ones that didn't go bankrupt filled up with Latino families. By the late eighties, a lot of Salvadorans were moving in. Crime skyrocketed with overcrowding, and the rest of Houston started calling it the Gulfton Ghetto. This was a stone's throw from an ex-president, right down Chimney Rock Road. I drove down there while Sarah was dozing and Annie was watching a movie with Mom."

Jack has leaned back against his door and is staring at me with something like wonder. "You're your father's son, you know that?"

"I hope so." I close my eyes for a second, blotting out my anxiety over my father and letting that long-ago pilgrimage fill my head. "They still lived in the same apartment complex, Napoleon Square. When he was murdered, Dominic Avila had been working hard to earn the money to move his family out of there and over to Northside, where some Hispanics were making inroads into safer neighborhoods. But after Dom was killed, Rosabel never saved the money to get out. Napoleon Square had been built as a seventies swingers' haven. Thirteen swimming pools, a disco. Now it was wall-to-wall immigrants with shops on the lower floors, and *paleteros* everywhere— Salvadoran ice cream vendors on bicycles."

"How did the mother react when she saw you?"

"Rosa broke down the second she opened the door. Praying and crying all at once. Then she warned me not to show any reaction, and led me back to Maribel's room. The girl was in rough shape, but she was still strikingly pretty, which was probably what had drawn Conley to her. She'd gotten some kind of associate degree in accounting, then gone to work at the trucking company. She was trying to fulfill her father's dream of getting her mother out of Gulfton and into a real house somewhere. She tried to put up a good front for me, but I saw through it. Rape is a weird crime, Jack. People handle it different ways, but it always scars you for life. I figured that photo would be scaring her, the idea that it would turn up on walls all over town, but she wasn't even thinking about that. Vargas had got it wrong about the internal damage. There was apparently some question about whether Maribel would be able to have kids. That was all the poor girl was thinking about by then. Old school, you know? What good man would want her if she couldn't have kids?"

"And the other siblings?"

"Two older girls. Both had moved away, one to L.A., the other to Miami. The eldest was doing okay, the middle child had drug problems. Maribel had been given her notice at the trucking company by this time, of course. She and Rosa were already eating through her savings."

"Did she tell you her story?"

I nod once. "Every word was gospel. It was another version of the horror I'd heard far too many times during my years at the office. I'd listened to a lot of victims and witnesses in my time, and heard all kinds of lies.

Exaggeration, shock-induced memory distortion, outright deception. But Maribel's story was straight from the abyss. Soul-withering truth. She never varied in one detail. That Conley bastard had been furious that a Latina girl had rejected him, and he went back to hurt her. If I'd been the prosecutor, I'd have taken it to court and put her on the stand."

"Even without the DNA evidence?"

"I think so. She was that compelling. But Mitch Gaines was immune to that kind of emotion. For him, it came down to a simple calculation. Could he win the case on the merits or not? Purely on the evidence."

"So what did you do?"

"I gave Rosabel some money and told her I'd look into it. I didn't promise anything. I really didn't think I could do much. The thing was done. Gaines would have been livid if he'd known I even visited that apartment, and Joe Cantor, too. I was way off the reservation. But like Felix Vargas, I couldn't let it go."

At the northern edge of the Garden District, I start up the long, gradual incline that leads to the high ground of the Natchez City Cemetery. To our right, in a low hollow, an oil well pumps lazily in the first shadows of dusk, but then we crest the hill and break back into the sunlight, where the redbrick pile of the Charity Hospital once towered over the vast cemetery like a factory providing corpses for the hungry fields below. As an overly imaginative boy, I had nightmares of orderlies shoving newly dead patients into the old-fashioned tubular fire escapes and sliding them down to waiting gravediggers, or worse, body snatchers. As crazy as it sounds, I was almost relieved when an arsonist burned down the antebellum hospital in 1984.

Passing the empty slab that once supported the massive building, I drive down to the second of four wrought-iron gates that offer access to the cemetery. This is the place where real life and my novels meet, deep in the overgrown shadows where the small stones of the anonymous dead trail out into the woods and the proud obelisks erected for forgotten bishops and generals rise into the rays of the dying sun. Taking one of the narrow lanes, I make for Jewish Hill, an earthen promontory that rises twenty feet above the rim of the two-hundred-foot bluff facing the Mississippi River.

Jack is staring past me, into the seemingly limitless reach of space over the river and the delta lands of Louisiana, but his mind is still in Texas, which also lies in that direction. "So did you finally call your old boss?"

"No. On my way home, I called a cop I knew and found out who'd worked the Avila case. Turned out to be a female detective, Eve Washington. I gave her a call, and Washington confirmed my instinct. She believed the Conley kid had done the rape. She didn't buy his alibi about getting stoned out by the airport. She didn't believe his friends, either. But she had no way to break their alibi. She'd searched every place she could think of for that Sony Mavica and the picture of Maribel, but it was nowhere on any property owned by Conley, his relatives, or his friends. 'The forensic findings fucked us,' she said. That's what I remember. I asked her to go back over all the evidence and see if they might have missed anything, and especially to keep hunting for that picture. She promised to do it, and to keep quiet about my call—and she probably did, for a few hours. But most detectives at the HPD knew me, and after talking to me, Washington knew that I might be making some waves. If I was going to do anything quietly, I had to move fast."

"So what did you do?"

"I didn't have any choice. I went home and took my shift at Sarah's bed. I spent some time with Annie and my folks. Then I drove over to the motel and updated Sarah's father, who was pretty close to the edge. Stone drunk and cold sober at the same time, if you can imagine. Like a drunk man facing a firing squad."

Jack looks out at the passing gravestones. "I can't even imagine being in his position. Not really. When Frances's attacks have been their worst, I've seen hints of what the end might be like. But to imagine my daughter dying before my eyes . . . no."

I could not speak of this with anyone other than my father or his brother. "You know what it was like?" I almost whisper. "When Sarah was in that half-drugged state, between sleep and wakefulness, and I looked into her eyes . . . it was like watching someone drift away from you in a boat on the open sea, with nothing you can do to reach them."

Jack nods slowly, saying nothing.

"That night, as I sat by the bed, holding her clammy hand, everything I'd seen and heard that day went to work on me. And while I sat there, the unalterable reality finally settled into my bones. No matter what I did, Sarah was going to die. But Maribel Avila was different. I couldn't turn back time and prevent that rape, but I could make sure she didn't have to worry about that son of a bitch coming back and getting her again—which rapists sometimes do—or raping anybody else. And once I got that thought in my head, I felt a little like my old self. My younger self. Righteous anger, you know? A man on a mission."

"Oh, hell. Nothing gets you in trouble quicker than self-righteousness."

"Yeah, I know. At about eleven, after Mom came in to relieve me, I called Vargas's cell number. 'I want to see the crime lab,' I told him. 'If it's so bad over there, I want to see it with my own eyes.'

"By that time Felix wanted no part of what he'd started. He was in survival mode. But I shamed him into going."

A faint smile touches Jack's mouth.

"He was scared shitless, but he took me up there. Hell, the security guard recognized me from the old days, waved me right in."

"How bad was it?"

"It was a defense lawyer's wet dream." I shake my head at the memory. "In one room alone, the roof leaked so badly that specimens were obviously contaminated. There was diluted blood on the floor. Some evidence was stored in such a way that cross-contamination was inevitable. Houston's hot as hell in the summer, and they had oscillating fans on the tables. In rooms where they analyzed hair and fiber evidence! It was a disgrace. I'd had no idea, really. None of us did. I guess Dr. Kirmani had the place cleaned up whenever he knew ADAs were coming over."

"But surely the police knew about this?"

"They claim they didn't."

"Shit." Jack looks incredulous. "And you had *no* suspicions prior to this?"

"I'd always had a weird feeling about Dr. Kirmani. He seemed to enjoy testifying a little too much. You know, putting on the suit and playing the part of condescending expert to a bunch of laymen on the jury. And about a year before Vargas came to see me, there'd been a public scandal over a guy who'd gotten left in the county jail for seven months while awaiting DNA analysis in his case. And he was innocent."

"Christ."

"Yeah. Anyway, because of that feeling about Kirmani, I'd always made absolutely sure of my forensic evidence. When I had DNA evidence in capital cases, I always made Joe pay for outside geneticists to do the testimony. I wanted my cases bulletproof, so that when Barry Scheck or Alan Dershowitz came down the pike with some pro bono appeal years later—which was inevitable in Harris County—they wouldn't find one hair out of place."

"Penn, it really stretches credibility that no one in authority knew about this."

"Not as much as you think. Kirmani was a master at manipulation. He hired people who were either barely qualified or lacked credentials, so they didn't have the courage to challenge him. He kept a few competent people to whom he channeled the bulk of the work he didn't understand. And his superiors had less technical knowledge than he did. They were awed by his advanced degree. Think about it. How often do you look under your hood to check your engine? Only when some problem gets so bad you can't ignore it, right? There's a major independent investigation of that lab going on as we speak. But I honestly don't think we'll ever know who knew what, and when. I think Felix knew a hell of a lot more than he told me about, but he kept quiet for fear of incriminating himself."

I park the BMW at the top of Jewish Hill, and we get out and walk to the end of the promontory, where a wire bench stands beneath a lonely flagpole. Behind the well-tended brick walls up here stand the graves of the Jews who came to Natchez in the nineteenth century and did as much as anyone to build the thriving mercantile business that eventually competed with cotton farming. We sit on the bench, but the vast panorama laid out before us seems to hold little interest for Jack.

"Let's hear it," he says. "Tell me you blew the story wide open."

"Nope. By the time I got home from the crime lab, I was exhausted. Still, I couldn't sleep. I went into Annie's room and kissed her forehead, then went into the sickroom. Mom and Sarah's mother were sitting on opposite sides of Sarah's bed, hunched over her skeletal figure in the half-light. In that moment they looked like ancient women tending a leper in biblical times. I asked them to give me some time alone with her, and they vanished without a sound. Sarah was in that narcotized trance that substituted for sleep near the end. I'd wanted to talk to her, but she only had a few lucid moments before dawn. She couldn't focus long. The brain metastases had initially caused only hand weakness, things like that. But by the end, her memory was severely affected. That was one of the most frightening things for her. For me, too, to be honest. It's as though certain things you've done together never really happened, because they've been erased from the other person's memory.

"At some point during the night, I fell asleep. After dawn, I started awake in a cold sweat, certain that Sarah was dead. I leaned down over her face, the way you do with an infant sometimes, and I heard nothing. But when I touched her face, she stirred, then gasped.

"'Everything's okay,' I told her. 'Are you there? Are you with me?'

"She nodded uncertainly. 'Is Annie all right?'

"'Yes, she's sleeping. What about you? Are you all right?'

"Somehow, through the thick fog in her eyes, I saw the girl I'd married. 'Hey,' I said. 'I see you.'

"She stared back at me for a long time. Then she said, 'This isn't fair.'

"This was literally the first time she'd said anything like that.

"'You're right,' I said. 'It fucking sucks.'

"'Did I do something to deserve this?' she asked, looking as though she really believed she might have.

"'Absolutely not,' I told her. 'What you *deserve* is to live to be ninety-five and have ten grandchildren.'

"What she did next almost killed me. Her eyes were as clear as they'd been in weeks. She clenched my hand weakly and whispered, 'Penn, I'm scared.'

"I pretty much lost it then. I *wanted* Dad to knock her out. I was like her father, in a way. I could stand seeing her in pain, but I couldn't stand seeing her *afraid*."

Jack touches my arm and says, "I've been there, brother. Believe me."

His understanding gives me a feeling of comfort I don't quite understand—the luxury of not having to explain, I suppose. "Not long after that, Mitch Gaines called me back. He said he'd heard I was talking to cops about the Avila case, and he was doing me the favor of saving my ass by warning me off it. He actually told me that if I persisted, I might be charged with obstruction of justice. As you might imagine, I was in no mood to be threatened. I told him he was the one whose ass was hanging in the wind, and he'd better stay out of my fucking way. Then I hung up. I was raging mad, but I couldn't bring myself to leave Sarah's bedside.

"About ten that morning, her pain worsened significantly. She was moaning and crying, and Annie got freaked out. Dad could no longer keep the pain at bay without drugging Sarah senseless, which would have been a blessing. At this point, Mrs. Spencer was worn down to a shadow of herself. Only Mom and Dad were holding it together. It really looked like Sarah was going to die that day, but somehow she held on. About three P.M., she lapsed into what looked like a coma. But her vitals were still reasonably strong."

While Jack stares at me, waiting, I let my eyes track a quarter-mile-long string of barges moving downstream far below us. The burnt-orange containers are riding low in the water, and the rumble of the massive engines of the tugboat pushing them is but a hum from this height. Yet that steady hum enters into me like a tranquilizer, and I feel my mind coming unmoored from the present again.

"Penn . . . ?" Jack prompts.

"Sorry. I was going crazy just waiting, so I took that chance to call Joe Cantor. I'll give Joe credit: he didn't try to avoid me. We met in a quiet restaurant near my house, one we used to use during murder trials. The owner gave us a private table in the back. Joe told me it was good to see me, and he meant it. We'd tried some major cases together and put some very bad guys behind bars. It was sort of like two old soldiers meeting years after a war. He asked about Sarah, and I soft-pedaled that. I didn't want to get into it."

"What kind of guy is Cantor?"

"Unique. He's half Jewish, but nonpracticing and fully assimilated. About the only thing Jewish about Joe Cantor is his Old Testament sense of justice. He's not a big guy, but he's a Texan down to his boots and bones. He looks like Rod Serling. Black hair, iron jaw, and as steely a pair of eyes as you ever saw. He never had much accent, either, which was surprising. His paternal grandfather was a Texas Ranger, and the other was a lawyer who became a judge up in Abilene. Joe himself served two tours in Vietnam before going to Rice and majoring in history. He was decorated for bravery."

"I guess he came by his legal philosophy honestly."

"He doesn't mince words about it, either. He'll tell you he doesn't know whether the death penalty's a deterrent or not, and he doesn't care. He sees capital punishment as legal retribution by society."

"Got it. So how'd he take your bad news?"

The memory of that meeting is burned into my cerebral cortex—not merely the words, but the unsettling feeling of seeing the face of one of my heroes revealed to be a mask of sorts. "Not well."

I remember sliding into the chair in the little private room, watching those eyes I had always seen as the personification of tough-but-fair. Joe started with small talk, some office gossip, and I sat listening to that voice the reporters loved, the one that never dodged a question, that fired off million-dollar quotes faster than you could scribble them down. The voice that even defense lawyers trusted. I was listening the way I listened to witnesses, alert to the slightest emotional dissonance, the faintest tell.

"What put a burr under your saddle over this Avila business?" he asked suddenly.

"I know the family," I said. "That Conley kid raped Mirabel Avila, and Gaines pled it down because it didn't look like a slam dunk." Cantor didn't look surprised, so I gave it to him straight: "You've got problems at the crime lab, Joe. Real problems. Daman Kirmani's an asshole. I don't think he's even qualified to be doing the science he's doing."

"Are you qualified to make that judgment?" Joe asked gently. "Dr. K has a Ph.D., for God's sake."

"Not in chemistry. And he had no forensic experience when he was hired for that job. If I'd known that when I worked in the office, I'd have been screaming about it back then. When was the last time you went over there?"

"The HPD crime lab? Hell . . . it's been a good while. Years."

"Take my advice: pay them a visit. An unannounced visit."

Joe looked wary. "Why would I do that?"

"Because I went up there last night, and it's a mess. Rainwater is leaking through the roof, contaminating samples. I saw blood on the floor. Open samples, overheating, you name it. Flagrant violation of standard procedures for preserving the integrity of evidence."

Cantor was clearly perturbed, but he held himself in check. "You went to the crime lab last night? How the hell did you do that?"

"Is that really the issue here, Joe?"

"It might be. Penn, you resigned from my office. You're no longer part of my staff, and you have no right to be in that crime lab."

I felt my face getting hot. "Who gives a shit? Wes Conley's semen is on that carpet. Dr. Kirmani fucked up. That's a scientific fact, like it or not."

"What makes you say that? The kid has a solid alibi, and the cops never found any trace of the perp's Sony camera or the photo he shot. If Conley had taken that picture, he'd keep it close, so he could use it to whack off."

I thought about Felix Vargas, who was probably swallowing Valium by the handful in the crime lab restroom. "My word isn't enough anymore, Joe? I tell you what I just did about your crime lab, and this is your response?"

"It's not my crime lab. That's HPD, and you know they're always stretched for resources over there. If they have problems, they'll be fixed in due course."

"No, they won't. Kirmani has set up a fiefdom that operates on the Peter Principle. Everybody rises to his or her level of incompetence. Obvious problems are being ignored, and cases are being tried on their findings. The Avila plea is a perfect example of that negligence!"

"Negligence is a pretty strong word, Penn. I need more than unsupported accusations."

I told him about Dr. Kirmani failing to chemically test the carpet. Then I continued, being careful with my pronouns. "A tech in that lab saw Kirmani's mistake and couldn't live with it. They confronted Kirmani and got threatened with termination. This person knew that would be the likely response, but they did it anyway. The case meant that much. When that failed, and Mitch refused to do anything, the tech came to me."

Joe smiled, his eyes filled with a strange mixture of goodwill and regret. "To Penn Cage, the white knight."

"Hey, you're the one who let everybody call me Marshal Earp."

A waitress came into our private room, but Joe brusquely waved her away.

"How do you know this whistle-blower is trustworthy?" he asked.

"Gut feeling. And you always trusted my gut, boss."

"Did you gut-test his alcohol level?"

As I looked back into Joe's eyes, my head began to spin. "You already know about this. All of it."

Cantor shrugged noncommittally. "I found out this morning. Mitch Gaines is shitting M-80s, he's so pissed off. He wants to charge you with breaking-and-entering and obstruction of justice, and that's just to start."

"I know you cut that idea off at the knees."

Cantor waved his hand. "You don't have to worry about Mitch. But this plea deal is signed, Penn. The Conley kid's already gone before the judge. The film's in the can. It can't be edited anymore."

"You've got to find a way, Joe. Get the plea vacated."

Cantor's mouth fell open. "You know I can't do that! That's like unbreaking an egg. Look, it's a raw deal for the girl, but sometimes cases slip through the cracks."

"Not often in your office, I was always proud to say. I saw you prosecute crooked bankers like they were crack dealers, and crack whores like they were human beings."

I could see that my open respect for him was moving him, yet still he resisted me. He was hoping I'd give up, but I wasn't about to. "Joe, listen. If that kid gets off this time, he's going to do the same thing to some other girl."

Cantor stared back at me without speaking, silently taking the measure of something within me. For a few seconds I saw what I thought he must have looked like as a soldier in Vietnam, peering into the shadowy depths beneath some jungle canopy. He was making a threat assessment.

"What's really going on here?" I asked softly. "Conley's old man has money, but I know that doesn't mean shit to you. Mitch said you've got a big case coming down the pipeline, and suggested you don't want the integrity of the DNA lab questioned just now. Is he right?"

Joe took a sip of lukewarm coffee. Then he laid his elbows on the table and leaned toward me. "I've wanted Victor Luna's ass for a long time, you know that. And you know why. He's a goddamn killer and worse. You couldn't tally up the lives that drug-smuggling bastard has ruined." Cantor's eyes flashed cold fire. "Now I've got him by the short hairs, and I'm not about to let go. Yes, I need DNA evidence to convict him, but I believe the DNA lab is solid. Hell, you tried cases yourself based on their findings."

"Yes, but I always brought in an outside geneticist to review them on capital cases, and to testify."

Joe raised his forefinger. "Usually. Not always."

I bristled at this implied threat. "I'll stand by every case I ever tried. I doubt Mitch Gaines would be excited about doing the same."

Cantor closed his eyes and slowly exhaled. "You've got to let this go, Penn. For the greater good."

"I can't do that."

When his eyes opened, they were full of sincerity. "I'll check out the HPD lab, I promise you that. And if that Conley punk is guilty, he'll get nailed down the road. They always do."

This stunned me. "After how many more girls have been hurt? Maybe killed?" I shook my head. "This family's suffering. Maribel Avila may never be able to have kids."

"I didn't know that," he said.

At last, I thought, I've reached him. "Now you do."

"What do you want, Penn?" he asked in a weary voice. "Seriously. I can't try to vacate that plea agreement without setting off a firestorm in the defense bar. It'll raise too many questions."

In that moment, with those words, our relationship changed forever.

"Joe, you're a good man. Probably a great one. Don't let your legacy be tainted by something like this. It's not worth it, not even to nail Victor Luna."

His eyes hardened. "That's not your decision to make, is it?"

"No, it's yours." I let some of my anger and disillusionment enter my own voice. "But I'm going to be straight with you. If I don't hear within twenty-four hours that you're moving to get that plea vacated, I'm going to call a press conference. We both know the media loves you, they always have. And not too many people seem to care what happens down in Gulfton these days. But Mirabel Avila is a very telegenic young lady—especially with the stitches in her face. And I'm not without a certain level of celebrity. If I take Mirabel in front of the cameras and talk about the crime lab, the Hispanic leaders in southeast Houston are going to pick up her cause, and that you don't want."

Cantor's face went white, then red. It had been a long time since anybody challenged him. A DA in Harris County has a lot of power. He answers to almost no one. I gave him time to process what I'd said. He didn't yell and scream. He thought about all I'd told him, long and hard.

When he finally spoke, he said, "You don't seem to care that a lot of your stellar cases were tried based on evidence that came out of that crime lab. But if you throw hundreds of convictions into doubt, you'll create chaos for the office. You could clog up the appeals courts for years."

When this didn't move me, he tried to make it personal again.

"Now that you've got another career, I guess you're not worried about having your most famous cases reversed. But think about the two hundred good lawyers you left behind in my office. The people in the trenches."

"I have, Joe. And I'd like to believe that none of them wanted to put anybody innocent in prison, or to let anybody guilty go free. You don't want that, either. And look, maybe the lab isn't that bad. But you need to find out, one way or the other."

He just stared back at me like a disappointed older brother.

"By the way," I added, "your office isn't the trenches. Gulfton is."

He knew I was telling the truth, but it didn't matter. "Penn," he said, "let the Avila case be the trigger that started us fixing whatever problems HPD has over there. That's how we get blood from the stone on this one. But for God's sake, be content with that. Don't blow up years of casework that we both know is solid."

"If the work was solid, the verdicts will stand."

"But at what cost in time and money?"

"That's not my problem," I said. "It's yours. If you don't want to be buried in requests for retrials, then find *a loophole in the plea-bargaining system. Use your influence. A hell of a lot of judges and lawyers owe you favors, and you can be pretty damned intimidating when you want to be. I don't care how you do it, but find a way to balance the scales for the Avila girl. As for the crime lab, that's on your head."*

I took out my wallet and left money on the table for our check. "Twenty-four hours, Joe. I've got to go. I've left Sarah alone too long."

He started to get up and come after me, but in the end, he didn't. There was nothing he could say, and he knew it.

"Penn?" Jack says. "Penn! Are you with me?"

"I'm here," I mutter, not quite sure myself. Down on the river, the long barge has passed far downstream and is rounding the bend that leads to Baton Rouge and New Orleans. "I'm sorry, Jack. I've been losing it a little over the past few hours. Last week was pretty rough, and Dad's coronary on top of it . . ."

"I know." He squeezes my shoulder and gives me an empathetic smile. "You want to give the story a rest? Go back and see him?"

"In a minute. I need to get this out. Are you okay?"

"Hell, yeah. I want to know what happened. I'm betting Detective Washington found the picture of the girl. That's how they nailed Conley, right?"

"Nope." I wish I had a bottle of water to wet my throat. "When I got home from meeting Joe, Sarah was still out. After being out in the real world—even for just that one hour—I could see how exhausted everyone was, even Annie. Everyone sensed we were on our last lap. If we weren't, some of us wouldn't reach the finish line. Mom and Mrs. Spencer no longer looked like nurses tending a patient. They looked like old angels hovering by the bed, waiting to collect a soul.

"While Sarah slept, I took Annie outside to play with a neighbor's dog. All I could think was that in a matter of days, maybe even hours, there would only be the two of us. She seemed to understand that, too, but she didn't want to talk about it. I didn't, either. So long as Sarah's heart beat, so long as there was one breath in her body, her presence filled that house.

"Late that day, she came out of her haze. With wakefulness came the pain—bone pain in her legs—and she got very agitated again. Worse than the morning, even. Something had changed in her. The iron self-control I'd seen slip just after dawn had finally given way altogether. There was an animal fear in her eyes. Nobody knew what to do. There's nothing worse than seeing someone you love in pain and being unable to take the pain away. Dad filled a syringe to knock her out again, but Sarah slapped it out of his hand. I think she was afraid that if he gave it to her, she'd never wake up again.

"That was the worst night. Annie was crying, and Mom had to take her upstairs. Sarah's mother finally cracked. We were in the final stage of the struggle. The Avila case never once entered my head. Dad titrated morphine for pain, but Sarah refused to be fully sedated, and he was losing the battle by then. Half the time she wasn't coherent, and when she was, she was terrified. I couldn't understand it. She'd been so accepting all along, so heroically stoic. I think she was like an army that had finally outrun all its lines of supply and was disintegrating on the battlefield.

"At that point I asked everyone to leave her room. With just the two of us, I tried to bring Sarah back to herself, to get her centered again. I talked about the simplest things from our past, things I didn't think she could ever forget. I realized then that a lot of her fear was caused by the brain mets, terror generated by having no control over anything, not even her thoughts. After a while, she let Dad give her a shot of fentanyl. She calmed down a little then. I felt enormous relief, but when the pain subsided, she took my hand and in a very clear voice said, 'I don't think I can do it anymore.'

"'Do what?' I asked.

"'This. Being awake is . . . worse than nothing. I don't want Annie to see me like this.'

"I said everything I could think of to reassure her, but nothing was getting through. I don't know how much time passed, but when the pain started climbing the scale again, she asked me to get Dad. I did. Then I went upstairs and watched *The Little Mermaid* with Annie. She fell asleep on my shoulder. Very carefully, I put her to bed, then went down to check on Sarah."

"She was gone?" Jack asks quietly.

"No. The opposite, in fact. Dad seemed to have worked some kind of miracle, because all her anxiety was gone. Her pain, too. I found out later he'd rolled her over and given her an epidural, like they do for pregnant women. He wasn't an anesthesiologist, but he knew how to do it, and he got my mother to assist him. It was an extraordinary measure, trying that at home—crazy by any conventional standard—but God knows he wasn't worried about any rules at that point. And the result was miraculous. It was as though this doom we'd all been fighting had magically been lifted, as though fate itself had been suspended, and time stopped. I woke Annie, and we all gathered around the bed. Sarah smiled and smiled, and even laughed a couple of times. Then our parents went out, and it was just the three of us. Annie was euphoric, seeing her mother like that, with the terrible weight lifted, the pain gone from her eyes. For an hour we were just a normal family, the family we'd been in Disney World four months earlier, before the diagnosis.

"Eventually, though, Sarah tired. I asked Mom to take Annie, and then it was just the two of us. For the thousandth time, Sarah made me promise to take care of Annie. And I did, like I'd never said the words before. She told me she loved me. And then she said I shouldn't let her death be an excuse to stop living. That I needed someone, and Annie would need a mother in her life. You'd think we would have talked about that long before, but we hadn't. I tried to stop her, but she wouldn't let me. She seemed to feel this was her last duty, to give me that permission. She was speaking straight from the heart, pure truth, without fear or regret."

I shake my head, trying to push away the memory. "You don't need to hear all this."

"It's okay," Jack says. "Was that the last time you spoke to her?"

I nod slowly. "I didn't know it, though it seems obvious now. Dad spelled me after a while, and I fell asleep on the sofa, watching an old Sherlock Holmes movie. Basil Rathbone and Nigel Bruce. I've always remembered that."

"There's nothing like a mystery to distract you from reality."

"Dad woke me about five hours later. The second I saw his eyes, I knew she was gone. Then I felt it. There was an emptiness in the house that hadn't been there when I lay down."

"Who was with her when she died?"

"Dad. Just Dad."

Jack nods slowly. "And Annie?"

"Asleep, thank God, which gave me time to prepare for telling her. It also gave me a little time alone with Sarah. I just sat on the bed and held her hand. I'd thought it was cold the night before, but death brings a coldness all its own. After a while, I felt somebody beside me. I looked up, and it was Dad.

"'She stood it as long as she could,' he said, and I heard a crack in his voice. Then he said, 'She was a trouper, son.'"

"Jesus," Jack whispers. "You know what that means, coming from Tom?"

"Uh-huh."

"What do you think he meant by that first line? Do you think . . . he helped her at the end?"

"Yes. She'd been suffering so much the night before, and then after she spoke to Dad, she was almost blissful. I think she made her decision right before that epidural.

That procedure alone could have killed her, given her brain metastases and the possibility of elevated pressure in her spinal canal. And Dad would have told her that. She wanted a few last hours of clarity before she left us."

Jack considers this for a while. "Whatever happened, it was her choice."

I nod silently. "I think her mother sensed it, too. When Mrs. Spencer left to get her husband, she hugged Dad and said, 'Sarah was so lucky to have you through this, Tom. We'll never forget you.' "

I shake my head, almost unable to continue. "After Mrs. Spencer left, I woke Annie and told her. That was the hardest thing I'd ever done, up to that point. Sarah had prepared her as well as she could. Not by saying she was going to heaven or any of that. Believe it or not, she used *The Lion King* to explain it. How she was going back to be part of the earth and then the grass and finally the stars again. Annie seemed okay with it. At first, anyway. But that's another story."

I get up and wipe my eyes on my shirt. "It's getting kind of cold. You want to get back in the car?"

"Can we pull it out here on the grass?" Jack asks. "Watch the sun go down with the heat on?"

"We're not supposed to. But I did it all the time as a teenager. Hey, the mayor ought to get *some* perks, right?"

Walking back toward the car, I say, "We were waiting for the funeral home people to collect Sarah's body, and the doorbell rang. When I answered it, I found Joe Cantor standing there. Joe had no idea Sarah had died. I'd finessed her condition the day before. He was stunned.

He asked to come in and pay his respects, but I told him no. I took him over to the porch swing where I'd sat when I talked to Felix Vargas two days earlier. That already seemed like weeks ago.

"'I'm so goddamn sorry,' Joe said. 'To intrude like this, I mean. But you gave me that deadline. I wanted you to know I'm moving to get that plea vacated.'

"'What do you mean, "moving to"?'

"'You know that's not an overnight process. But I've spoken to Conley's defense lawyer, and I've spoken to the judge, and I can tell you we're going to get to a new result.'

"'Which is . . . ?'

"'I think they might be willing to take a seven-year sentence for aggravated battery.'

"I forced myself to think about that. 'No sexual component? No registering as a sex offender?'

"Cantor shook his head. 'No. But a sure seven years in Huntsville. No federal country club. The alternative would be to try the case. I told them that's what would happen if they didn't take the prison deal. In fact, I told him I'd try the case personally, and I'd nail the kid's ass to the barn door. Between you and me, though, I'd rather not do that, if I can avoid it.'

"'So you don't risk the crime lab being looked at too closely?'

"'For a lot of reasons, honestly. For one, I hinted that we might have that picture.'

"My heart thumped in my chest. 'They didn't start screaming that was impossible?'

"Cantor gave me his cagey look. 'Not as quickly as they should have, in my estimation. But I'd like to close this out before Evan White gets too curious and starts calling my bluffs.'"

Jack stops beside the passenger door of the BMW and looks at me over the roof. "Who's Evan White?"

"One of the top criminal defense lawyers in Houston. I told Cantor that White must be curious already. Then I asked him how the hell he was getting this new deal arranged. 'You can't really get a plea vacated simply by calling in favors, can you?'

"'Let me worry about that,' he said. 'You just give me the okay.'

"I thought about it. The offer was tempting, but it wasn't up to me to say yes or no. 'I'm not sure the Avilas would settle for the guy not admitting the rape.' I told him.

"'Surely you can influence them on that?'

"'That's not my place, Joe. Maribel Avila was the one who got raped, not me. And not you, either, no matter how you may feel right now.'

"Joe was about to argue with me when a long black hearse rolled down the street and turned into our driveway. He shook his head, then got up and started to give me a hug, but I couldn't do it. 'Christ,' he said awkwardly. 'I can't tell you how sorry I am about Sarah. I wouldn't have come if I'd known.'"

"Goddamn," Jack says, opening the passenger door and climbing into Dad's car.

I get in and start the engine, then pull the big sedan out within a few yards of the edge of Jewish Hill and park, leaving the motor running. In the distance, the sun seems to be dropping faster, flaming orange filling the clouds above the river where it winds through the still-green fields.

"The next days were a blur," I recall aloud. "Sarah's wish was to be cremated, and Annie started having nightmares about fire. I wasn't sure what to do. I comforted her as best I could, and we all tried to explain that Sarah was beyond feeling any physical pain, but it was tough. That was a harbinger of things to come.

"They cremated her on Wednesday, and we planned a memorial service for Friday. I didn't know how many people to expect. I had so many cell calls I started to ignore them, and eventually I shut the thing off. After that four-month war of attrition, Sarah's death had left us in a state of utter exhaustion. I don't think Maribel Avila even crossed my mind during those days. I didn't know what Cantor was doing on her case, and I didn't much care.

"When Friday came, nearly five hundred people showed up. Most of the lawyers from the DA's office came, tons of cops, teachers and kids from Annie's school, all the neighbors. We were overwhelmed. Friends I hadn't seen in years flew in from Mississippi. Rosa and Maribel Avila even showed up. Thank God it wasn't raining. The entire backyard was filled with people. I lit a fire in the pit, and people took turns telling stories about Sarah. A friend of hers from college sang Joni Mitchell's 'Both

Sides Now,' which Annie loved. Then we had food, or spread what we had around as best we could.

"While this was going on, Joe Cantor suddenly showed up and asked if he could speak to me in private. We went into my study, and he wasted no time getting to the point.

"He said he'd been busting his ass on the Avila case, but we were out of time. He laid out two options. One, Conley would do nine years in Huntsville, no time off for good behavior, but no sexual component, either. Two, the case would be tried in open court. That meant no guaranteed result. An independent crime lab had verified Conley's DNA on the carpet, but Joe felt that if they took it to trial, Conley's legal team might make the HPD crime lab an issue in the case, and the kid could get off because of it. Evan White had already heard some rumors about Kirmani, and he had made some noise about it. To keep him in check, Joe had threatened to go for the maximum sentence for aggravated sexual battery: ninety-nine years."

"That'd make anybody think twice," Jack says.

"And you can bet Joe delivered that message without any subtlety whatever. I've seen him turn legal pit bulls into quivering puddles of Jell-O. Evan White was tough enough to test Joe's resolve, but I think Conley's old man was afraid to."

"Did you let the Avilas make the choice?"

"Yes. I told Joe to go get himself a drink while I spoke to them. Then I found Rosa and Maribel and brought them into my study. They sat holding hands while I explained their choice. When I was finished, they spoke in Spanish for a couple of minutes. I think Rosa asked Maribel if she wanted to go through a trial. Maribel asked in English if I thought Joe Cantor could win a trial, given all the circumstances. I said there was a good chance, but Wes Conley had a top-flight lawyer, and there were no guarantees. In the end, they decided that putting Conley away for nine years was enough. It would ensure that he wouldn't hurt any other women for a long time, and maybe he'd learn a lesson while he was inside. I told them he'd probably get some firsthand knowledge of what Maribel had been through, and I saw some satisfaction in Rosa's eyes. Then we all hugged each other, Rosa blessed me, and they left.

"When I gave Joe the news, the relief in his eyes was palpable. He did *not* want to take that case to trial. He left almost immediately, to close the deal before Evan White had time to persuade Old Man Conley to change his mind."

"Was that really the end of it?" Jack asks.

"Not quite. It took another hour for all the guests to clear out. Our close friends and relatives were still hanging around. There was also a woman I didn't recognize, about thirty, and black. I had the feeling she was waiting for a chance to speak to me, so I went over to her.

"She introduced herself as Detective Eve Washington, the woman I'd called on the day Vargas contacted me. She'd worked the Avila case from the beginning. I thanked her for coming, but she told me she was there because she'd heard things were in play on the Avila case, and that most of the office lawyers were coming to the service. She'd seen Joe go into my study with me, and then the Avilas. When I told her the result of our talks, she didn't look surprised. Then she asked what Cantor had told me about getting Conley's plea deal vacated.

"'Nothing,' I said. 'I figured he must have called in a year's worth of favors downtown. A lot of people owe him.'

"Detective Washington shook her head. 'Uh-uh,' she said. 'He's getting it vacated on material breach of the agreement by the defendant.'

"This stunned me. 'How could he manage that?' I asked her. 'What did Conley do?'

"Eve Washington smiled. 'Remember you asked me to go back over the case and see whether we might have missed anything?'

"A chill raced up my back, and—"

"They found the picture!" Jack cries.

I shake my head.

"The camera, then."

"No."

"Then what did they miss? Had the crime lab screwed up something else?"

I smile in remembrance of Eve Washington's satisfaction. "Detective Washington never believed Conley's five friends with their alibi about the airport. So she got a warrant and traced all their parents' credit cards for the day of the crime. They already had the records on the boys, but she figured, why not? Sure enough, one had bought gas at a station near Hobby Airport about ten minutes prior to the time of the rape. Washington and her partner drove out to that station and took a look at their security tapes. The station had been having a spate of drive-offs out there, so they had a great camera setup.

There was beautiful footage of those five boys buying gas for a jacked-up dually pickup truck. They were all outside the vehicle, horsing around, drinking beer and acting fools."

"What about Conley?" Jack asks.

"No sign of him. He wasn't in the vehicle, either. And their story was that they had all ridden to the airport together, after leaving Conley's truck at a friend's house."

"How could the police be sure Conley wasn't inside the truck?"

"Once Washington had that footage, she took another run at his friends. The second one folded in five minutes. He was on probation for a drug charge. He didn't know anything about the missing camera, but he admitted Conley had never been with them that night, and that he'd asked them to cover for him after the fact. Part of the initial plea agreement was that Conley swore to the judge that he'd been at Hobby with his friends during the rape. Washington had proved that was impossible, and that he'd lied. That gave Cantor grounds to get the plea vacated."

Jack gives a cynical smile and shakes his head. "And Cantor never said a word to you about that."

"As Eve Washington told me at the funeral, 'He's a politician.' Joe wanted me to think he'd called in major favors to help me out. Or moved heaven and earth to do the right thing. Take your pick.

"I told Washington it didn't matter, that the Avila family was okay with the new plea, and we'd got the best result we could. I thanked her for her work and told her

I was in her debt. She already knew that, but she looked grateful for the praise. You don't get much of it in her job. 'You, too,' she said. 'That was a stand-up thing, you getting into the case like that. Especially with all this other weight on you.'

"I almost ended the conversation there. But then I asked her how bad the crime lab really was. I told her from what I'd seen, it was pretty fucked up.

"She shrugged. 'That question's way above my pay grade. We work with what we have, you know? I hear weird stuff out of there. Crazy things have happened. But that's a problem for the brass, right?'

"'Are they aware of the problems?'

"'Got to be, by now. But . . . people see what they want to see, right?' She gave me a curious look. 'You gonna get into that next? Make some noise downtown?'

"I thought about it, then shook my head. 'I pushed Joe hard on the lab,' I told her. 'And he promised to check it out. I've got my hands full with my daughter.'

"Washington gave me a sad smile, and then she left. I never saw her again."

"Damn." Jack is smiling strangely. "What about Vargas?"

I shake my head. "Felix quit or was let go not long after all that. He moved his family out of town, never called me once."

"Huh. You know, it's funny that it *was* a picture that nailed Conley in the end. It just wasn't *the* picture."

"Yeah." I reach out and turn down the heat in the car. "You know what happened after that. The illusion of

Annie being okay fell away pretty quickly. She developed severe separation anxiety. Therapists didn't help. I had to start homeschooling her. And the house . . . Sarah had laid every tile, refinished ever floor, chosen every paint color. Her spirit invested the whole place, which you'd think would be comforting. Yet it felt like there was a hole that moved from room to room with us. Her absence was a palpable thing. I should have realized sooner that Annie needed to get out of there.

"I was experiencing my own disconnect. The book I'd been working on completely stalled, and the Avila case had tainted the city for me. I'd never loved Houston, but I had friends there. I'd done good work there. But my ultimatum to Joe had a strange ripple effect. I sensed a general feeling that I'd put people's careers at risk. If I hadn't been dealing with Annie's problems, and my own grief, I might have made a battle of it. Tried to pull down the whole temple. But I didn't have the strength for that. Investigations into the crime lab began soon enough. But fixing the problems proved harder than anyone could have imagined. They were so endemic to the system, to the city culture . . . the DNA section had to be closed altogether for a while. And they *still* haven't straightened it all out."

"Joe Cantor is leading that investigation?"

"No. Joe gracefully retired less than a year after I left Houston. Long before it all became a national scandal."

"He knew enough to get out while the getting was good."

"Maybe. I still believe he had more personal integrity than most DAs I've met in my life. And while quite a few convictions for lesser crimes have been reversed for flawed serology or DNA evidence in Harris County—most tried under Joe's successors—there's yet to be a capital case overturned. So Joe was right, in a way: the lab wasn't as bad as Felix Vargas had feared. But the investigations are far from over, and I worry that reversals on capital cases may be coming. Think about that, Jack: a truly innocent man rotting in Huntsville Prison for murder. How do you ever make that right?"

"You can't. Not with all the money in the world."

"God forbid they ever go back and find we executed an innocent man."

Jack whistles softly. "Amen."

"A lot of good lawyers became cynical fast in that ADA job. I never did. But over time . . . what I saw changed how I felt about the death penalty in this country. Eleven years ago I shot a man because he was trying to kidnap my child. No picnic, by any means, but at least that was clean. A necessity." I point out at the broad channel of the Mississippi. "A week ago I drowned a man twenty yards out in that river. He was trying to kill me. Not much gray area there, either. I sleep fine at night." A rush of tangled memories flashes behind my eyes: a gasping mouth beneath eyes filled with hatred, and blood in the water. "But when you kill people with paper—with a stacked deck of cards—it starts getting easy. And when it's easy, eventually you kill somebody who just happened to be in the wrong place at the wrong time."

Jack sighs deeply, then gives me a look that forgives everything without a word being spoken. "You think we'd better head back to the hospital?"

"Yeah. Maybe you can persuade Mom to give you a turn at the bedside now."

"Tom's going to make it," Jack says, his eyes filled with faith. "I know it."

I nod, but I'm far from feeling his certainty. "So you think I should just let it go, about Dad telling Mom he had something important to tell me before he died?"

Jack gives me his enigmatic look. "Let's talk about it on the way back."

As I PULL through the massive wrought-iron gate of the cemetery and turn south, toward town, Jack says, "If you thought you were going to die in half an hour, would you be at peace with it? Or would you maybe need to make a call or two? Maybe ask for forgiveness, or grant it to somebody?"

"I hear you. I think it's only the fact that this is Dad that's rattled me. Of all the men I've ever known, he's the one where you felt like what you saw was what you got. Somehow, his integrity has held up through every storm."

Jack nods. "Oh, I know. But Tom's human, too." He picks up the McDonald's bag with the sandwich wrapper and loudly crushes it. "You probably never knew this, but when I was in my early forties, Frances and I nearly got divorced. It was a bad time. This was after I'd quit Hughes Aircraft and joined Argus Minicom. I'd made too much money for my age; I was drinking way too much and . . . overdoing some other things as well. When things hit the crisis point, Tom flew out to California and spent three days with me. He wasn't overbearing about it, but he'd come to talk me back down to earth. I was out of control. Worst of all, I felt like there was no way to go back to Frances, after the things I'd done.

"The last night he was there, Tom got to drinking with me. And then he did what we all do when we're trying to make somebody on the low end of the downslope feel like there's still hope. We tell them they're not the only ones carrying heavy baggage."

My pulse quickens. "What did he tell you?"

"That he'd done some things in the past that he didn't think he could be forgiven for. He'd felt for years that he was damned because of them. Literally beyond redemption, beyond any happiness. But eventually, he got past them. I think you and your sister had a lot to do with that. And your mother."

"What was he talking about, Jack?"

My uncle shrugs. "Tom stopped short of telling me. He just couldn't bring himself to do it." Jack looks up at me, his eyes as sober as I've ever seen them. "But my feeling was, it had to do with the war."

"What made you think that?"

"I was only a toddler when Tom came back from Korea. But years later I talked to Phil, who was nineteen when Tom got back. Phil said Tom wouldn't tell him a damned thing about what happened over there. But when Phil enlisted in the Marines, Tom nearly killed him. Later on, Mom and I found a couple of medals Tom had won over there. Not small stuff, either. But whatever he'd done to get them, he kept to himself."

"I know he was wounded, but only because of the shrapnel scars on his back and belly. When I asked how he got those, he just said he'd been in the wrong place at the wrong time. I don't think he ever even told Mom the real story."

Jack shrugs. "There you go. If I had to lay money, I'd bet he did some things over there that no man should have to do. That was a brutal war, and he was in the thick of it. The retreat from Chosin, for God's sake. And he was a medic. There's no telling what he saw. So, if Tom has decided he doesn't want to talk about whatever it was, I say let him be. He's alive; that's all that matters."

"I know. My mind's been running wild with speculation, but Korea's the black hole in his life, as far as the family is concerned. That must be it."

Jack gives me a bittersweet smile. "Let it go, Penn."

"Let the dead bury the dead?"

He raises one eyebrow. "Actually, no. Jesus supposedly said that to a disciple who asked to be excused from his spiritual work to go and bury his father. In reality, the disciple wanted to leave Jesus and go live with his aging father until he died. Jesus wanted the man to focus on his spiritual calling. As an atheist, my advice is the exact opposite: go home and live with your aging father until he dies. And take him as he is. Let the past die, and let the future take care of itself." Jack pats me on the thigh. "But I'm just an old hippie. What do I know?"

More than most, I answer silently. As the *Examiner* building comes into view, I'm overwhelmed by an impulse to see my daughter and fiancée. "Do you mind if we stop and see Annie and Caitlin before going back to the hospital?"

"Of course not," Jack says. "I'd love to see them."

Taking out my BlackBerry, I text Caitlin that Jack and I are about to pull into the front parking lot. Only moments after I finish sending my message, the ringer goes off.

My heart thumps when I see my mother's number on the screen. "It's Mom," I tell Jack.

"It's okay," he says in a steady voice. "It's going to be good news."

"How do you know?"

He smiles. "Because we're due some, by God."

"Hello?"

"We got another troponin level back," my mother says, her voice tremulous with excitement. "The damage is serious, but Dr. Bruen says he's cautiously optimistic."

"Did he say what that means in concrete terms?"

I ask this without quite thinking about what I'm making my mother face to answer me. After a long silence, she says, "A year, probably. Two or three if Tom will straighten up. He's going to be in congestive failure soon, if he doesn't."

"Then we'll make him straighten up," I say quickly, with some of Jack's certainty.

"That's right," Mom says. "Now you and Jack come back. Tom's been asking for you."

"We'll be there in fifteen minutes."

I relay the information to Jack as we pull into the *Examiner* lot.

"I told you," he says, looking more relieved than satisfied.

Before we can get out of the car, Annie pushes open the front door of the building and looks around in confusion. Then her eyes settle on the black BMW and her face lights up.

"My God," Jack whispers, seeing her willowy form run toward us. "She looks exactly like Sarah."

"Yep," I say, a hitch in my voice. "It's a mixed blessing, brother."

He squeezes my arm in empathy, but then Annie yanks open my door and says, "Where's Papa, Daddy? What are you doing in Papa's car?"

Before I can answer, her eyes light on Jack. "Oh," she says. "I'm sorry. Who are you?"

Jack smiles. "I'm Papa's little brother," he says, reaching out to shake her hand.

"You don't look very little," Annie says, her eyes still wide with curiosity. "What's going on?" Her mouth tightens with anxiety. "Has something happened?"

By this time Caitlin has walked up behind Annie. She leans down and smiles at Jack. "So what's going on?" she asks in a casual voice that belies the concern in her green eyes.

"We've got good news," I tell her. "Get in."

Her eyelids close with relief at this promise of deliverance. We've both seen enough death recently to last us quite some time. After a moment, Caitlin wipes her eyes with her sleeve and then opens the back door for Annie, whose sudden laughter fills the backseat like warm light. "Let's go see Papa!" she cries. "I made a one hundred on my history test, and I want to show him."

Jack turns and smiles, then gives her a thumbs-up. "Sounds like a plan, kid." He winks at me. "Let's go, Dad. Show us what this baby can do."

EXCERPT FROM *NATCHEZ BURNING*

Prologue

"IF A MAN is forced to choose between the truth and his father, only a fool chooses the truth." A great writer said that, and for a long time I agreed with him. But put into practice, this adage could cloak almost any sin. My mother would agree with it, but I doubt my older sister would, and my fiancée would scoff at the idea. Perhaps we expect too much of our fathers. Nothing frightens me more than the faith in my daughter's eyes. How many men deserve that kind of trust? One by one, the mentors I've most admired eventually revealed chinks in their armor, cracks in their façades, and tired feet of clay—or worse.

But not my father.

A child of the Great Depression, Tom Cage knew hunger. At eighteen, he was drafted and served as a combat medic during the worst fighting in Korea. After surviving that war, he went to medical school, then paid off his loans by serving in the army in West Germany. When he returned home to Mississippi, he practiced family medicine for more than forty years, treating some of the most underprivileged in our community with little thought of financial reward. The *Natchez Examiner* has named him an "Unsung Hero" more times than I can remember. If small towns still have saints, then he is surely one of them.

And yet . . .

As the cynical governor created by my distant relation, Robert Penn Warren, once said: *"Man is conceived in sin and born in corruption and he passeth from the stink of the didie to the stench of the shroud. There is always something."* My younger self sometimes wondered whether this might be true about my father, but time slowly reassured me that he was the exception to Willie Stark's cynical rule. Like poor Jack Burden, my hopeful heart answered: *"Maybe not on the Judge."* But Robert Penn Warren had the kind of courage I've only begun to discover: the will to dig to the bottom of the mine, to shine his pitiless light downward, and to stare unflinchingly at what he found there. And what I found by following his example was proof of Willie Stark's eternal rule: *There is always something.*

It's tempting to think that I might never have learned any of this—that my mother, my sister, and I might mercifully have escaped the consequences of acts committed deep in the haze of history (a time before cell phones and digital cameras and reporters who honor no bounds of propriety, when *N-word* meant nothing to anybody and *nigger* was as common in the vernacular as *tractor*)—but to yearn for ignorance is to embrace the wishful thinking of a child. For once the stone hits the surface of the pond, the ripples never really stop. The waves diminish, and all seems to return to its previous state, but that's an illusion. Disturbed fish change their patterns, a snake slides off the muddy bank into the water, a deer bolts into the open to be shot. And the stone remains on the slimy bottom, out of sight but inarguably there, dense and permanent, sediment settling over it, turtles and catfish prodding it, the sun heating it through all the layers of water until that far-off day when, whether lifted by the fingers of a curious boy diving fifty years after it was cast or uncovered by a bone-dumb farmer draining the pond to plant another half acre of cotton, that stone finds its way back up to the light.

And the man who cast it trembles. Or if he is dead, his sons tremble. They tremble by an unwritten law, one that a fellow Mississippian understood long before I was born and casually revealed to a reporter in a French hotel room in 1956, dispensing eternal truths as effortlessly as a man tossing coins to beggars in the road. He said, "*The past is never dead; it's not even past. If it were, there would be no grief or sorrow.*" And ten years before him, my distant relation wrote, "*There is always something.*" And six decades after that, I thought: *Please, no, let me remain in my carefully constructed cocoon of Not-Knowing. Let me keep my untarnished idol, my humble war hero, the one healer who has not killed, the one husband who has not lied, the one father who has not betrayed the faith of his children*. But as I know now, and hate the knowing . . . Willie was right: there *is* always something. So let us begin in 1964, with three murders. Three stones cast into a pond no one had cared about since the siege of Vicksburg, but which was soon to become the center of the world's attention. A place most people in the United States liked to think was somehow different from the rest of the country, but which was in fact the very incarnation of America's tortured soul.

Mississippi.

PART ONE

_____

1964–1968

At his best, man is the noblest of all animals;
separated from law and justice he is the worst.
—ARISTOTLE

Chapter One

ALBERT NORRIS SANG a few bars of Howlin' Wolf's
"Natchez Burnin'" to cover the sounds of the couple
making love in the back of his shop. The front door was
locked. It was after seven, the streets deserted. But today
had been a bad day. Albert had tried to cancel the rendezvous by switching on the light in the side room where
he taught piano during the week—he'd even sent a boy
to warn the man to stay away from the shop—but the
two lovers had ignored his warnings and come anyway.
He'd set up their rendezvous a week ago, by sending out
a coded message during his gospel radio show, which was
his usual method. But lovers who saw each other only
twice a month—if they were lucky—weren't going to be
deterred by a warning light in a window, not even if their
lives were at risk.

The white woman had arrived first, rapping lightly
at the alley door. Albert had tried to run her off—whites

were supposed to use the front—but she'd refused to budge. Terrified that a passerby might see her, Albert had let her in. Mary Shivers was a skinny white schoolteacher with more hormones than sense. Even before he could chastise her, he heard his side door open. Moments later, six-foot-three-inch Willie Hooks barged into the store. The big carpenter stuffed five dollars into Albert's hand, ran to the woman, seized her up in one arm, and carried her to the back of the shop. Albert had followed, desperately trying to explain about the visit he'd gotten from the furious white men that afternoon, but Hooks and the schoolteacher were deaf to all appeals. Three seconds after the door slammed in his face, Albert heard the sounds of people shedding clothes. A moment later, the woman yelped, and then the springs in the old sofa in the back room went to singing.

"Five minutes!" Albert had shouted through the door. "I'm kicking open this door in five minutes. I ain't dying for you two!"

The couple took no notice.

Albert cursed and walked toward his display window. Third Street looked blessedly empty, but within five seconds Deputy John DeLillo's cruiser rolled into view, moving at walking speed. Acid flooded Albert's stomach. He wondered where the schoolteacher had parked her car. Deputy DeLillo was even bigger than Willie Hooks, and he had a fearsome temper. He'd killed at least four black men Albert knew about, and he'd beaten countless others with rods, phone books, and a leather strap spiked with roofing tacks.

Big John's cruiser stopped in the middle of the street. His big head leaned out of the car to gaze into Albert's shop window. Albert couldn't see the deputy's eyes, thanks to the mirrored sunglasses he wore, but he knew what DeLillo was looking for. Pooky Wilson was the most wanted man in Concordia Parish tonight. Just eighteen, Pooky had gained that dubious distinction by bedding the eighteen-year-old daughter of one of the richest men in the parish. Since he'd worked at Albert's store for nearly a year, Pooky had naturally run to Albert when he learned that the Klan and the police—often one and the same—were combing the parish for him. Knowing that local "justice" for Pooky would mean a tall tree and a short rope, Albert had hidden the boy in the safe box he'd constructed for illegal whiskey, which he sold on a seasonal basis. For the past two hours, Pooky had been sitting cramped in the shell of a Hammond spinet organ in Albert's workshop. Positioned against a wall, the A-105 looked like it weighed five hundred pounds, but the hollow housing could hold a full load of moonshine, and even a man in a pinch. There was a trapdoor beneath it for dumping contraband during emergencies (and a hidey-hole dug in the earth below), but since the music store sat up on blocks, Pooky couldn't use that for escape until after dark.

Albert raised his hand and gave Deputy DeLillo an exaggerated shake of his head, indicating that he'd seen neither hide nor hair of his employee. For a few paralyzed seconds, Albert worried that DeLillo would come inside to question him again, which would lead to the big deputy kicking open the door that separated him from the loudly copulating couple, and then to death for either DeLillo or Willie Hooks. The violent repercussions of Willie killing the deputy were almost unthinkable. Thankfully, after a few awful seconds, Big John waved his mitt and drove on. An invisible band around Albert's chest loosened, and he remembered to breathe.

He wondered how Pooky was doing. The fool of a boy had been hiding in the Hammond when his girlfriend's father and a Klansman named Frank Knox had burst into the store, cursing Albert for "fomenting miscegenation" and threatening to kill him if he didn't produce Pooky Wilson. Albert had summoned all his courage and lied with the sincerity of Lucifer himself; if he hadn't, both he and Pooky would already be dead.

As the bedsprings sang in the back of the store, Albert prayed as he never had before. He prayed that the Klan hadn't stationed anybody outside to watch his store. He prayed that Willie and the schoolteacher would finish soon, would get away clean, and that darkness would fall. Anything less meant the end for all of them, except maybe the white woman.

The sofa springs groaned at about E above middle C, so Albert tuned his voice to their accompaniment. "*There was two hundred folks a-dancin',*" he belted as he negotiated his way through the pianos in the display room, "*laughin', singin' to beat the band.*" He'd already run out of verses, so he'd taken to making up his own, describing the tragic fire that would likely have killed him, had he not been away in the navy. "*Yeah, there was two hundred*

souls a-dancin', lawd—laughin', singin' to beat the band."
Entering his workshop, he sat beside the Hammond organ, picked up a tonewheel, and pretended to work on it. *"Two hundred souls on fire, locked indoors by the devil's hand."*

After a quick look back at the display window, he tapped on the Hammond and said, "How you doin' in there, Pook?"

"Not good. I'm 'bout to pee in my pants, Mr. Albert."

"You got to hold it, boy. And don't even think about lifting that trapdoor. Somebody outside might see your water hit the ground."

"I can't breathe, neither. I don't like small spaces. Can't you let me out for a minute? It feels like a coffin in here."

"There's plenty of air in there. That small space is the only thing that's gonna keep you *out* of a coffin tonight."

Albert heard a ripping sound. Then part of the grille cover beneath the organ's keyboard was pulled back, and an eye appeared in the hole. It looked like the eye of a catfish gasping in the bottom of a boat.

"Quit tearing that cloth!" Albert snapped.

The eye vanished, and two dark fingers took its place. "Hold my hand, Mr. Albert. Just for a minute."

With a lump in his throat, Albert reached out and hooked his forefinger in Pooky's. The boy hung on like Albert was the only thing still tying him to the earth.

"Is there somebody else in the store?" Pooky asked.

"Willie Hooks. He'll be gone soon. Listen, now. When it gets dark, I'm gonna turn on the lights in the display room and start playing piano. That'll draw any eyes watching the place. Once I get goin' good, open that trapdoor and drop down to the hole. If the coast looks clear, make your way two blocks over to Widow Nichols's house. She'll hide you in her attic till tomorrow. When I think the time is right, I'll pick you up in my panel truck and carry you to the train station at Brookhaven. From there, it's the Illinois Central straight up to Chicago. You got that?"

"I guess so. What I'm 'posed to use for money? Man can't ride the train for free."

Albert leaned over and slid five twenty-dollar bills under the bottom of the organ.

"Tuck that in your pants. That foldin' money's gonna get you started in Chi-town."

Pooky whistled in amazement inside the organ box. "Can we really make it, Mr. Albert? Them fellas mean to lynch me for sure."

"We'll make it. But we wouldn't even *be* in this mess if you'd listened to me. I told you that girl was just trying to prove something to her daddy, messing with you."

Pooky whimpered like a frightened dog. "I can't he'p it, Mr. Albert. I love Katy. She loves me, too."

The boy sounded like he was barely holding himself together. Albert shook his head, then got up and returned to the display room, once more belting the blues like a bored man working alone.

He'd met Howlin' Wolf back in '55, at Haney's Big House up the street, back when the Wolf was playing the chitlin circuit. Wolf's keyboard man had been sick, so Haney called Albert down from his store to fill in.

Albert had met most of the great ones that way, over the years. They'd all swung through Ferriday at one time or another, since it lay so close to the Mississippi River and Highway 61. Ray Charles, Little Walter, B.B., even Muddy himself. White boys, too. Albert had taught Jerry Lee Lewis more than a few licks on piano. Some of the black acts had tried to lure Albert onto the road with them, but Albert had learned one true thing by watching musicians pass through his store: the road broke a man down fast— especially a black man.

The white woman screamed in the back. Albert prayed nobody was walking through the alley. Willie was working her hard. Mary Shivers had been married five years and had two kids, but that wasn't enough to keep her at home. Two months ago, she'd struck up a conversation with Willie while he was working on a house next door. Next thing you know, Willie was asking Albert to set up a meeting somewhere. That was the way it went, most times. The black half of the couple would ask Albert to set something up. Might be the man, might be the woman. A few times over the years, a particularly bold white woman had set up a rendezvous in the store, whispering over the sheet music for some hymn or other she was buying. Albert had reluctantly accommodated most of them. That was what a businessman did, after all. Filled a need. Supplied a demand. And Lord knew there was demand for a place where black and white could meet away from prying eyes.

Albert had set up a couple of places where couples could meet discreetly, far away from his shop. But if the white half of the couple had a legitimate interest in music—and enough ready cash—he occasionally allowed a hasty rendezvous in the back of the store. He'd got the idea for using his radio show to set up the meetings from his stint in the navy. He'd only been a cook—that's about all they'd let you be in World War II, if you were black— but a white officer had told him how the Brits had used simple codes during music programs to send messages out to French Resistance agents in the field. They'd play a certain song, or quote a piece of poetry, and different groups would know what the signal meant. Blow up this railroad bridge, or shoot that German officer. Using his Sunday gospel show, Albert had found it easy to send coded messages to the couples waiting to hear their meeting times. And since whites could tune in to his gospel show as easily as blacks, the system was just about perfect. Each person in an illicit couple had a particular song, and each knew the song of his or her partner. As disc jockey of his own show, Albert could say something like "Next Sunday at seven o'clock, I'm gonna be playing a one-two punch with 'Steal Away to Jesus,' by the Mighty Clouds of Joy, followed by 'He Cares for Me,' by the Dixie Hummingbirds. Lord, you can't beat that." And they would know.

Credits

Cover design by Amy Halperin

Cover photograph © by Stephen Helstowski/Shutterstock
Images